The Art of Teaching Adults

The Art of Teaching Adults

HOW TO BECOME AN
EXCEPTIONAL INSTRUCTOR
AND FACILITATOR

Expanded
Tenth Anniversary
Edition
with an Introduction
by Daniel D. Pratt

Peter Renner, EdD

Training Associates, Vancouver

The publisher gratefully acknowledges the permission given to use previously copyrighted materials on pages 47-53 by Training House, Inc.; last known address Box 3090, Princeton, NJ 08543; telephone (609) 452-1505.

National Library of Canada cataloguing in publication

Renner, Peter F., 1943-
    The art of teaching adults: how to become an exceptional instructor and facilitator / Peter Renner; with an introduction by Daniel D. Pratt.—Expanded tenth anniversary ed.

Includes bibliographical references and index.

ISBN 0-9697319-2-2

    1. Adult education—Study and teaching. I. PFR Training Associates Ltd. II. Title.

LC5225.T4R45 2004   374'13   C2003-907125-1

Edited by Elaine Jones
Designed by George Vaitkunas
Typeset in Stone Serif and Stone Sans
Proofread by Virginia Ulrich
Printed by Hignell Book Printing of Winnipeg, MB
on acid-free, 100% process chlorine free paper.

9 8 7

Training Associates
o/a MPS Executive Suites *(A Division of Davenport Management Ltd.)*
Suite 720, 999 West Broadway
Vancouver BC V5Z 1K5 Canada
Telephone (604) 732-4552   Fax (604) 738-4080
Email: Books@OfficeSpaceVcr.com   www.peter-renner.com

Contents

Appreciations

After thirty-odd years of teaching others how to teach, my path has taken a turn toward more contemplative pursuits. To mark this shift and to give back some of what has been given to me, I present this revised and expanded edition of *The Art of Teaching Adults*. As attractive as I find Lao-Tzu's observation that "he who talks does not know, he who knows does not talk," I've added almost fifty new pages, thus proving the sage's point by displaying my ignorance once more.[1]

This expanded book reflects some of what I know "works" to help adult learners prosper. Most of it I've learned by borrowing from others, from watching students at work, and from continually observing and tinkering. If I did anything consistently during hundreds of workshops and classes, it was to ask for participants' feedback; standard questions were always "What just happened?" and "What did you learn?" Without their generous readiness to do what I asked them to, their direct criticism, occasional rebellion, and generous compliments, I would not have become the teacher that I am. To the thousands who thus taught me, I dedicate this book.

If there's anything clever in these pages, it rests in the fact I found time and determination to sit down and write. My role—as a teacher for all these years, and now as the book's compiler—has been that of "a harvester of grain, borrowing from others and making one bundle out of many that [have] gone before," as a ninth-century commentator said of Saint Benedict, the author of the *Rule* that continues to govern monastic life in the West.[2] I have acknowledged sources as diligently as I could and promise to make corrections in future printings if errors are brought to the publisher's attention.

Throughout our long friendship, Dan Pratt of the University of British Columbia has been a teacher, colleague, and research supervisor to me and I gratefully acknowledge his learned introduction to this book. Two colleagues at the University of Nebraska generously contributed original chapters: Irene Karpiak on autobiographical learning and Kathryne Roden on using PowerPoint. As with the first edition a decade ago, I have again relied on the superb skills and patient support of Elaine Jones as editor and George Vaitkunas as designer. Deep bows to you all.

P. R.

Notes

1 Quoted in Mitchell, S. (1988). *Tao te ching*. New York: HarperPerennial, p. 85.
2 With this exception, footnotes are shown chapter by chapter, starting on page 174. The source for this quote is De Waal, E. (1997). *Living with contradiction: an introduction to Benedictine spirituality.* Harrisburg, PA: Morehouse Publishing, p. 21.

Introduction
by Daniel D. Pratt

Imagine you are in an interview, or in front of a class of adult learners, and someone asks you to explain your approach to teaching. How would you reply? It's a difficult question. And, although most of us spend a good deal of time thinking about *how* we teach, we spend comparatively less time thinking about our approach; that is, the underlying biases, preferences, and values that guide our teaching. This introduction should help you clarify your overall approach to teaching. It should also help you make more constructive and reflective use of *The Art of Teaching Adults*.

En route to clarifying your approach to teaching we need to go on a brief tour of a rather large and complex landscape. The tour is distilled from several years of research, representing different lands and different points of view. Yet, the insights and findings about teaching are consistent and should prove useful as you explore and make use of *The Art of Teaching Adults*. Throughout, you will see the terms *teacher* and *teaching*. Substitute *instructor/instructing*, *facilitator/facilitating*, or any other words that suit your preference or your circumstance. The issues are the same.

Teaching BIASes

We all come to teaching with our biases, but not the kind of biases you might imagine. For over twenty years, my students and I have been exploring the way teachers of adults go about their work. We have observed the teaching and explored the thinking of hundreds of teachers, trying to understand teaching from their point of view. We started our research in Canada, but our work soon expanded to include several other countries.[1] Across a wide range of people, disciplines, and contexts, we found that teachers vary on four dimensions that we call their BIASes.

B – Beliefs about learners, about the process of learning, about the content or skills to be learned; and beliefs about the role and responsibilities of a teacher.

I – Intentions as to what learners are to learn or what the person teaching them is trying to accomplish.

A – Actions, or ways in which the teacher enacts the role of teacher using techniques and methods in particular ways to help people learn.

S – Strategies, or ways in which a teacher combines beliefs, intentions, and actions into strategic thinking and decision-making.

Although teachers have their own ways of teaching, we did not find hundreds of different BIASes. In fact, there was a great deal of commonality. Among the teachers whom we studied, we found five significant sets of BIASes. Each set defined a different philosophical orientation to teaching. These different orientations are called *perspectives on teaching*. The five perspectives are: *transmission, developmental, apprenticeship, nurturing* and *social reform.*

Our findings were not unique; they correspond to the findings of many other researchers around the world whose works span twenty years and several countries. In reviewing most of that research, David Kember found a surprisingly high level of correspondence across time, context, and disciplines.[2] What is important here is to recognize that no single perspective dominated what might be called "good teaching." Researchers found both effective and ineffective teaching in each of the five perspectives. This notion of a plurality of good teaching is important for two reasons: first, because it supports authenticity as a basic tenet—to be an effective teacher, you must be yourself; and second, because it means there is no single "best way" to use the techniques and ideas in this book. All the materials should be adapted to your own perspective on teaching.

Perspectives on teaching

A perspective on teaching is a lens through which we view our work as educators. We may not be aware of our perspective because it is something we look through, rather than at, when teaching. It is a way of "being" in relation to the content, the learners, and the work we do as teachers. Each perspective represents a different way of thinking about adults as learners, the process of learning, the content to be learned, and the context within which learning and teaching are to take place. Each perspective is a unique blend of BIASes; yet there is overlap between them. Similar actions, intentions, and even beliefs can be found in more than one perspective. Educators holding different perspectives may, for example, have similar beliefs about the importance of critical thinking in the preparation of learners for professional practice. To this end, all of them may espouse the use of case studies and thought-provoking questions as a means of promoting critical thinking. However, the way they use case studies or ask questions, and the way in which they listen and respond when learners consider those cases or questions, will vary considerably across perspectives. These variations are directly related to underlying beliefs and strategies about how best to help people learn critical thinking.

Contrasting perspectives on teaching

An important principle of learning is based on the idea of contrast. It suggests that learning is enhanced when people can examine contrasting examples of the same thing. In other words, we learn about something by comparing it to other things that are of like kind, but different in some important way. For example, if you want to understand your own culture, it's important that you learn about at least one other culture.

This same principle holds when we talk about teaching perspectives. We learn about our own perspective by comparing it to other perspectives on teaching. Through comparison, we are able to see those things that are hidden from our view, aspects of our approach to teaching that we may never have questioned or examined. Using this principle, we can look inside each of the five perspectives and see, for example, how the adult learner, the process of learning, and the product of learning are characterized. As you look at the beliefs outlined below, remember two things: First, each perspective is an amalgamation of many people. The teachers whom we studied may not have given us this particular metaphor, or any metaphor for the adult learner. The metaphors are part of our interpretation of how teachers holding that perspective *tend* to think about adult learners. Second, it's important to remember that the beliefs about learning represent only one aspect of each perspective. The perspectives are more complex than can be fully represented here.

Consider the different beliefs and representations and imagine how each of them might influence (differently) the use of the tools in this book. Look also for the perspective that best represents your own beliefs. Remember, from the point of view of those teachers we studied, each of these metaphors is a legitimate representation of the learner, the process, and the product of learning.

Transmission perspective: learner as a container

The **learner** is a container to be filled.
The **learning process** is an additive process.
The **product of learning** is an increase in knowledge.

Containers (learners) are to be filled with something (knowledge). The knowledge with which learners are to be filled resides in the text or in the person of the teacher. In other words, it exists outside the learner. The educational goal is to efficiently and effectively pass along (teach) a common body of foundational knowledge and way of thinking similar to what is in the text or the teacher. The process of learning is additive, which means that teachers should take care not to overload their students with too much information. To increase the amount that is learned, teachers may focus on the internal structure of the new knowledge. The structure of the content can then be used as an efficient means of storing and retrieving the material when needed. With proper delivery by the teacher, and proper receptivity by the learner, knowledge can be transferred from the teacher to the learner.

Developmental perspective: learner as a computer

The **learner's** mind is like a computer network.
The **learning process** starts with what the learner already knows.
The **product of learning** is a qualitative change in the way of thinking.

This metaphor assumes that we need to know how people are "programmed," i.e., how they think and what they value in relation to our subject. With that information, we can bridge from our knowledge of that subject to their ways of thinking about it. It is based on the notion of cognitive schemas as ways in which we organize, interpret, and summarize our experiences. Learning affects the schemas in one of two ways: when a new experience fits within existing schemas, we build stronger links and commitments to those ways of thinking or valuing; when a new experience does not fit within current ways of thinking or valuing, either we must discard older ways of thinking and build new schemas, or reject the new experience. The process of educating is based on building bridges between what learners already know or value and what we would like them to know or value.

Apprenticeship perspective: learner as a member of a community

The **learner** is understood in relation to a community.
The **learning** process is one of socialization into the community.
The **product of learning** is a change in the learner's identity and social role.

Here, learning is more than the building of cognitive structures; it is the development of skilled performance and a change in identity that occurs as a person adopts the language, values, and practices of a community (e.g., a profession or vocation). Through observation, participation, and practice, it is assumed that learners will fine-tune their skills.

The goal is to refine existing knowledge and/or performing abilities. Yet, at the same time, the individual is developing a sense of identity and place in relation to other members of the community. The learners' progresses are marked by movement from the outside or periphery (as novice or beginner) to the inside (as experienced member) of the social life and practices of a community. As new members come into the community, the community itself changes. Thus, learning is both an individual phenomenon and a social phenomenon.

Nurturing perspective: learner as a self-concept

The **learner** is understood both emotionally and intellectually.
The **learning process** is enhanced by caring relationships.
The **product of learning** is a more confident, self-directing person.

This metaphor assumes that long-term, hard, persistent efforts to achieve come from the heart, not the head. People will be motivated and productive learners when they are working on issues, problems, or needs that are important to them. Learners are nurtured by knowing that (a) their achievement is a product of their own effort and ability, rather than the benevolence of a teacher; and (b) their efforts to learn will be supported through caring and committed relationships with their teacher and their peers. The more pressure to achieve and the more difficult the material to be learned, the more important it is that social support come from caring relationships. As such, this metaphor assumes a central role for the learners' self-concepts. When the learners' self-concepts are under threat or diminished in any way, learning will be blocked, diverted, or halted altogether. Learning outcomes, therefore, include more self-sufficient and confident learners, believing in the power of their own actions to achieve the learning they seek.

Social reform perspective: learner as a product of society

The **learner** is understood to be a product of larger social structures.
The **learning process** is activated by creating dissonance with current views.
The **product of learning** is directed toward society as much as the individual.

Within this metaphor we move beyond the individual toward larger social structures as the context for understanding learners, learning, and learning outcomes. Learners are nested within particular social, cultural, and historical values. These values are reflected in dominant discourses that influence both the process and product of learning. Most importantly, many of these discourses are taken for granted and never named, questioned, or seriously examined; they are simply assumed to be a form of common sense. Effective teaching requires people to examine the assumption that dominant ideas and practices are normal or natural. It also challenges the use of language that describes those practices and assumptions as a form of common sense. The goals of learning, therefore, are concerned with changing social, cultural, and political values as well as individual ways of thinking.

Discovering your perspective on teaching

How might you discover your perspective(s) on teaching? The *Teaching Perspectives Inventory* (TPI), which is freely available on the Internet, is meant to help people identify their perspectives on teaching. As of 2004, over 15,000 educators from 85 countries have taken this inventory. Some have taken it as part of a course requirement; others have taken it out of personal or professional interest. It takes approximately 15 minutes to complete and is available at www.TeachingPerspectives.com. When taking the TPI, be sure to focus on a single group of learners, in a specific setting, as you respond to the questions. This will make your results more meaningful and more valid. You are welcome to take it as many times as you wish. There are also a number of documents that can be downloaded from the TPI Web site to help you interpret your TPI profile and learn more about the five perspectives.

Perspectives vs. tools vs. styles of teaching

I must add a caution at this point: It is common for people to confuse *perspectives on teaching* with *methods* or *techniques of teaching*. This book is about methods and techniques of teaching—the tools of teaching. Perspectives are the philosophical orientation you bring to those tools. Your perspective influences what tools you select to use, how you use them, and how you interpret their success or failure.

There is a third dimension to teaching that can cause confusion: style. It is not uncommon to hear people confuse *perspectives on teaching* with *styles of teaching*. Style, as I am using it, is the personal dimension of teaching; it is the unique expression of your person in the role of teacher. If the first rule of teaching is to "be yourself," that means we have to incorporate and trust Parker Palmer's admonition that, "We teach who we are."[3] To neglect our personal style by taking on some other role or persona is to jeopardize our authenticity, and thus our effectiveness as teachers.

This book is, however, also about the *art* of teaching adults. Artistry requires more than the simple use of techniques and methods; it flows from a comfortable blend of experience and harmony. Experience is the accumulated knowledge we acquired over time, through trial and error and through reflecting on what we have done. Harmony comes from the insight we gain from reflecting on the relationship between our personal style, our philosophical perspectives; and the tools we use as teachers. When we reach the stage of artistic teaching, we have moved from *technical knowledge* to *craft knowledge* in how we use the tools in this book. When we have craft knowledge, the tools are no longer separate from us; they have been adapted, not adopted, to become part and parcel of the answer to the question, "What is my approach to teaching?"

Closing and opening

As with any book, there is a stowaway aboard the good ship *Art*—its author, Peter Renner. It could not be otherwise; authors cannot entirely retreat from themselves. Having known Peter for over thirty years, it's not difficult to find his perspective on teaching among the offerings of this book. In quiet tones and gentle manner, he suggests that we respect the learner; that we be honest to all who come within our teaching reach; and that we care deeply about those who entrust themselves as learners to our teaching guidance. His perspective, his style, and his manner are evident in the selection of tools, the narration of how we might use those tools, and in the artistic design and layout of the whole enterprise. I trust you will enjoy the wealth of experience and harmony that awaits you in the pages ahead.

1

Planning a session

The Art of Teaching Adults describes ways in which learners and teachers can cooperate to come to terms with course content. However, the countless decisions that precede their encounter in the classroom – the course planning process – are beyond the scope of this book.[1] In your work, you either inherit an existing course design, take the time to devise your own, or simply go in cold. In any case, you'll benefit from having prepared a minute-by-minute schedule, traditionally called a *lesson plan.*

Such a plan, in a nutshell, should outline your objectives, describe your plan of action to reach these objectives, indicate the timing of various segments, list facilities, materials and equipment needed, and provide for ways to measure progress.

A simple lesson plan might look like this:

Time in minutes	(1) Activity
10 (2)	Greet participants and introduce myself: name, qualifications, brief work history, why I like to teach.
10	Hand out the course outlines and briefly explain the course objectives and session plans.
11	Ask participants to form groups of five. Have them go around the group and first introduce themselves by name and affiliation, and then share their reasons for signing up for the course. Each person has two minutes.
6	Ask groups to arrange a flip chart or wall-mounted newsprint. Ask them to take five minutes to record their ideas about the course outline: additions, deletions, comments. Tell them to just list their ideas, not to edit or prioritize. One person to act as recorder.
9	Help recorders to post their sheets on a wall, side by side. Invite everyone to get out of their seats and gather around. Briefly review the lists and respond. Be clear on which you can accommodate and which you can't. This is important contracting.

Comments

(1) *This first session includes some quick introductions and a discussion of course outline and expectations. The lesson plan denotes who will do and say what.*

You'll soon develop your own shorthand. For instance, if I want to do a warmup activity during which people team up, interview each other, and then introduce their partner to the whole group, the notation will read: Do interviews. If you are designing the session for someone else, instructions have to be more explicit.

(2) *Estimate the amount of time each component will take. At first try, the time needed rarely matches the actual time available and you have to rework your design. Until I have run through a sequence several times, I make it a habit to jot down the actual time each segment takes as the session progresses; this is of immense help when checking progress and evaluating the design for future use.*

A more detailed plan

Min (1)	Obj (2)	Instructor's Activities (3)	Text Page (4)	Learners' Activities (5)	Instructional Devices
10	3.1	Introduce topic of reservations. Ask why they are necessary – and what would happen if there was no such thing. Develop list on board or flipchart. Ask if anyone had experience with making a reservation at a hotel: good or bad experience?		Contribute ideas.	Flip chart, feltpen. Chalkboard, chalk.
5		Describe functions a reservation system must be able to handle, regardless of type of operation, clientele and volume.	p. 81		
10		Explain the routes by which potential guest can reach an operation to make reservation. Explain role of various "agents," the cost and benefits to the hotel.	p. 82		OT #3
20	3.2	Using actual forms for each pair of students, lead them through the filling out of a basic reservation form. Different forms are used, but the basic reason for basic information remains.	p. 86-8	Working in twos will fill out res. forms from information provided by their partner. (7)	OT #4
		Explain terminology and abbreviations used: GTD, 6 pm, VIP, special rate, etc.			
	3.3	Explain differences in handling individual & group bookings. Who should handle them?	p. 102		OT #5
10	3.1	Explain how/why reservations are charted and how this will differ in approach from one op. to another. The following charting exercise will give students a chance to learn the skills involved.	p. 93		OT # 6 OT #7, 7a
60		Charting exercise: instructions in package.		Following instructions and working through the exercise.	HO: *Reservations Charting Exercise*
		Be available for consultation: it is not necessary that everyone finishes it, but that s/he has a good understanding how/why this is done and must be done with precision/care. (6)		(6)	

From a course on hotel operations

Comments

(1) *This column refers to two types of objectives. A* learning objective *spells out the educational intent in terms of measurable progress of knowledge, skills, and feelings.[2] For instance: The learner will be able to distinguish a hawk from an eagle. A* process objective, *on the other hand, describes desired benefits that are not as easy to quantify. For instance: Learners will work in cooperative teams.*

(2) *A step-by-step description of content and process. Teaching points are given in some detail to ensure the course content is covered. This segment is heavily weighted towards information-giving by the teacher, but in a short time it incorporates two practice sessions.*

(3) *Page references to the textbook help teacher and learner.*

(4) *Planned activities involve participants at different levels of complexity.*

(5) *Materials and equipment are shown with specific references to prepared overhead transparencies (OT) and handouts (HO).*

(6) *A lesson plan shows who will do the work. Try to balance activities that are led by the teacher with those in which participants take an active role.*

(7) *This session includes a practical test to assess learners' comprehension and to flush out questions.*

2 *Planning a session*

2

Declaring objectives

Stating your destination before setting out will serve you well along the journey of course planning and delivery. It will help to communicate your intentions to your organization, the students, and other trainers. It will function as a reference point when selecting teaching techniques, instructional aids, and resource materials. It will form the basis for student and course evaluation. Yet, as I worked with hundreds of train-the-trainer course participants over the years, I noticed that most resisted this part. They were more at ease with "Here's what I want to teach" or "This is the material we need to cover" than with tackling such questions as "What do I want students to learn?" or "How will we know that instruction has been successful?" Considering the unpredictability of the teaching-learning process, I understand their hesitation. However, not defining objectives is akin to boarding a plane without a ticket or known destination, hoping that somehow we'll all arrive at a desired, yet unspecified, place—in time, in one piece, and on budget. I'm suggesting that we aim for somewhere between the extremes: start with clearly worded objectives, keeping in mind that they can (and must) be adjusted en route.

A good place to begin planning or renovating a unit of instruction is with an investigation of whether instruction, as such, is the way to go. Quite frequently, when there are organizational problems or deficiencies, the first reaction is to send people to a course. Off they go to plan or purchase an educational product—often considering little outside of costs and logistics. Robert Mager[1] suggests we begin with a **performance analysis** "to determine whether there is an important difference between what someone is *already* able to do and what it is *intended* for [them] to be able to do, and, if an important difference does exist, whether instruction or some other course of action (inform, manage, ignore) is appropriate." If indeed "instruction" seems the right way to proceed, Mager proposes a **task analysis** to determine "what the competent person does or is supposed to do when ... doing a job. From this description, it is possible to describe *outcomes* for instruction that are tied closely to the *reason* for instruction."[2] Which logically brings us to outcomes, or objectives, grounded in real-life needs.

Goals vs. Objectives: crossing the stream by feeling the stones with your feet by Daniel D. Pratt[3]

I find it difficult to start planning from the point of view of setting objectives, but useful to try to specify my goals. For me, the difference is one of level—goals are broad and objectives are specific. I usually know what I want to accomplish (goals); it's usually harder fro me to state what I want people to learn (objectives). For example, in a one-semester course on adult learning I had written the following goals:

- **Compare and contrast three perspectives on adult learning.**
- **Develop a set of learning principles that illustrate each perspective on adult learning.**
- **Study one adult learner and explain his or her approach to learning from one or more perspectives of learning.**

As you can see, these are very broad goals. They say something about the overall course and its intended outcomes. They answer the question, "What are you hoping to accomplish in this course?" You might also see how the goals are related to each other. The first goal is related to studying about perspectives on learning. This could be accomplished just by reading and discussing within the class. It might also result in an assignment, like a paper, that requires students to compare and contrast different perspectives. The second goal asks participants to distill the principles from the readings and discussions about perspectives on learning. Participants will have to go beyond the descriptive literature on learning perspectives by synthesizing it into statements that have implications for practice. Finally, the third goal requires that they apply the readings, comparisons, and distillation of principles to the task of studying an adult attempting to learn something. These goals build sequentially from comprehending what is read, to synthesizing it, and finally evaluating its place in practice. [See Bloom's chart on page 7.]

When the goal is clear, it is easier to identify objectives. Where goals apply to several sessions or cut across the entire course, objectives are usually specified for each session. In the case of the example above, I set the following objectives for the session:

By the end of this session you should be able to:
- *State at least three main tenets of a constructivist[4] view of learning.*
- *Identify at least one adult learning situation well suited to a constructivist view.*
- *Identify at least one underlying problem with a constructivist view of learning.*
- *Explain why a constructivist view of learning is or is not helpful to you.*

It was a lot easier to identify these objectives after I had declared my goals. Some learning, however, does not lend itself to this type of evaluation. Some examples are an appreciation of artistic creativity, critical thinking about political changes, a change in social attitudes, or an examination of personal beliefs or values. In these cases, it may be impossible to precisely specify behavior that would be an adequate indication of learning.

An objective (sometimes called a learning, behavioral, or instructional objective) expresses a desired outcome—what a successful learner is able to do or know at the end of the event. For instance, the student will be able to "describe a systematic approach to the design of instruction" or "discuss and illustrate the principle of a solar eclipse" or "start an intravenous injection in the arm of a patient." Note how the focus is on **observable and measurable behavior** (describe, discuss, start) and that such behavior concerns the learner, not the instructor. Statements of teacher behavior, using such phrases as "to provide the students with the opportunity to explore ..." or "show learners how to perform..." interfere with the usefulness of an objective as a reference point for planning, instruction, and evaluation. Mager also cautions against **false performance objectives** as ones which contain words and phrases with little or no meaning, such as "to demonstrate a thorough understanding" or "to increase one's capacity for contained self-growth through understanding, self-direction, and self-education" or "to think critically."[5] Clear language is the key to a useful and meaningful objective. It is useful and meaningful when it "succeeds in communicating your intent ... [and] excludes the greatest number of possible meanings *other than* your intent."[6] Here's a comparison of words which are open to—

—many interpretations	—fewer interpretations
to know	to write
to appreciate	to contrast
to develop	to construct
to have	to compare
to understand	to recite
to really understand	to list

Ideally, an objective answers three questions: 1. What should the learner be able to do to demonstrate successful completion of this objective? ⇨ PERFORMANCE. 2. Under what circumstances (in what setting) do you want the learner to be able to do it? ⇨ CONDITION. How well must it be done? What quality or level of performance will constitute success? ⇨ CRITERION.

It may not always be possible, desirable, or necessary to include the second or third component, but the first is a must. The more you can define these components, the better students (and co-teachers) know what is expected of them. And don't feel restricted to just one sentence in stating an objective. Mager gives the following example from a course where learners are required to engage in a creative activity. Learners will be able "to prepare within twenty-four hours analyses

Learning is improved when learners have a clear purpose for learning.

– Daniel D. Pratt

of any five of the given case studies. These analyses should discuss the cases according to the principles presented during the course, and should describe each problem from the points of view of at least two of the participants. References and notes may be used."[7]

Limitations of behavioral objectives

- *Too much of a good thing?* During the 60s and 70s, behavioral objectives became a central component of the drive for accountability and efficiency. Mager's books popularized the process to such an extent that teachers in virtually every subject area, from kindergarten to graduate school, nursing education to management training, were kept busy writing endless lists of objectives. Eventually people became overwhelmed by too many details and the whole approach fell out of favor—another case of a good idea instructionally turning bad operationally.

Use objectives for their strengths: as tools to help refine and express intent, to select teaching and assessment techniques, and to communicate with transparency among the participants in the educational enterprise.

- *Much learning occurs subconsciously.* Michael Polanyi offers the notion of tacit knowing as knowing that involves more than can be told in words, more than what we are conscious of.[8] No matter how carefully crafted an objective may be, it simply cannot account for learning that occurs below the surface, in the individual's inner, or personal, landscape. Much of what is meaningful arises from everyday living, from making mistakes, from figuring things out, from coping with life's ups and downs. As teachers, we can play our part in supporting learners to tap this rich source of their lived experiences.[9]

At the beginning of a course, turn customary rounds of introductions into meaningful conversations about people's lives. During the course, use learning logs or journals to assist students in connecting personal learning with the formal curriculum.

- *Some objectives evolve as we go.* Behavioral objectives are unsuitable for the creative aspects of human expression. They may be "crisp, unambiguous, and precise," writes Elliot Eisner, "but what about the rhetorical force of a student's essay? ... the aesthetic quality of her painting? ... the cogency of his verbal argumentation? ... her intellectual style, the ways she interprets the evidence in a science experiment ... the way in which historical material is analyzed?"[10] Eisner proposes *expressive outcomes* in anticipation of learning that results from personal experience. "Outcomes are essentially what one ends up with, intended or

Learners prefer to have a clear sense of progress toward their goals.

– Daniel D. Pratt

Levels of cognitive understanding

Benjamin Bloom[11] identified six distinct levels of cognitive understanding and organized them into a taxonomy of objectives from knowledge to evaluation, basic to complex. Here's a list of action verbs arranged according to a taxonomy. Use them to construct learning objectives and assessment strategies.

levels

descriptions

action verbs

Knowledge	Comprehension	Application	Analysis	Synthesis	Evaluation
the ability to remember material previously learned	the ability to grasp the meaning of material	the ability to use learned material in new situations	the ability to break material into components so that its structure can be understood	the ability to put parts together to form a new whole	the ability to judge the value of materials for a given purpose
tell	translate	solve	uncover	invent	appraise
list	define	adopt	dissect	compose	assess
show	interpret	use	examine	combine	debate
find	outline	try	take apart	reorganize	evaluate
label	expand	illustrate	classify	develop	grade
recite	qualify	diagram	simplify	produce	select
check	alter	report	categorize	design	reject
locate	account for	apply	compare	predict	judge
choose	associate	calculate	contrast	arrange	recommend
select	classify	complete	analyze	collect	rank
name	compare	demonstrate	appraise	construct	critique
order	contrast	examine	criticize	generalize	estimate
identify	describe	illustrate	debate	integrate	measure
write	differentiate	interpret	differentiate	manage	rank
recall	discuss	locate	distinguish	organize	rate
match	distinguish	operate	infer	prescribe	revise
count	explain	predict	inspect	propose	test
define	estimate	practice	question	specify	
draw	predict	relate	separate		
quote		report	summarize		
relate		restate			
repeat		review			
state					
tabulate					

not, after some form of engagement. Expressive outcomes are the consequences ... that are intentionally planned to provide a fertile field for personal purposing and experience."[12] You may want to review the objectives of your course(s) and distinguish between behavioral (their outcome can be specified, measured, taught, tested) and expressive (they can be anticipated, supported, documented in some way). Match each type of objective/outcome with one or two teaching techniques that are best suited to promote significant learning.

Activities

- Review a unit of instruction (all or part of a course, workshop, or similar module) and do a simple performance analysis. Is there an important difference between what someone is *already* able to do and what it is *intended* for (them) to be able to do. If an important difference does exist, is instruction the best course of action? Might another approach be more appropriate, cost-effective, helpful? What might that approach be? Who might be able to help with this? Could you ask colleagues, learners, other experts?

- Try a task analysis to determine what a competent person does or is supposed to do when performing this function. If you can't do it alone, who could assist you? From this description, it is possible to describe *outcomes* for instruction that are tied closely to the *reason* for instruction.

- Look over existing descriptions of outcome (goals, objectives) to see whether they describe the expected performance, using active verbs and clear language; indicate the conditions under which the behavior must be performed; and state the criterion for measurement of success.

- Write or rewrite objectives for a unit of instruction that you're responsible for. Show the list to an expert in the subject matter, another teacher, and one or two prospective students. Listen carefully to their interpretation of what's expected. How do their interpretations differ from yours? How could you rephrase the objectives to communicate more precisely your intent?

A large part of instruction lies in making the difficulty of new problems large enough to challenge thought, and small enough so that, in addition to the confusion naturally attending the novel elements, there shall be luminous familiar spots from which helpful suggestions may spring.

– John Dewey, *Democracy and education.*

The collaborative classroom

Margaret Tinzmann and colleagues have published detailed guidelines and techniques for what they call collaborative classrooms.[13] At their core, such spaces share the following characteristics:

Knowledge is shared. In traditional classrooms, the primary roles of the teacher are that of content expert, information giver, and process definer. Knowledge flows from the teacher to the student. This deficiency model (where students' deficiencies are rectified by the teacher's expertise and hard work) is also known by Freire's term as "banking method," in which passive learners receive deposits of preselected, ready-made knowledge. Their minds are seen as an empty vault into which the riches of approved knowledge are placed.[14] The collaborative classroom, by con-

trast, is based on the premise that knowledge is shared by all. Teachers offer vital knowledge about content, skills, and process, but they also value and build upon the know-how, experience, previous training, culture, and curiosity brought by the students.

Authority is shared. Traditionally, the teacher is responsible for setting goals, designing learning tasks, and assessing what is learned. Collaborative teachers invite students to set specific goals within the framework of a prescribed curriculum with options for activities and assignments that reflect and build on students' individuality. They encourage students to use their own knowledge and provide opportunities for participants to share that knowledge. They create an environment that encourages and nurtures mutual

respect, diverse opinions, creative thinking, and open dialogue.

Teacher is mediator and facilitator. As the collaborative classroom evolves, the role of the teacher emphasizes mediated learning. As mediator, the teacher helps students to connect new information to prior experiences and learnings on the job, at home, and in the community. As facilitator, the teacher encourages them to "recall, value, talk about, and perhaps critically analyse their lived experience to construct knowledge from it."[15] The teacher aims to help students take charge of their own learning.

3

Setting up the room

By arranging tables and chairs in a certain way, you set the tone for things to come. A careful setup also communicates your attention to detail and makes that important first impression as participants arrive.

Arrange the room to suit your plan

If you plan to lecture, then rows of seats are fine. If you intend to use small-group activities, ensure the furniture supports your plan. But even if the existing layout is awkward, you can often work around it. If the seats are bolted to the floor, for instance, people can turn around and form a group with the three sitting behind them. If that's your plan, ensure that participants seat themselves in a way that leaves no gaps of empty seats. If the chairs are loosely placed in rows, then groupings can be arranged spontaneously when you give the word.

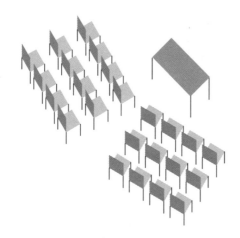

Take inventory – well in advance

Inspect the facilities, count furniture, notice electrical outlets, examine audio-visual equipment, note windows and doors. Then sketch your desired room setup and discuss it with the person who is in a position to get what you need. But be prepared for surprises: you may arrive and find that things aren't as expected – which brings us to the next point.

Be prepared to arrange at the last moment

In spite of good intentions and advance planning, your room may not be in the condition you expected. You now have to shift furniture yourself and, with a sketch in hand, recruit willing helpers on a moment's notice. Allow extra time for this so that the room is ready when participants arrive. If scheduling does not allow early entry to the room, recruit the first arrivals to help with the setup. There's a warm-up activity for you!

Layout examples

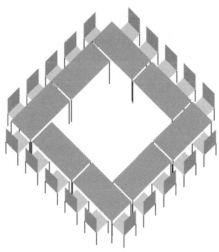

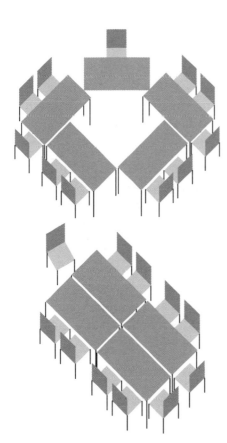

This is a similar setup, but with no designated head table. This layout is ideal when all support materials are in front of the learners. Using a flip chart or overhead projector is possible, but awkward, since one row of participants would have to crane their necks to see.

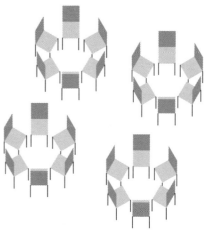

Here are two setups that simulate a round table, using rectangular tables. This arrangement gives everyone a clear field to see and hear everyone else. Your spot is obviously at the head, next to flip chart or white board.

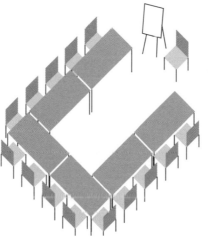

The popular U-shaped arrangement has several advantages. Participants can see each other when listening and speaking; visual devices are well located; and the facilitator can move into the square to intervene or withdraw to the outside to let the situation flow unhampered. A spare table holds teaching resources and can easily be inserted to create a closed square.

For group activities that focus on discussion, role-playing, problem-solving, and personal sharing, tables are a hindrance. Removing them takes away the "security blanket." By opening up the circle so that everyone is equally exposed, you create a setting that invites participation and interaction.

4

Getting packed

These points are worth considering, especially if you are working in an unfamiliar setting:

☐ Book the room and inspect beforehand. Get to know by name the person who is in charge of room booking and the one who looks after the physical setup. Even when all arrangements are confirmed, you can arrive to find the building locked.

☐ Sketch the room layout to show the desired placement of furniture and audio-visual devices. Discuss it with the person responsible. If possible, confirm in writing. Locate the front of the room away from entrance doors to allow for a traffic flow that will not interfere with the proceedings. To reduce distractions, arrange seating to face a blank wall, rather than doors and windows.

☐ Find and test light switches and electrical outlets. A room that's cool in the morning may heat up considerably when filled with fifty active people. Where are the temperature controls? Can you let in some fresh air?

☐ Check soundproofing. If you'll be working in a room with a portable division, noise may spill over from next door.

☐ Determine whether you can use the walls to post newsprint sheets. Ask to have pictures removed. Assure your hosts that masking tape leaves no marks and that you'll double-sheet and use water-based pens to avoid staining the walls.

☐ Check out availability of refreshments. If participants are on their own, determine the distance to vending machines, an in-house cafeteria, or the nearest restaurant. You can reduce confusion and save time by suggesting specific places for people to go and setting realistic break times.

If refreshments are provided to your group, contact the caterer and coordinate timing and variety. Breaks must include decaffeinated beverages as well as coffee; more and more people look for soft drinks and fruit juices.

☐ Clarify parking arrangements. Determine tow-away zones and parking fees. Find out about special rates for participants of your organization.

Let your group know in advance where to park; send maps and clear directions if possible.

☐ Locate access to public telephones and incoming messages. Cellphones and pagers can interrupt the proceedings; ask participants to arrange for no interruptions.

☐ Identify entrance and exits for regular and emergency use. Prepare and post directional signs.

A few words of caution

Always come early and expect the full force of Murphy's Law to descend on you: What can go wrong, will! The possibilities are endless. The person you talk to could go on holidays and leave someone else to set up the room "the way we always do." Frequently you inherit someone else's arrangements (and their mess on the walls and boards). Come prepared for a quick makeover and don't hesitate to ask early arrivals to lend a hand.

Even the best-laid plans are no guarantee. When I was asked to be an after-lunch presenter at a conference, my host had agreed to arrange the furniture to suit brainstorming. I arrived thirty minutes before my allotted time to find that the previous speaker was running late, participants were getting restless, the room was hot and stuffy, sixty instead of forty people were present, chairs stood in rows theater-style with stacks of tables to one side, and an unexpected video crew with bright lights and lapel microphones was adding heat in the room. Some quick thinking, a few laughs, and many helping hands were needed to create a suitable space.

Materials checklist

☐ Flip-chart easel (two are better than one).

☐ Plenty of newsprint paper; have at least one extra pad.

☐ Masking tape.

☐ Felt pens to make notes on flip charts. Use the water-based type (such as Mr. Sketch brand); they smell better and stain less. Test pens and discard old ones.

☐ Transparency pens: water-based ones erase, alcohol-based ones do not. Test pens and discard old ones.

☐ Overhead projector, movable screen, extension cord, spare bulb.

☐ Transparencies: bring blanks as well as prepared ones.

☐ Equipment to play videotapes and films.

Give us the tools and we will do the work.

– Winston Churchill

☐ Video setup for taping and play-back.

☐ PowerPoint projector, cables, and spare bulb.

☐ Class registration list.

☐ Handout materials: sorted, stapled, and three-hole-punched.

☐ Name tags and name cards.

☐ Your notes and manuals.

☐ Course-related books and magazines. Place them on a side table for browsing and reference.

☐ Tools: three-hole punch, stapler, staples, pens, pencils, blank writing paper, file cards, clear tape, rubber bands, pliers, (the latter to remove picture hooks and nails, in order to clear a wall to hang flip charts).

☐ Miscellaneous items: band-aids (for nasty paper cuts), headache tablets, breath freshener, comfortable shoes, toiletry kit, personal snacks (fresh fruit, chocolate, or whatever feels good when you work hard).

FUNDAMENTALS

Focus on the learner

Psychologist Carl Rogers conceptualized "client-centered therapy" and later developed a parallel theory about adult education. Based on his observations that "therapy is a learning process," he puts forth some basic hypotheses of "student-centered teaching:"[1]

- We cannot teach anyone directly; we can only facilitate a person's learning.

- A person learns significantly only those things which are perceived as applicable in the maintenance or enhancement of the structure of self.

- If an experience involves a change in the organization of the self, learners are likely to resist it. A person's boundaries tend to become rigid when threatened, relaxed when free from threat.

- Any experience perceived as inconsistent with the self can only be assimilated if the current organization of self is relaxed and expanded to include it.

- The educational situation that most effectively promotes significant learning is one in which threat to the self of the learner is reduced to a minimum.

Rogers suggests we shift the spotlight from teacher to individual learners. Throughout the entire course design, he calls on us to question the relevance of every course requirement, entrance exam, assignment, project, classroom activity, lecture topic, and evaluation procedure.

Rogers proposes we involve learners in the important aspects of course design and management. He advocates delineation of accountability so that teacher and learner become jointly responsible for a positive outcome.

Rogers also directs us to the creation of an environment perceived as safe and supportive by all participants – a climate that encourages risk-taking, questioning the old, and trying out the new. Directions and feedback, to be most helpful, must be given with caring attention to individual needs.

5 Using icebreakers and energizers

When a new group first assembles, participants are usually somewhat awkward and full of questions. Who is here? What's going to happen? Where do I fit in? How safe a place is this? Is this worth my trouble, time, and money? Try to anticipate these concerns by starting off with a warmup activity.

Most adults function best in an atmosphere of respect and support, and even the most self-assured person appreciates some sort of ice-breaking activities. Whichever technique you decide to use, make sure it helps to get people settled in, create a sense of welcome, and establish an atmosphere of collegial cooperation.

Select your activity with care. An exercise that works in one group may bomb in the next. With perfect hindsight, I recall working with a group of health-care managers; my choice of warmup activity fitted them perfectly and they were working together in no time. When I introduced the same activity to an assembly of corrections officers, I sensed trouble right away: my cheerful instructions were met with cold stares and very reluctant responses.

Activity 1: Hello, my name is ...

Names are important to all of us. It is comforting to be addressed by name in a strange environment. The pin-on type is a good beginning to the matching of names and faces. The problem with these tags is that they fall off, are obscured by people's clothing, and usually disappear by the second and third session.

Use double-folded sheets of paper or old file cards as desk-top name cards. Have each person print (in bold letters) the name they want to be called. This should be done on both sides of the card so that it can be seen from different directions. Have brightly colored felt pens on hand. This activity gets you past the awkward Mr./Mrs./Ms./first name/last name quandary. Also, the cards can be brought back for the next session.

What do people want in a first session?

As children, the first day of classes was usually taken up with room assignments, textbook distribution, and timetable discussions; we were pleased to be let out early and have as little instruction as possible. However, adults have different expectations. Good use of time and value for money are important concerns.

Researchers asked adult learners at two Canadian universities about their expectations for a first session.[1] The results suggest that students are more interested in content and the instructor than classmates during the first session. Information about course content, objectives, and expectations rated the highest priority.

But students also wanted to get to know their instructor during that first session. They wanted to know about their instructor's professional and academic background, teaching style, expectations, and availability. They were also interested in each other's backgrounds and reasons for taking a course.

Respondents were split equally between those who wanted early introductions and those who preferred to get acquainted more naturally during refreshment breaks and through group tasks.

Variations

- Ask participants to put their present occupation, affiliation, or anything they consider relevant for identification in small letters in the corners of their name card.

- Ask them to turn the card inside-out and jot down the completion of statements you supply. Use the following examples or improvise your own:

  - Right now, I'd rather …
  - I hope this course won't be …
  - I would like to learn …

  While this information is confidential at this stage, you may later wish to ask volunteers to share it with the class. You may also come back to it towards the end of a session or course, when you prompt participants to assess their progress.

Activity 2: Remember me?

This is a further variation of the go-around naming routine. It is best done partway into the course or just before the end of the first session.

- Ask participants to place their chairs in a circle or sit on the table edges. You, too, join the circle.

- Introduce the activity, using your own words along the following lines. "We have been together for a while now and I'd like us to use each other's names whenever possible. Let's play a game you may recall from earlier days. The rules are simple.

  "I'll start by telling you my name. The person next to me turns to the person on her right, repeats my name and adds hers, and so we'll go around the circle. When your turn comes you have to try to repeat all the names before yours and then add your own. Don't worry about forgetting a name – you simply ask the person."

- Allow for some reaction to your announcement of this activity, but don't hesitate to remind them that you'll be the last person and will have to remember all the names! This should be good for a few laughs.

How to remember names

- *Pay attention to a new name. If you don't remember it, or hear it clearly the first time, ask the person to repeat it.*

- *Repeat the name yourself. This will improve recall by 30 percent.*

- *Use the name in conversation. Repetition will engrave the name in your long-term memory.*

- *Observe faces. Most of us can remember faces better than names, so really study the face and choose one outstanding detail.*

- *Use the name when saying good-bye. This final reinforcer also ensures that you know the name.*

Activity 3: Press conference

This activity helps to develop team spirit among people who just minutes ago were strangers to each other. It makes useful information available and shows that playfulness is compatible with serious adult education.

1. Explain that group members should assume for a moment that they have been invited to a press conference. This is a chance to query the teacher about the course they're about to begin. Emphasize that the notion of "dumb questions" has been suspended for the duration.

2. Ask participants to form groups of four to five each and pool their questions.

> *Form groups of four to five*
> *Decide what questions you want to ask Peter about:*
> 1. My background   2. The course – Its hours
>   My experience   Its contents
>   My present activities,   Tests
>   etc.   Practicum
> PLEASE ASK ME ANY QUESTIONS THAT YOU FEEL
> ARE IMPORTANT TO YOU!!

3. Give them six minutes to compile their lists. Suggest that each group take one minute for a quick round of introductions and then use five minutes to work on the list. Ask one member to record the questions in point form.

4. Seat yourself in the "hot seat," ready to be quizzed.

5. When five minutes are up, invite the first representative to pose the first question. From there, proceed from group to group until all questions have been dealt with. Going from group to group and dealing with one question at a time avoids duplication and spreads the questions around the room.

Are ice-breakers necessary?

Researchers have given us the "uncertainty reduction theory" in support of ice-breakers and personal introductions.[2] They say that initial interactions between strangers are characterized by information-seeking aimed at reducing uncertainty through such reciprocal acts as self-disclosure and nonverbal warmth. If you feel like doing your own research with this theory, start your next class without warm-up activities and introductions. Later on, pause for introductions and, if appropriate, raise the issue of the delay by asking questions such as the following: Did you miss the customary introductions? How necessary are they? How important are ice-breakers in addressing uncertainty at the start of a course?

Activity 4: Show me

1. Ask each participant to take a blank 8" x 11" sheet of paper and boldly place "I AM ..." as the heading. Then ask everyone to complete the statement in five different ways. (See example at left.)

   Complete a sheet for yourself as well.

2. Once participants have completed their sheets, ask them to hold it in front of them so it can be read by others as they mill about the room.

3. Explain that the rest of the exercise will be done in silence.

4. Ask them to have a look around, mingle, and make nonverbal contact with at least three separate people. Participants should read the lists and gather any additional clues, spending at least thirty seconds with each person they encounter.

5. Some people will need encouragement to move around or reminders to remain silent.

6. After ten minutes of circulating, ask for the sheets to be hung on a wall. Participants may want to have another look during the refreshment break, connecting people and lists.

Variation A

1. Hand everyone a blank piece of paper and a short section of masking tape.

2. Ask participants to put their name in bold letters at the top of the sheet. Next ask them to print five or six words ending with "ing" below their names. These words will serve as their introduction. Examples: reading, cooking, traveling, caring.

   Other word endings may also be used:
   - "able," as in approachable, reasonable, capable, irritable.
   - "ist," as in optimist, pianist, cyclist, specialist.
   - "ful," as in playful, careful, hopeful, delightful.

3. Participants (including you) then hold the sheets up and mill about the room. You can try this with silence for the first two minutes, or you can invite people to meet with two others and share their lists.

Variation B

1. Change the heading to I AM A RESOURCE and invite participants to list their areas of expertise.

2. Stipulate whether or not the list should be confined to the course content or embrace a wider range of know-how and interests. Here's a sample sheet, at left.

Activity 5: Thelma meets Louise

1. Ask students to team up with one of their neighbors. Their task is to spend four minutes interviewing each other and find out at least three things (other than name) about their partner. When the time is up, each participant introduces his or her partner to the large group.

   If people need some help with interview questions, make some suggestions. Why are you taking this course? Where do you come from? How does this course relate to your job/family? What's exciting in your life right now? What do you do when you don't work?

2. After the time is up (gauge it by the amount of talking, but try to keep close to the announced limit), ask people to come back together as a class. You may want to go first, to model the introductions.

3. Ask the person being introduced to stand up so that all can see. Thank everyone for participating.

Activity 6: Listening triads

Ask participants to arrange themselves in groups of three, dispersed about the room for some privacy. Suggest they join with people they know the least.

Give the following instructions:

1. Decide who will be A, B and C in your group.

2. Person A will now tell the others why you are here (or what you expect to learn during this event). Share as much as you are comfortable with. You have two minutes for this.

3. When A's time is up, B and C report back to A what they have heard. A may restate or clarify until he or she is fully understood by B and C. Take no more than two minutes for the feedback phase.

4. Repeat the round until each of you has been in each role.

5. The total time will be twelve minutes. But don't worry about that, I'll call out the times.

Stay alert. Your lesson plan may call for a particular activity at a certain time, but the group may not be ready. Pay attention. Be flexible. Offer suggestions and options; always seek ways to maximize learning.

– based on the teachings of Lao Tzu.

Activity 7: Expectations revealed

This combines introductions with a sharing of expectations. The survey results provide valuable information for course planning or possible modification.

This activity can be completed in less than fifteen minutes, but will take longer if you expand it into an agenda-building or course-planning session.

There are at least two ways to proceed:

- The quickest and most contained way to gather data is with a questionnaire. Prepare it in advance, listing possible topics, issues, skills, etc.

  Ask participants to check off their most pressing needs, perhaps in order of priority. You can also ask them to add their own items and assign a ranking to them as well. Such a survey can be completed in a few minutes and will provide a quick feel of the communal pulse.

- A more open-ended and less controlled approach requires more time, but may yield unexpected results. Before asking, be clear how much flexibility you have to respond to individual needs.

  The following are samples of questions that will open Pandora's box:

  - I want to learn to ...
  - I learn best when I'm involved in the following activities: ...
  - My expectations of the teacher are ...
  - My expectations of the other participants are ...
  - My contribution to this course could be ...

Once everyone has responded, either in class or by way of a take-home assignment, compile the data or, better, delegate this task to small groups. Assign separate groups to each of the questions and ask them to present their summary to the whole class.

This activity shifts the focus from teacher to learners. You begin the course based on clearly understood expectations. Familiarity with everyone's interests, backgrounds, and needs is invaluable for future session planning.

Variation: Common concerns[3]

This activity takes between five and twenty minutes, depending on the number of participants and the amount of discussion.

Prepare a list of concerns in advance and distribute it at the start of the sessions. The items here are examples only – compose one to suit your

Seek cooperation at every step. You can no more teach without the learner than a merchant can sell without a willing buyer.

– based on the teachings of Lao Tzu.

occasion. As you hand out the list, invite participants to add their own items, or to circle the three items of greatest importance to them.

Which of these ideas has crossed your mind as you prepared for this workshop?
- I won't get my questions answered.
- We'll be doing too much small-group stuff.
- There will be too much lecturing.
- I won't have time to practice the new skills.
- The material will not apply to my situation.
- I'll be expected to make a presentation.
- Discussions will take up too much time.
- Breaks will go on for too long.
- Our backgrounds will be too diverse.
- I won't learn anything new.

Participants first work alone, marking their most important items. Then ask them to discuss the items with others. Depending on the group size, this can be done by the whole group, in pairs, or small groups of three to five. Write up the most-often-raised issues on a flip chart, respond to the concerns, and leave the list up as a reminder for all.

Use this activity only if you are prepared to discuss and even change some aspects of the course design. Inevitably, there will have to be some give and take between you and the participants. The beauty of this activity is that it starts a cooperative process that can carry on throughout the course.

Activity 8: Learning needs

Use this to establish the expectations of your group. But be fully prepared to respond and, if necessary, make changes to your instructional plans.

1. To begin, post the chart illustrated at left. If you have ten or fewer participants, one sheet will suffice: everyone can take turns recording ideas on it. Ask that they use key words and print boldly with colored felt pens. If your numbers are larger, ask small groups of five or six to work together.

2. Interrupt the recording when a good number of ideas has been recorded. If working in groups, post the sheets where everyone can see them.

Adults learn best in situations characterized by physical comfort, mutual trust and respect, and acceptance of differences.

– Daniel D. Pratt

By Friday I want to be able to:

DO: | KNOW:

HAVE EXPERIENCED:

3. Invite participants to form a semicircle and look over the sheets. Let the discussion run for a few minutes so that everyone has a chance to read all lists.

4. Respond to the posted expectations. Do they match what you have planned? Which can you accommodate and which lie outside the course parameters? Note all similarities between group lists and your own design. If possible, offer suggestions for individuals whose expectations cannot be met.

This activity will demonstrate your interest in everyone's needs and your approach to conflict.

In the early stages of learning, every desired response should be reinforced.

– Daniel D. Pratt

Activity 9: Agenda-building

If your course design is open to modifications, make the building of a joint agenda a warmup activity.

1. Present a summary of your course goals. Make it clear that they are here to guide the participants, not dictate to them.

2. Help the group to express its goals and to build an agenda for the next session(s).[4] Guided by consensus, the group might decide on content, assign responsibilities, and manage its own time. Here's an example of a group agenda.

AGENDA

CONTENT	WHO	PROCESS	TIME
What we've done since last week	Mary	Starting up	15'
Goals and agenda	Reg	Discussion	10'
Planning models	Reg	Lecturette	20'
Needs assessment	George	Group exercise	60'
Group critique	All	Round-the-room	12'
Goals for next session	Reg	Handout	3'

This chart was suggested by Reg Herman

Topics are listed down the left-hand column, with names of the person responsible. The right-hand columns show the techniques to be used and an approximation of the time available for each topic.

Activity 10: Unfinished statements

This one takes only ten minutes and is especially suitable for large assemblies.

1. Greet participants and tell them the activity will take about ten minutes.

2. Ask them to listen to an unfinished statement and think of ways to complete it. For example: the one thing I like about teaching ...; the main reason I'm here ...; the thing that frustrates me most about my current job .... (Choose a sentence that suits your group.)

3. Write the sentence stem on the board or overhead projector.

4. Ask participants to get up and make contact with one person at a time. Ask them to share their sentence completion and, if appropriate, seek elaboration. Instruct participants to move around the room and take no more than sixty seconds for each encounter.

5. Let the activity continue for five to ten minutes, enough time for everyone to meet at least five different people.

6. Monitor the process by moving around the room, listening inconspicuously to the encounters. If people wander off the topic, remind them to stick to the exchange of statements. If necessary, adjust the timing for each meeting.

7. Conclude the activity by asking participants to return to their seats. As an optional add-on, ask for volunteers to share their reactions to what they have just heard.

Activity 11: Predicting success

This has become a favorite opening with task-oriented groups; it subtly informs participants of their responsibility for the session's outcome.

1. Post the heading: What has to happen for this course (or session) to be a success?

2. Ask participants to call out descriptions of what they'd consider evidence of success. The chart on the next page shows some examples, recorded in such a way as to distinguish content from process issues. If the numbers warrant it, ask people to form groups of five to six members and have each group complete a sheet. Five minutes are probably enough.

Learning is facilitated when the learning environment is nonthreatening.
– Daniel D. Pratt

3. Post the sheets side-by-side and lead a brief discussion of the entries. Explore how these expectations relate to the course agenda.

4. Throughout the course, refer to the success statements to keep the group focused on their desired outcome.

Activity 12: How did I get here ?

This can be done during the first session or later in a course. Post the question on the board or flip chart. Ask participants to take a half-sheet of flip-chart paper, find a quiet spot in the room, and depict—in words, symbols, images—how they came to be here, on this day, to this workshop, as this person. Open the doors to this activity by suggesting some of the many ways to answer this question: I came by bus and got off at the corner of ... ; My family and I immigrated here in ...; I've wanted to learn about this ever since .... Give clear time lines (ten to fifteen minutes, at least), provide colored pens, ask that the activity be done in silence, explain that people will each have five minutes afterward to share their story with the class (or a small group of three to five), and consider playing some gentle, soothing music on your portable tape recorder.

Activity 13: Memorable teachers

This activity asks participants to think back on previous schooling and remember a teacher who left an impression. Explain that the memory doesn't necessarily need to be a happy one: it could be positive, negative, or bittersweet. This exercise helps unearth some of the preconceptions and expectations we all bring to new learning situations—usually unspoken but still clear in our consciousness. Storytelling can be a rich source of information and insights. Invite participants to take out pen and paper, sit comfortably, exhale, and become quiet. Ask them to

Learning is an active process of bringing past experience and knowledge to bear upon new situations.

– Daniel D. Pratt

think back to previous education experiences: kindergarten, elementary school, high school, vocational training, university, night school, on-the-job training, professional development, religious education, sports and leisure activities—any situation where there was someone in charge of instruction. Ask them to recall and record something a teacher did or said that made them memorable. Even small events can hold big memories—the mere fact of recall is worth noting. Give a time limit (ten minutes) and explain that there will be a sharing phase afterward. Create a talking circle or, if the class is large, divide into smaller groups. Propose a three-minute opening for each person to tell their story—without comments from others. Keep a close eye on the time and intervene, if necessary, as some stories will want to go beyond. You might want to ask for a volunteer timekeeper.

Learning is more easily remembered if emotions are involved.

– Daniel D. Pratt

Activity 14: Four (or more) corners

This one gets people off their seats, moving around, and talking to strangers in nonthreatening ways. In preparation, think of categories that might appeal to your group, then provide subgroups in each category. Here are a few samples.

Animals	Colors	Psychological types	Vehicles	Ethnic food
tiger	blue	sensing	pick-up truck	Japanese
porcupine	red	intuiting	SUV	Mexican
dolphin	green	feeling	sports car	French
greyhound	yellow	thinking	camper van	Fusion
dove			antique car	

I've also used printed images, such as photos, newspaper headlines, and art reproductions from discount calendars. Post the images or words in four corners of the meeting room and invite participants to go to the corner that attracts them. Allow some time for milling. Ask people to have a second choice in case a group is too small and needs to be combined with another. Once people have found their group, ask them to form a circle (sitting or standing), take turns introducing themselves, and share some of their reasons for choosing this subgroup. Next, ask them to take a few minutes speculating about what they have in common and what kind of learning activities they'd enjoy the most, and the least. Ask them to select a spokesperson who will report on their behalf. Finally, reconvene the large group for reports.

Activity 15: Mottos and metaphors

*What's in a name?
that which we call a rose,
By any other name would
smell as sweet.*

– William Shakespeare,
   Romeo and Juliet, Act II,
   Scene 2.

Think of cultural mottos as the sayings or truths that express your most basic ethical guidelines or world view. Michelangelo's motto, for instance, was "And still I am learning"; the Prince of Wales's is "I serve"; and in my own family, although this was never spelled out in Latin, it was "Work hard and know your station." A metaphor[5] is a figure of speech in which a word or phrase literally denoting one kind of object or idea is used in place of another to suggest a likeness or analogy between them (as in *drowning in money*).

Explain the concept of cultural motto and metaphor and how they are the storehouses for the beliefs and assumptions we hold about the world. "They guide our behavior and attitudes and they typically come to us from our ethnic background, our families, our religious education, and similar influences. This activity will help us individually and collectively give a name to these forces and serve to introduce ourselves to each other in an unusual way." Ask participants to take a 3 x 5-inch card, write their name on it, draw a line down the center, and label the left half with the words *Cultural motto* and the right with *Metaphor* (or *Being a teacher is like ...*). Use colored pens to embellish your words with drawings, highlight, and symbols. After about five minutes, ask for volunteers to briefly read out their cards. If the group is large and time is short, do this in small groups. Next, invite everyone to post their card on a wall space (using masking tape). Leave the cards up for informal visit during the breaks. Here are a few samples from a university course on teaching adults:

Cultural motto	Being a teacher is like...
Do your best! Don't give up. Learn from experience.	Teaching is like sculpting.

Cultural motto	Being a teacher is like ...
The sea of knowledge is infinite—only hard work can help you reach the shore.	... being at war with the learners.

Cultural motto	Being a teacher is like...
Don't rock the boat.	... giving them the colors to create a masterpiece.

Cultural motto	Being a teacher is like...
Hard work and caring for each other.	... planting a seed and making sure it can blossom.

Cultural motto	Being a teacher is like...
Don't waste time and energy. Be practical. Keep it simple.	... sharing a pie—sharing knowledge in pieces.

Cultural motto	Being a teacher is like...
Take the middle way in life ... and work hard, very hard.	... being a telescope that helps students see the complexity of the world.

Activity 16: Poster sessions

This is an idea borrowed from academic conferences, where researchers customarily display their findings on wall-mounted posters and then remain near to engage visitors in conversation. Ask participants to form groups of three to five, or assign people to groups if you're looking for a particular mix. Give each group a different topic or assign the same topic to all groups. Ask participants to pool their resources and create a poster on flip charts or poster boards, using colored pens to draw diagrams, flow charts, and illustrations. Allow sufficient time, depending on the complexity of the topic, and ask the groups to display their posters. If you do this activity in the first session, mention that the posters are a mere snapshot and that posters will look dramatically different by the course's end. Make sure also to comment on the depth and variety of knowledge already present. In a round-about way, posters can serve as a needs analysis, a sort of pretest. If possible, time this activity before a break so that people have a chance to visit each other's boards. Ask that posters be staffed during that time. Here are a few topics for different courses:

Nothing has meaning or is learned in isolation from prior experience.

– Daniel D. Pratt

Train-the-trainer workshop	Weekend course on baking bread	On-the-job training course for new restaurant staff
The instructional design process.	From raw flour to finished loaf— a flow chart.	Table settings for a full-service wedding banquet.
Good and poor furniture arrangements for group-based learning	Different glazes and scoring patterns.	Layout for a reservations book.
Matching learning objectives to teaching techniques.	Different ethnic breads and their characteristics.	Some Dos and Don'ts in wine service.

Activity 17: Creating a charter

By common custom, basic "rules" are spelled out by the teacher (punctuality; assigned readings; participation) or they are implied and subtly evolve over time. This activity aims to involve participants in setting the rules by creating a *charter of rights and freedoms* for the course. Doing this early in the proceedings sets a tone for cooperation, democracy, and shared responsibility. Here's a suggested sequence of events:

1. Explain the goal and process of the activity.

2. Ask everyone to write down three to five "rules" (or desired conditions for learning) on paper.

3. Ask the whole class to gather around a flip chart or white board. Have extra space and paper on hand should the list become long.

4. You can act as facilitator of the session as well as recorder—or ask for a volunteer scribe from the group. This would be an example of task-sharing.

5. Ask participants to call out an item from their list, one person at a time. Record them on a chart. Remind participants to listen so as to minimize duplications and ensure everyone can be heard.

6. When the flood of ideas subsides, invite everyone to sit in silence for a minute and look over the list. Ask, "Are all your written ideas represented?" and "What else comes to mind?" Invite the scribe to contribute as well. Offer your own contributions at this time.

7. Guide the group in tidying up the list by combining, deleting, and clarifying items, with the aim of paring down the list to a manageable six to ten maximum.

8. Create and post a clean sheet. Ask for possible headings, such as "our code of conduct," or whatever the group seems comfortable with.

9. Explain that these rules will guide the group's work during the workshop. Participants should feel free to alert the group to infringements. Explain that this is an open-ended list that may be edited over time.

Activity 18: Needs analysis

This activity offers an opportunity to explore the background of participants and engage them in looking at the course outline. In preparation, create a self-assessment sheet, based on course objectives (see next page). Hand the sheet out and ask participants to score their relative familiarity or expertise with each item. Ask that they put their names on the sheets, but explain that individual scores will remain anonymous.

Learning is enhanced when content and purposes for learning are relevant and meaningful to the learners.

– Daniel D. Pratt

You will, however, collect and summarize the sheets as your guide in further course planning. This exercise can open a conversation about how the course will unfold, how the ground might be covered, how in-class expertise might be utilized, what the expectations are, and so on. It may require the instructor to make adjustments to a pre-planned lesson plan—a wonderful opportunity for cooperative planning. Here's a partial handout I've used at the outset of a three-day train-the-trainer workshop (adapt it to suit your situation):

We learn in relation to what we already know.

– Daniel D. Pratt

Self-assessment

Please read this list of course objectives and then assess your pre-course familiarity on a five-point scale.

1	2	3	4	5

this is new
or quite unfamiliar
to me

familiar to the point
that I could
explain it to others

Kindly write your name at the bottom. I shall tabulate the results and post them as a summary. Your name and score will remain anonymous.

Thank you
(Name of instructor)

Degree of familiarity (circle one)	Learning objectives
1 2 3 4 5	Create behavioral objectives based on a job or task analysis.
1 2 3 4 5	Match learning objectives to teaching techniques.
1 2 3 4 5	Conduct an ice-breaker activity with a group of 10 people meeting for the first time.
1 2 3 4 5	Design a lesson plan for a one-hour class—with the emphasis on participatory activities.
1 2 3 4 5	Debrief a role-playing activity.
1 2 3 4 5	Act as recorder (scribe) during a brainstorming session.
1 2 3 4 5	etc.

Activity 19: Coat of arms

This is meant to be a playful activity that allows participants to introduce themselves and reveal aspects of their persona. In preparation, download[6] and duplicate this elaborate blank. (Note that coat of arms is the proper name for the whole thing; the decoration sitting on top of the helm is called the *crest*, the curlicues around the helmet the *mantling*, and the blank field in the middle the *shield*; the wavy banner below holds the family name, war cry, or *motto*.) You can, of course, draw a simple shield on the board and ask participants to transfer it to their own blank sheet. Next, ask them to divide the shield in four quadrants. Designate the upper left as "my craft, profession, how I make a living," the upper right as "what I do to relax, to play, to have fun," the bottom left as "where and how I live at home," and the bottom right as "something people don't usually know about me." Make crayons and colored pens available and ask everyone to take ten minutes to put depictions in the four fields of their shield. As this is only a draft, there's no need for artistic excellence or accuracy! Call "time," ask participants to write their name on the banner, and post their work along a wall. As a **variation**, introduce the concept of a "motto," a saying that sums up the world view or intention of a person, family, or organization. Be ready to give an example.

"And still I am learning" (*Ancora imparo*, Michelangelo)

"Be prepared" (Boy Scouts)

"I serve" (*Ich dien*, Prince of Wales)

"Mountaineers are always free" (*Montani semper liberi*, West Virginia)

"One from many parts" (*E pluribus unum*, first US motto).

"By following, one acquires" (*Sequitando si giunge*, Lambert family from Ireland)

"I remember" (*Je me souviens*, Province of Quebec).

Activity 20: Famous words

Select a quote that suits the group and course—similar to the ones in the margins of this book—and display it for all to see. Next to it, post two or three questions along the following lines:[7]

What does this mean?

Where does it have relevance in your life?

How might it relate to the study of [insert name of subject or course]?

Ask participants to find someone to talk to, introduce themselves, and begin exchanging responses to question #1 only. After three minutes, call "time" (or use some mechanical device, such as a chime or gong) and ask duos to meet up with another pair, introduce themselves, and share their views on question #2. Ask them to be mindful of the time, as they'll only have four minutes—one minute per person—for this round. After four minutes ask the groups to break up into pairs again, this time with a different partner, and tackle question #3 for four minutes. Finally, gather the class as a whole and ask for responses to question #3. The degree of controversy embedded in the quote will set the tone for the day. The pair/quartet/pair grouping is arbitrary, intended only to mix things up and get people talking to each other about themselves and some essential issues pertaining to course content.

The aging learner

With more and more older persons participating in adult education activities, the effects of physiological aging are a concern for planners and teachers. Patricia Cross has summarized research about the probable effect of certain physical changes on learning.[8]

- *Reaction time*

"As people grow older, they slow down. Speed of learning involves reaction time to perceive a stimulus, transmission time to transmit the message to the brain, and response time to carry out the action. On the average, older learners perceive more slowly, think more slowly, and act more slowly than younger people. In general, the time required for learning new things increases with age."

- *Vision*

"As eyes age, there is a loss of elasticity and transparency, pupils become smaller and react more feebly, and there is an increasing incidence of cataracts and defective color vision. While almost everyone recognizes the need for bifocals as a sign of aging, not everyone is aware of the need for increased illumination. A fifty-year old is likely to need 50 percent more light than a twenty-year old."

- *Hearing*

"Aging brings problems with pitch, volume, and rate of response. Rapid speech, for example, can result in loss of intelligibility of up to 45 percent of older people. Women seem to lose acuity for lower pitch, while men lose it for high pitch, making older women able to communicate more readily with women while older men can hear men's voices better."

A process is underway to advocate age-integrated, instead of age-segregated programs and policies in adult education.[9] One observer predicts that "gerontology is not going to last [because] chopping up the life cycle was not a very good idea to begin with."[10] Rather than planning separate programs, educators are urged to integrate the perspectives of older adults and what is known about their learning styles and preferences into ongoing programming. In age-integrated educational programs, older adults become both learners and teachers, sometimes imparting their existing skills and knowledge and sometimes continuing to engage in learning new things.[11] The information available over the Internet both about and for older adults is another trend with implications for educators. Many older adults are defying the stereotype that computers are for the young and are actively engaged in using the Internet as both consumers and producers of information. This is consistent with the kind of education in which they tend to engage—informal or noncredit—and educators need to consider how they can use it to support and/or deliver educational programming for older adults.

6

Contracting for learning

Motivation to learn is increased when the goals of the instructor are also the goals of the learners.

– Daniel D. Pratt

A contract is a written agreement specifying mutual expectations between two or more persons. The term "contract" underscores that such an accord is legitimate, fair, and possible.

Learning contracts can be used for a wide variety of subjects and course formats. They acknowledge that adult groups are not homogenous: participants arrive from widely differing backgrounds and are motivated by assorted needs. Contracts can provide choices to people who have separate aspirations and abilities.

If you are trying a contract for the first time, start with one that opens just a few components to negotiation. This way you and the participants can enter your new relationship with little anxiety. Here are some items that can easily be individualized:

- individual learning goals

- steps to be completed to reach the goals

- specified reading and out-of-class preparation

- nature of class participation

- method of evaluation or grading

- attendance requirements

- topic and format of individual projects

Learners and instructor each keep a signed and dated copy. At evaluation times, it forms the basis for assessment and possible changes. A learning contract is an important step towards establishing a community of learners. It reinforces participants' responsibility for their own learning. It also specifies the teacher's functions and responsibilities.

In addition to their use in short-term courses and workshops, contracts offer interesting possibilities in career and management development programs. In such circumstances, a learner might make an agreement with a teacher, mentor, supervisor, or even a support group. Such contracts could pertain to on-the-job training programs, independent learning projects, or any professional development sequence.

Case study: the contracting process

This contract lets the students decide the end-of-course evaluation and potential grade. It was used in a course called *Effective Interpersonal Relations*, where some came for professional development, others for university transfer, still others for personal growth alone. While course content and process were controlled by the faculty – and were not negotiable – students selected the workload associated with each potential grade. According to Malcolm Knowles, the contracting process should include nine steps:[1]

1. The learner selects a realistic goal for the undertaking and then breaks it into achievable subgoals.

2. A competency model is developed, consisting of the knowledge, attitudes, and skills required to meet each subgoal.

3. Present levels of competency are first documented, then contrasted with desired levels.

4. Based on the gaps between present and desired competencies, learning needs are identified.

5. Existing and potential learning resources are identified and matched to learning needs.

6. A practical schedule for completion is established.

7. Criteria and acceptable evidence for evaluation are specified.

8. A support network and reward structure is identified and agreed upon.

9. The contract is carried out and evaluated.

Sample learning contract

1. What you can expect to gain from the course
- knowledge of communication and helping skills
- ability to attend, observe, listen, and respond more accurately
- ability to express yourself more clearly and constructively
- increased awareness of your self, feelings, thoughts

2. What you can expect from the instructor
- to model the skills and qualities being taught so you can see how they work
- to lecture clearly so the skills and the theory can be understood
- to train you (in small groups) in the use of the skills
- to be available for consultation about personal concerns related to the course outside class (not long-term counseling)

3. What the course expects of you
- to attend all forty-five hours of the course; anyone absent for nine hours or more may be asked to take the course over
- to read assigned readings outside of class and complete the pre-discussion questions
- to participate in small groups and share some personal, but not deep, issues
- to practice skills outside of class

4. Grading criteria and procedures
If you do not want a grade
- you can choose to audit. As an audit student you pay fees, and attend classes, and participate fully, but are not required to submit a videotape for evaluation.

You can expect a "pass"
- if you demonstrate your skills in class

at the "C" level (described below); you are not required to do a videotape for final evaluation.

You can expect to receive an "A" if you are able to
- attend, observe, listen, and respond specifically (as described in the manual)
- help others personalize a problem (as described in the manual)
- demonstrate an overall understanding of the helping model presented in this course in a written essay exam
- help someone personalize a problem on the video final

You can expect to receive a "B" if you are able to
- attend, observe, listen, respond effectively (as described in the manual)
- demonstrate an overall understanding of the helping model presented in this course in a written essay exam (final)
- help someone personalize a problem on the video final

You can expect to receive a "C" if you are able to
- attend, observe and listen accurately and respond specifically to others in the class
- demonstrate an overall understanding of the helping model presented in this course in a written exam (final)

7

Working in groups

Buzz groups are the workhorse of interactive teaching. "Buzz" refers to the sound emitted by groups of adults concentrating on a task. Occasionally the label "Phillips 66" is used, acknowledging the colleague who first wrote about "small groups of six people working together for six minutes."

Buzz groups are spontaneously formed teams with a task to be accomplished in a short time. Their assignments may be about idea-generating, brainstorming, information-sharing, question-gathering, list-making, or problem-solving.

Typically, one person acts as recorder, noting and summarizing the group's output, and reporting to the larger group afterwards. The teacher stays out of the way, but monitors the progress of the groups and offers procedural guidance and content suggestions as needed.

Buzz groups are best used to:
- stimulate individual input
- break the ice at the outset
- warm up the class to a new topic
- measure previous knowledge and experience
- generate lists of questions
- gather opinions and identify preconceived ideas
- rank-order items to create an agenda
- obtain feedback on virtually any topic
- tackle a wide range of problems
- elicit ideas on classroom procedures
- ensure individual "air time," regardless of class size and time restraints

Group size

The size of a basic buzz group is best kept between three and six members. If groups are larger, members tend to seek smaller, less confusing subgroups. But even your largest class can be divided into several small groups; it's quite possible, for instance, to divide 120 people into 20 small groups and spread them across a meeting room.

Time required

Allow four to six minutes for the buzz, as well as time for your initial instructions, the grouping process, and subsequent reporting. As participants become better acquainted with this technique, they also become more efficient and very little time is wasted.

Materials needed

Depending on the reporting procedure (see step 9 below), each group may need newsprint, felt pens, and masking tape.

Room setup

If chairs are movable, ask learners to shift so they can face each other. If seats are fixed to the floor (in an auditorium), two to three people turn to those seated behind them to form buzz groups.

How to proceed

1. Explain the procedure.

Most adults are familiar with teacher-centered schooling, and they appreciate a few words of explanation whenever you ask them to become active participants. Be quite explicit in your introduction: "Now that I have laid out my plan for the day, I'd like to hear what you think. Since we are quite a large group it would take too long for everyone to be heard in turn, so let's do it in small groups. You'll be sitting with four or five other members for a few minutes to respond to a question I shall post. One of you will be the recorder and be asked to report to the large group on what you've each had to say. This way everybody will be heard, first in the small group, then by way of the recorder. How does that sound? Do you have any questions before we proceed?"

2. Form buzz groups.

Have participants turn to others sitting nearby and form groups of four to six. Give specific directions, such as "Turn to the people sitting near you," or "Get together with someone you know least," or "This time, I'd like you to team up with people who work in settings similar to yours." Initially, this grouping will take a bit of time, but don't let that deter you. The benefits of learner-involvement compensate for the time spent; adults become quite adept at choosing groups and on subsequent occasions groups are formed with little delay.

3. Describe the task.

The task must be something that can be accomplished in five or six minutes. If it is larger, divide it up and deal with each piece in turn. If, by design or accident, a task is larger than the time available, you'll

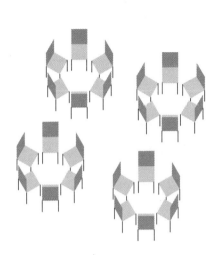

The space between people working together is filled with conflict, friction, strife, exhilaration, delight, and vast creative potential.

– Bruce Mau, designer.

AS A GROUP,

MAKE A LIST OF ITEMS THAT YOU'D LIKE TO ADD TO THE PROPOSED AGENDA.

THE RECORDER'S JOB
- Keep track of the group's output.
- Write it on a sheet of paper (for a verbal report) or in large print on newsprint (for posting).
- It's OK to abbreviate – but edit only with consent.
- Recorder can add his or her own comments.

have to think of ways to deal with the loose ends. With all the commotion in the room, it is best to write the task on the board, flip chart, or overhead. Leave it in plain view throughout the discussion; groups frequently refer to it to stay on track. Clear language is important, as in the example at left.

4. Specify a time limit.
Four to six minutes are typical time spans for small tasks. On average, each group member has a minute of air time. Anything less leads to crowding; anything longer invites tuning-out, wandering off topic, and social chit-chat. Time restraints help groups focus on the task. You must gauge this element carefully and expand and contract the time allowance to suit the task and the maturity of the participants.

5. Ask for recorders.
Suggest that each group select a recorder and explain the recorder's job.

6. Recommend a process.
This applies mainly to inexperienced groups. Following the previous example of agenda-building groups, ask participants to take a moment to introduce themselves, then go around the circle so that each person can state one item to be added to the agenda. Those who are satisfied with the existing agenda should say so. Then it's the next person's turn, until every member has had equal air time. If a group has spare time, go around again to catch additional ideas. Ask groups to assist their recorder in registering each contribution.

You may ask that recorders add contributors' names in brackets next to each item for future reference. To sharpen the focus on the task, you can further stipulate a specific number of items to be generated.

7. Monitor progress.
Circulate from group to group to unobtrusively listen in as they go about their work. This is not a time to relax: it is vital that you are alert to monitor each group's progress, ready to make brief interventions to steer groups and recorders towards the accomplishment of their task. But take care not to interfere too much, since a group quickly develops its own personality.

8. Act as timekeeper.
Time does fly when buzz groups get together. By announcing "half-way through" or "two minutes remaining" you help groups with their task and remind everyone of their share of air time. Should you sense that more time would be of benefit, feel free to announce a schedule change. Example: "You are all working so hard – please take an extra three minutes to complete the list. I remind each group member to

The questions-only rule

Suppose an individual was given the task of making a presentation to the group and is about to sit down to receive feedback. Or, in a different scenario, the class has expressed unhappiness about an aspect of course procedure. Instead of trying to "have a discussion," you and the class may benefit from experimenting with the "questions-only" rule. For a specified time period, anyone may ask any question of the "key witness" (the presenter, yourself, or another designated person), but may not give advice or suggestions. "The questions-only rule is radical," writes Parker Palmer, "We need ways to listen more openly to each other; to judge and advise and 'fix' each other much less; to find the strengths—not just the weaknesses—in each other's proposals; to leave each other feeling heard and affirmed as well as stretched and challenged when our conversations end." [1]

ensure that your views have been accurately recorded"; "If your group is already finished, please look over your list once more, and make any additions you think are important."

9. Invite the recorders to report.
If you are working with just a handful of groups, the simplest procedure is to ask one recorder after another to stand up and report. Alternatively, ask the recorders to post the summary sheets of their group's findings on a blank wall.

10. Process the information.
If you want people's input, you need to acknowledge their contributions and then act on them. In the agenda-building example we have used here, the negotiations could now center on incorporating the learners' agendas with that of the teacher.

Variations

Multiple uses for buzz groups

- Buzz groups can be used as a warmup with new groups. Ask group members to first introduce themselves and then share one or two expectations for the course. This serves as a starting point for a discussion on what is desirable and possible to accomplish. Adults appreciate being involved from the outset and in having a say in how time is spent.

- Use buzz groups prior to a lecture. Buzz groups can tell you what's already known about the topic, what people expect to learn, and which aspects are of particular interest.

- Intersperse a lecture with buzz groups to foster comprehension and bring out questions.

- Conclude a lecture by asking groups to integrate new information with previous learning. They can be asked to identify remaining problem areas or explore practical applications of theoretical material.

- Preceding or following a complex course component, ask buzz groups to collect questions and issues that need clarification.

- Buzz groups are an ideal vehicle for various assessments. In a supportive climate, people will make constructive comments on course content and instructor performance, as long as there is a safe way to do this. Working in small groups, free-style or with an evaluation form, participants can provide valuable information – without having to face the teacher directly. Recorders, speaking on behalf of others, are more at ease in reporting sensitive information.

Reporting techniques

- Not all groups need to report individually, only those who have something new to contribute. This reduces repetition and encourages enthusiastic participation the next time you ask the class to work in groups.

- If the task involves list-making, ask groups to collect their ideas first, and then rank the items in some order – by importance or urgency, for example. During subsequent reporting and action-planning, rankings simplify the processing.

- Have recorders report only one point per turn. This avoids situations where the first group reports the bulk of the information, preventing others from contributing.

- Ask various recorders to post their reports side-by-side on a wall. Have recorders briefly describe their lists, elaborate as necessary, and answer questions from the audience. It'll be hard work for them. Ask them to skip items that have already been mentioned. Throughout, you act as process consultant – let the group do the work.

- Reverse the flow of information: instead of taking it to the group at large, have participants circulate from posting to posting. Ask that one member stay behind and act as interpreter. After participants have had time to check out other lists, they return to their own.

There they briefly report what they have learned and then make any changes and additions to their own work. Conclude this round by asking for verbal reports on significant learnings.[2]

Group size

Asking participants to arrange themselves into small groups is easily said, but the novice participant may be hesitant or uncertain and hold back. However, if handled with some sensitivity, small-group activities yield valuable benefits in the form of increased participation and commitment.

Small-group activities offer several advantages. While lectures and other instructor-centered activities invite learner passivity, small-group tasks require and encourage active engagement of all participants. In small groups people have less chance to hide or get lost.

Researchers have found that participants tend to speak more freely in small groups than in large ones; that in large groups people feel little or no personal responsibility for the success of the course; and that participating in small-group tasks increases individual commitment dramatically.

- **Two people (dyads)**
  This size of group works only with people who know and trust each other. Members tend to feel intensely responsible to one another, avoid expressing disagreement or antagonism, and feel obliged to adjust to the other's preferences and style of behavior. If one member withdraws, the group becomes ineffective.

- **Three people (triads)**
  This is the minimum-sized group where a coalition can form; the group can still function (as a diad) if one member withdraws or does not cooperate. Creative and innovative ideas are more likely to develop here than in a group of two.

- **Two to five people (small groups)**
  From all indications this is the ideal size for task-oriented groups.

- **Six to ten people (medium-sized groups)**
  Once a group exceeds five members, there is a tendency for subgroups to form and go off on tangents. Participants may then complain of a lack of coordination, insufficient opportunity to have a say, and poor use of time. Accomplishments tend to be of poorer quality. Face-to-face interactions and the care and consideration that are associated with them become difficult if there are more than eight people. Personal statements are not made, and people tend to experience less personal satisfaction and involvement with the group's activities.

Small-group dynamics

M. E. Shaw[3], after searching the literature on small group behavior, reported the following.

- **Seating arrangements**
  People followed the person across from them in speaking more often than those in any other position.

- **Table shapes**
  Interesting behavior was observed with rectangular tables. Those sitting at the two ends of the table participated more than others in the group.

- **Eye contact**
  The possibility of having eye contact with group members tends to increase interaction, regardless of relative seating distance. Women communicate with eye contact more frequently than men.

- **Leadership**
  The probability that a leader will emerge increases with increasing group size. The individual with special skills relating to the group task is usually more active in the group, makes more contributions towards the task, and has more influence on group decisions. The anxious group member inhibits group functioning, and (you guessed it) the well-adjusted member contributes to the group's functioning.

- **Age**
  Social participation increases with increasing chronological age. Group leaders tend to be older than other group members; there is a slight tendency for physically superior individuals to become leaders.

8

Delivering lively lectures

The teacher's words are like fingers pointing to the moon. If you watch the fingers, you won't see the moon.

– Buddhist saying.

Why does lecturing have such a poor reputation? You probably have your own recollection of past events: boring, inefficient, a waste of time. Just a few are remembered favorably: they captured our imagination, stimulated our thinking, and propelled us to explore the topic on our own. The content of others, less helpful and downright annoying, we have long forgotten, although the memory lingers. Yet, in spite of its controversial reputation, the lecture remains the mainstay of educational practice.

Few instructors seem to be comfortable with lecturing, and even fewer adult participants look forward to it; it is simply endured as part of classroom learning. Yet we also know that a good presentation can bring even the most complicated or dry subject to life and turn passive listeners into active participants. So, what do we need to understand about this technique, in order to turn dreaded lectures into delightful discourses?

Best use of the lecture

Institutional traditions often suggest that you use the lecture as the primary teaching technique. Before you automatically succumb to these expectations, be sure that it's the best method for the task. The lecture's best uses are in the following situations:

- To establish the general outlines of your subject matter. Use the lecture to provide an overview of the topic.

- To arouse interest in a topic. Use it to share your general enthusiasm for the subject. Make important connections between the students' needs, your own interests, and the topic. Show how the participants might benefit from a further exploration of the material.

- To demonstrate how to approach a field of study and make sense of much data. By the structure of your lecture and the way you present your material, you show participants how to deal with a vast body of information.

- To provide information. If you are clear on the learning needs of your audience and present information with clarity and enthusiasm, the lecture may be the most efficient method.

- To mix passive and active techniques. Listening to someone speak to a large group for an extended period of time is essentially a passive activity. The average attention span in such a setting has been estimated at somewhere between twelve and twenty minutes.[1] Even if your schedule calls for a one-hour lecture, you are still free to cut it into short segments peppered with some of the involvement techniques mentioned in this book.

When not to lecture

The lecture is of limited value if students are expected to master complex, abstract, or very detailed material. The lecture also has limitations when dealing with matters pertaining to participants' feelings and attitudes. It can be used to describe and argue such matters theoretically and give the lecturer a chance to share personal experiences, but it does not allow for individual interaction.

What students expect from us

When asked for their opinions on lecturers,[2] adult learners tell us that they look for someone who can:

- demonstrate knowledge of the topic
- follow a well-organized presentation
- capture and hold attention
- use relevant examples and applications
- show genuine enthusiasm
- involve the audience, directly or indirectly
- respond to questions with respect
- use humor

The AIDA format makes it easy to address most of these points.[3] The acronym stands for "attention," "interest," "desire," and "action."

To gain the group's *attention*, allow a few minutes at the outset of the lecture for people to settle in. Begin right away to establish your competence as speaker as well as content specialist. Restate the topic of the lecture and outline your plan for the amount of time you have allotted. If applicable, spell out learning objectives and make reference to previous materials and events. A story, an anecdote, a cartoon, or a startling statistic can all help to draw attention to you and your presentation.

Teachers as actors

To distinguish good from poor, Californian researchers arranged for regular teachers as well as briefed actors to give a series of college lectures. Students were unaware of the experiment, and when end-of-term results were compared, those taught by the actors did better than those with regular teachers. Another study, at Tel Aviv University, showed that in courses taught by professors who had been coached to use humor, students fared 15 percent better on exams than their colleagues in laugh-free classrooms.

Next, get the group *interested* in what you have to say, by showing the relevance of your presentation to their situation. Offer a preview and touch on highlights of things to come. Address unspoken questions about content and procedures. Why is this important? What are the qualifications of the lecturer? What can I expect to learn? What is expected of me? Will we be able to ask questions? What else will we do during this session? Will there be a break? Should I take notes?

The *desire* part of AIDA alludes to your personal commitment to the topic and how you present it. This is reflected in the thoroughness of your preparation, the use of visuals, relevant examples, and your enthusiasm. The latter is conveyed especially by your alert posture, sweeping eye contact, timing, and use of voice. Ignite participants' desire by making repeated connections between your material and their knowledge and experience.

Once you preach, the point is gone.

– Zen saying.

Finally, *action* describes the way you act before the group. Be conscious of the standards you set by being prompt, prepared, organized, attentive, respectful, sensitive, and honest. You can encourage learners to take an active role in several ways:[4]

- Interrupt the lecture to ask for examples of the concepts you have presented or answer spot quiz questions.
- Ask them to briefly turn to their neighbors to compare notes, pool questions, solve puzzles, and teach each other.
- Assign specific listening tasks to individuals or small groups. Following a lecture segment, teams gather to share concerns, generate questions, and work on applications.
- Lecture for a while, then stop. Pose a case study and invite small groups to analyze it in the context of the material you have just presented.

Time required

Experience suggests that no lecture should last longer than thirty minutes. In other words, try to limit your straight lecturing to between twenty and thirty minutes. At that point utilize any technique that requires participants to switch from passive to active behavior, from listening to doing. There is no reason why you could not have a one- or even two-hour lecture, as long as you mix up the techniques and keep your participants involved.

Variation

A *lecturette* is a short lecture lasting not more than ten minutes. It is a handy way to break a complex topic into several small ones, interspersing other learning activities to aid in understanding and comprehension. If this variation appeals to you, but you aren't sure that you can stick to the ten-minute limitation, try something that's worked for me. Set a kitchen timer, place it in full view of the group, and explain what you are attempting. By letting your group in on the experiment, you not only get their attention, but also involve them in the mechanics of teaching.

Materials needed

None for the lecture, unless you think visual aids would help you make the point better.

Room setup

Each participant should have a full view of the lecturer. You can enhance this by moving around, either on the designated platform or throughout the room.

Nine ways to renovate your lectures

1. Set limits.
Limit the scope of the lecture: six major points are enough for half an hour.

2. Outline your plan.
Specify what you plan to cover, how long it will take, and how you plan to proceed. This helps participants anticipate events, prepare for change in technique, and allot their energy accordingly.

3. Provide summaries.
At the beginning, the end, and occasionally in the middle, pause to give listeners a chance to catch up and summarize for themselves.

4. Use visual supports.
Use flip charts, overheads, skits, models, demonstrations, and critical incidents to grab learners' attention and support your points.

5. Utilize handouts.
Save time and disruptions when handing out materials. Instead of one sheet at a time, give it all out at once, with pages numbered or color-coded. Or situate materials in strategic spots and, on your request, ask volunteers to distribute to their group or row of seats.

6. Pace yourself.
Adjust your rate of speaking and choose your vocabulary to fit the experience level of your group. Build in checks to see if everybody understands the points you are making. Do this by asking questions, posing hypothetical cases, or assigning small-group tasks.

7. Keep 'em interested.
Mix activities so that students can be alternately passive (sit, hear, see) and active (problem-solve, write, construct, discuss, move, walk, speak, operate equipment).

8. Sequence deliberately.
Structure material in a logical way: go from the general to the specific, the simple to the complex, the old to the unfamiliar. And every so often – just to keep everyone from becoming stale – reverse this order.

9. Attend to questions.
Clearly state how and when questions will be dealt with. Do you want to hear questions any time something is unclear or do you want them held until you ask for them? You might suggest that participants jot down their questions and raise them at a designated time. But if you say you'll handle questions, do so and allow sufficient time

Just how funny are you?

Used at the right moment and without giving offence, humor certainly lightens up the day. I don't tell jokes, but rely on situational humor and anecdotes to connect with my audience. Humor research (yes!) is inconclusive on the beneficial effects of humor on learning and retention, but "appropriate self-disparaging humor" can reduce students' anxiety by letting them know that the teacher is human and fallible.[6]

Communications professor Charles Gruner suggests that humor may increase your "character" rating, but have little impact on the "authoritativeness" of what you say. If you think you have a good joke or anecdote, he offers this test. Unless you can say "yes" to every question, cut it out![7]

- *Will it fit the subject and mood of my lecture?*

- *Will every person feel comfortable with it?*

- *Is it fresh, short, and uncomplicated?*

- *Can I deliver it with confidence and perfect timing?*

Spirited question-and-answer sessions

When addressing large groups, the opportunities for individual attention are limited ... until you get to questions. Here are some tips used by seasoned speakers:[5]

- Take questions from all parts of the room. Don't restrict yourself to people sitting in the front row. Don't let special interest groups monopolize you.

- Listen carefully to each question. Don't frown or smile as you listen – reserve your response until you answer.

- Mind your body language. Avoid motions that might convey uncertainty or lack of interest. Try not to show your approval or disapproval of the questioner's viewpoint or manner of asking.

- Look at each questioner until you understand the question, then direct your answer to the whole audience. This keeps you from getting stuck in an exchange with just one person and invites others to join in.

- Treat each questioner as equal. Avoid the "Good question!" compliment; however sincere, it suggests that you are evaluating the quality of the question and some are better than others. Show respect and curiosity for each question. You did ask for them!

- Repeat questions in full or at least paraphrase them. This ensures that you have understood, gives others a chance to fully hear it, and even gives you a moment to collect your thoughts.

- Respond simply and directly. Use the time to clarify and reinforce points you made during the lecture, not to make impromptu speeches or major additions. If the questions go too far off the topic, state limitations to refocus the group. If questions are slow in coming, be prepared to prime the pump – or move on to other activities.

- Encourage questions right up to the time limit, but avoid saying, "We have time for one more question." If it turns out to be a difficult one or one that raises important further points, you'd end on a "down" tone. Instead, choose a question and answer that makes a good ending and simply end there.

- Use buzz groups. If you are working with a large audience and you expect more questions than time permits, consider asking people to turn to their neighbors and form groups of three to four. Ask them to quickly pool their questions on a piece of paper and assign a priority rating to the list. One person acts as spokesperson for each group, raising one question at a time. Group by group, you ask for their next-most-important question. Those already posed by others are deleted from the list as you proceed.

How to get everyone's attention

- Change your position. Move around, speak from the back of the room, the front, the left or the right of the room. I have been known to stand on top of a table to make a point.

- Use gestures. Hand, head, and body movements can serve as supporters (and distracters) for verbal output.

- Focus attention. Say something like, "I was shocked to read that …," or, "Look at this peculiar graph …."

- Vary the style of interaction. Use questions, student-student interactions, buzz groups, demonstrations, problem-solving, tasks, discussions.

- Let silence work for you. Use it to encourage reflection, question formulation, and concentration.

- Change tempo. With voice tone, volume, and speed, fluctuate between loud and mellow, fast and slow, happy and sad, matter-of-fact and personal, fluent and hesitant.

A public speaker is one who talks in someone else's sleep.

– Hugh Auden

Please take notes

"Fill in the blanks" is a useful way to assist learners in note-taking and ensure that they focus on your main points. As you make your important points, participants can fill in the blanks on the handout you have prepared. They learn by seeing and hearing as you speak, but also by repeating in writing.

Fill in the blanks

Topic: Managing Conflict

Principles:

    1. Conflict is _____.

    2. Conflict can be desirable when it is _____.

    3. Uncontrolled conflict is

    _____.

Controlled Conflict:

    1. Deal with conflict _____.

    2. Identify the _____ problem.

    3. Handle _____.

    4. Consider the _____ traits involved.

    5. Ask for _____ and proposed solutions.

    6. Avoid _____, use logic.

    7. Think it _____.

    8. Schedule a _____ session.

Contributed by Susan Reuthe.

9

Asking beautiful questions

*Always the beautiful
answer
who asks a more beautiful
question.*

– e.e. cummings

John Dewey has said that the aim of education must be "the formation of careful, alert, and thorough habits of thinking." The best questions, those that are truly instructive, are formulated with care and posed with sensitivity. In this section you'll find some essential dos and don'ts, along with proven techniques to assist you in developing your questioning skills.

The best question has as its primary goal the promotion of thinking. As the ancient proverb states:

> I hear, I forget.
> I see, I remember.
> I do, I understand.
> I think, I learn.

In one study, researchers found that two-thirds of the questions asked in a typical classroom required only recitation of a memorized text as a satisfactory answer. A subsequent investigation concluded that the overwhelming proportion of questions asked by college professors were on the memory level. The first study was conducted in 1912 and the second, more than seventy years later.[1] Apparently little has changed. Through the ages, most teachers have asked rote questions designed to get the "right" answer, to "cover the text," and "prepare students for exams."

When we become teachers ourselves, we often draw on our own educational experiences for guidance. And since most of our teachers (in schools and on the job) rewarded the "right answer" above all else, trainers and adult educators unconsciously continue that tradition. Can we break the mold? Yes, if we have the courage and the stamina. The tools have been around for at least forty years. In 1956 Benjamin Bloom and his associates published a six-level model for use with achievement tests and classroom questions.[2] They proposed a taxonomy with six cognitive (thinking) operations arranged in a hierarchy, each level subsuming those preceding it. Here they are, in ascending order. Use them to vary the complexity of your questions.

Level 1: Knowledge – the ability to remember material previously learned.

Level 2: Comprehension – the ability to grasp the meaning of material.

Level 3: Application – the ability to use learned material in new, concrete situations.

Level 4: Analysis – the ability to break down material into its components so that its organizational structure can be understood.

Level 5: Synthesis – the ability to put parts together to form a new whole.

Level 6: Evaluation – the ability to judge the value of material for a given purpose.

My greatest strength as a consultant is to be ignorant and ask a few questions.

– Peter Drucker

Lecturing usually covers the material faster than the more ponderous asking of questions. But questioning shifts the focus from teacher to learners; instead of monopolizing discussions, the teacher becomes a facilitator and participants gradually increase responsibility for their own learning.

One colleague, after experimenting with higher-order questioning, reported that his learners "pay attention; they listen to each other and give answers that show that they are thinking about what they are going to say. I find that the quality of their questioning has also improved; they seem to have a better understanding of the concepts and are showing improvements in tests and written work."[3]

Questions about questions ... with answers by Dr. Scott Parry[4]

The way you ask a question has a lot to do with the answer you get. For a group to work together effectively, everyone's ideas must be heard. Effective questioning is a necessary skill for facilitating a training seminar. To get everyone involved and learning, you have to know what to ask, how, and of whom. You have to know how to give every learner a chance to come up with her or his own solutions.

Questions are one of your most valuable tools – for making points, for assessing understanding, for arousing interest, and for testing understanding. Most trainers would agree. Still, many are uncomfortable using questions as a means of converting lectures to dialogues. Here are the answers to some of the most common questions about questions.

• **Is it better to call on participants by name or ask "overhead questions" and hope for volunteers?**

If you are trying to create a free flow of conversation and dialogue between learners and instructor, then it's better not to call on individuals

by name. Naming a respondent in advance can have several negative effects.
- The person may be embarrassed.
- Someone else may be better qualified to answer and thus be of greater benefit to the group.
- Others may feel that they are "off the hook" and may not think through their own answers.
- The climate may become one of classroom recitation, a "parent-to-child" series of transactions in which the instructor plays the role of judge.

An effective teacher can call on participants by name without encountering any of those negative side effects. One way is to let a person know why you're calling on her or him in particular. Example: Sandy, I know you've had some experience with this problem at your location. What do you think about this?

The danger of hoping for volunteers, of course, is that you may get none – or that the same people will respond, leaving the silent majority behind, not contributing and perhaps even resentful.

- **How do you get learners involved who never volunteer? What about that silent majority who see learning as a passive activity – a spectator sport?**

The much-cited 20/80 ratio probably applies to classroom behavior as well as to so many other phenomena. Namely, 80 percent of volunteered responses come from 20 percent of the learners. In a class of twenty people, the same three or four people may be answering all the time. Since people learn best by being actively involved, you want everyone to respond. How can you accomplish that?

There are many ways. After you've posed a question, have people turn to their neighbors and respond to them. On short answers, have each person write his or her response on notepaper, then discuss the responses. On polarized issues (on which the responses are yes/no, more/less, and so forth), ask for a show of hands for each response. Once you've broken the ice with such techniques, learners will be more willing to volunteer.

- **Is it a good idea to repeat participants' questions to make sure everybody understood?**

In general, yes, although repeating every question can become tiresome. Most questions shouldn't need repeating. But if the question was not worded clearly, was spoken too softly for everyone to hear, or came "out of the blue," then it may be a good idea to repeat it.

Formulate your questions so they demand longish answers. By referring to areas of knowledge – rather than simple facts – you encourage more than yes and no answers.

– Peter Renner

- **How should I deal with someone who has just given me a wrong answer, especially if the person has rank or status in the group? I'm thinking of the regional manager attending a local management seminar, or someone who's the in-house expert on the topic.**

There are two issues here. First, those with rank or status have no corner on the market when it comes to intelligence or understanding. Everyone in your class is entitled to make mistakes and have misconceptions. By the same token, everyone is entitled to respect; it is the instructor's job to "save face" for everyone.

If someone provides a wrong answer, it may be an indication that others are having difficulty. It's not likely that you picked the only person who did not understand. You may want to turn to the group after a wrong answer and ask, "How do the rest of you feel about Jackie's response? Is your own answer similar?" Such neutral wording will let you know how widespread the problem is, and may get another person who has an acceptable answer to explain the reasoning behind it to Jackie and anyone else who is having trouble. That relieves you from always being the one to correct wrong answers and gets your trainees to view one another as resources.

- **Sometimes I just don't understand an answer enough to know whether it's right. What should I do in such cases?**

You have several options:
- Tell the respondent that you don't understand what she or he is saying; ask the person to word it differently.
- If you think you understand some of what the trainee is saying, try restating it. The respondent will step in with clarification as needed.
- Ask the rest of the group for help: "Do all of you understand Thomas's response? I'm not sure I do. Can someone interpret it for me?"

- **What if someone takes forever to answer, is repetitive, rambling, or has trouble organizing his or her thoughts?**

Allow a reasonable time to organize an answer. If you see that the person is in trouble and that you're wasting group time, you may want to interrupt and summarize: "Let me see, Chris, if I understand what you're saying. You feel that ..." If you are at a loss to understand Chris well enough to attempt a summary, you may want to ask the group, "Can someone summarize Chris's response?" Or, you might simply interrupt, thank Chris, and say, "I'd like to get answers from several people on this question, since it's a difficult one."

React to "false" answers with acceptance, even if you had hoped for a different response. Do everything, short of giving the "right" answer, to lead the learner to the solution.

– based on the teachings of Lao Tzu.

- **What if no one answers my question?**

  Let's examine some of the possible reasons:

  - The question may have been so obvious or simple that no one wants to look like the class idiot by answering it.
  - You may not have broken the ice yet, in which case you may want to try some of the techniques discussed earlier in this section.
  - It's possible that no one knows the answer, in which case the question was premature or your instruction was inadequate.
  - Perhaps no one understood the question. You might say, "Do you understand what I'm asking?" Ask trainees why this question seems to be giving them trouble. Or try rephrasing the question, which gives them new wording and additional time to think through the answer.

- **How should I deal with a learner who asks irrelevant questions that interfere with the flow of my instruction?**

  If a question can be answered in a sentence or so, it might be easier to deal with the question rather than with the disruptive behavior. If the questions are making it hard for the other participants and you to keep on track, you might say, "I'm not sure how your question relates to the point we've been discussing ... Can you make the link for us?" This gives the person a chance to explain the relevance or graciously drop the question altogether.

- **What if a learner asks a question that is irrelevant but of great interest to the group, or a question that will be addressed later in the course but that is premature at this point?**

  Sometimes a learner's question may be irrelevant or disruptive to you but of interest to the group (for example, a gripe they all have or a hidden agenda that is now exposed). At the beginning of the session, you might tape a sheet of flip-chart paper to the wall and give it the heading, "To be taken up later" or "Things to do."

  As people ask questions that you'll be dealing with in subsequent sessions, you can write reminder notes for all to see. Sometimes participants bring up questions of a policy nature that you'll want to check with someone in authority before answering. The chart buys you time to do so.

  If you've shared the schedule and the course objectives with the participants in advance, you're less likely to get irrelevant or premature questions. When you do, you can simply refer to the posted schedule or to the objectives.

The way a problem is posed determines the way in which it is solved.

– Daniel D. Pratt

THINGS TO DO:

- •
- •
- •
- •

- **If no one else answers, is there anything wrong with me answering my own question?**

  If you asked the question to test understanding or to get the group's input, you're defeating your purpose by answering it yourself. Learners' failure to answer is a symptom, and you should try to analyze the problem underlying it. Was your question understood? Was it relevant? Do they know the answer?

  Many teachers feel embarrassed if no one answers within a few seconds. You may have to wait five to ten seconds for an answer, especially to a complex question. Rephrase it to increase understanding of what you want. This also gives participants more time to think through their answers. If no one volunteers, ask trainees to turn to their neighbors and discuss their answers. You can then circulate, listening in on a half-dozen answers to find out where the group had trouble with your initial question.

- **What if I don't know the answer to a question? Doesn't that cause a loss of credibility?**

  You'll lose more credibility by trying to bluff an answer than by stating that you don't know it but will try to find out before the next class. You might ask the group if anyone knows the answer. It's far more important to be a good facilitator than to be the one with all the answers.

- **How should I deal with someone who asks a question that is really a statement of opinion?**

  One of the most common ways a participant will try to make a point is by asking a question. Such questions often begin with wording like, "Don't you think that the best way to ...." When you recognize that someone is really expressing an opinion or making a point, it's a good idea to throw it back to her or him: "That's a good question, Lee. What do you think?" In short, give the trainee the chance to make the point. Don't take it away by answering the question yourself or by throwing it to the group.

- **What if someone asks a question about something I covered ten minutes earlier? Should I take the time to answer?**

  That depends. You might acknowledge for the group's benefit that you discussed the subject earlier, and reiterate the question. Ask if anyone else is having trouble. If no one is, you have a good reason to suggest that the learner see you during the break. Of course, if the question can be answered in half a minute or so, it's easier to do so and not make an issue of it.

It is better to have enough ideas for some of them to be wrong, than to be always right by having no ideas at all.

– Edward de Bono

There are some questions Donald Fairbairn calls "the seven deadly sins."[5] You'll probably recognize them from your own experience; they all seem legitimate, but not all challenge adult learners to think. These examples from my wine-appreciation course illustrate the seven types.

1. Factual and yes-no questions

Name three wine districts in Burgundy.

Which grape variety is legally permitted for the making of French Chablis?

This is probably the most common question type; unfortunately, it relegates learners to guessing and reciting. To reveal understanding, rephrase the question: If a customer asked you to explain the difference between a French and a Californian Chablis, what would you say?

2. Overlaid or multiple questions

Which two districts produce more **vin ordinaire** than any other and how much of it is turned into industrial alcohol?

This question asks for too much at once and confuses the listener. Even someone with the correct information can easily get muddled trying to respond to both issues. And if the question were divided into two separate ones, it still doesn't require more than the reciting of facts. How about a rephrasing that asks for a sifting of facts and an informed opinion: Why do you think so much wine ends up as industrial alcohol?

3. Ambiguous questions

Which wines are the best for everyday consumption?

Which are better, corks or screw caps?

Similar to the previous type, these questions confuse by being unclear. When asking for opinions and judgments, we must also provide criteria for such assessments. How about: What are the advantages of a screw cap from a consumer's point of view?

4. Chorus response questions

OK class, name the eleven German wine-growing regions, from the largest one down.

How do we pronounce the place name on this label?

No real harm is done, but such questions hardly challenge anyone to think, only to recite in the midst of other voices.

5. Leading questions

Which one is likely to be more expensive, a regional blend or a wine bottled by a château?

Watch me pull this cork. It doesn't matter whether I first remove the capsule, does it?

Objection, Your Honor, my learned friend is leading the witness. If you really want to determine what someone does or does not know, ask them! Otherwise, expect obliging replies that prove little in terms of individual understanding. They may also be seen as condescending by some and work against the positive effect of question-asking.

6. Ambush questions

The wine maker determines potential alcohol content by dividing the amount of grape sugar ... by what?

These start out as statements and suddenly become questions, catching participants off-guard. The disconcerting aspect of such questions is their sudden appearance when least expected. One moment participants listen passively to an explanation, the next they are expected to participate. It's much better to provide the explanation first and then, distinctly separately, pose the question.

7. Teacher-pleasing questions

What are we going to talk about tonight?

Who knows why I have selected these wines for tonight's tasting?

Some would argue that such questions, similar to most of the above, cause no harm. Perhaps. But adult education should be about making students think. Asking questions affords precious opportunities to detect areas of confusion and to flush out misunderstanding. Answering them provides participants with a clear sense of progress and accomplishment.

- **What if participants don't accept my answer and are fighting it? This often happens when I'm teaching company policy or procedures.**

  Don't take sides by either defending or knocking the organization. Simply acknowledge that what you're explaining may not be popular, but that it is the way things are. If you know in advance that you'll be facing resistance, it's good to have the responsible persons there to explain and sell the new things you're teaching. You may jeopardize your effectiveness as an instructor if you question or defend your content. If the answer that is being resisted is not a matter of policy or procedure, you might try asking for help from the group. "Has anyone tried the technique I'm describing? What's been your experience?" Or, you may be able to relate a personal experience in which you found it useful to do what you just described in your answer.

  In certain types of courses, you may want to state at the start that some of the suggestions and answers you'll be sharing won't be appropriate or acceptable to everyone. It is the job of each learner to select what is relevant and reject what isn't. Once you've said that, you can easily deal with participants who are fighting you: simply point out that if your answer isn't relevant, they shouldn't act on it.

F U N D A M E N T A L S

The inquiry method

The teacher's attitudes and beliefs have a strong influence on the composition of the learning environment, write Neil Postman and Charles Weingartner.[6] Their six principles show how to create a climate of inquiry in your classroom.

- *Principle #1: Rarely tell students what you think they ought to know. Telling as the main mode of instructing deprives the learner of the excitement and opportunity of self-directed and powerful learning.*

- *Principle #2: Use questioning as your major method of interacting. Rather than trying to seduce participants into reciting what you (or some other authority) consider the right answers,*

use questions as instruments that can open minds to unexpected possibilities.

- *Principle #3: Generally, don't accept a single statement as an answer to a question – not because you prefer right answers, but because too often the "right answer" only serves to discourage further thought.*

- *Principle #4: Encourage student-student interaction as opposed to teacher-student interaction. Aim to minimize your role as the sole arbiter of what is acceptable and what is not.*

- *Principle #5: Rarely sum up the position taken by a participant. Instead, see learning as a process, not a finished product. There's a danger that your*

"closures" will deter others from developing and expressing further thought.

- *Principle #6: Measure your own success in terms of behavioral changes in the learners. Do this by observing the frequency with which they ask questions; the increase in relevance of their questions; the frequency and conviction of their challenges to statements by others, yourself, or the text. Look also at their willingness to modify their positions when new data warrants it; their increased ability to observe, classify, generalize, and apply the results in an original way.*

10

Flexing learning styles

What would happen if in your workshop "not knowing" and "not understanding" were considered honorable behaviors?

– Peter Renner

"As a result of our hereditary equipment, our life experience, and the demands of our present environment, most people develop learning styles that emphasize some learning abilities over others," writes educational psychologist David Kolb. He and his research colleagues have developed the experiential learning model and the Learning Style Inventory.[1]

A bit of theory

Kolb makes three assumptions about experiential learning. First, the experiential learning cycle occurs continuously and a learner repeatedly tests concepts in daily experiences in order to confirm or modify them as a result of reflection on the experience. Therefore, all learning becomes relearning and all education, reeducation.

Second, Kolb believes the direction learning takes is governed by a person's needs and goals. We seek experiences that are related to our goals, interpret them in the light of these goals, and form concepts (and test the implication of these concepts) that are relevant to our felt needs and goals. Therefore, when educational objectives are unclear, the process of learning is erratic and inefficient.

Third, since the individual learning process is directed by goals and needs, learning styles become highly individual in both direction and process.

Each person develops a personal learning style that has weak and strong points. We may be ready to jump into new experiences, but fail to observe the lessons to be learned. We may be good at forming theoretical concepts, but fail to test their validity. The ability to analyze learning styles can be useful – or even crucial – to those involved in a variety of educational fields, including course design, personalized coaching, team building, and personal development.

Four learning styles

Several theorists have developed instruments that purport to assess an individual's unique style. Kolb's Learning Style Inventory (LSI) is probably the most widely used device; it helps to identify a person's preference for certain learning behavior, grouping the behavior into four statistically different styles.

- **Converger.** People who rate high on this style do best in activities that require the practical application of ideas. As they focus on specific problems, they organize knowledge through hypothetical deductive reasoning. Research has shown Convergers to be relatively unemotional, preferring to work with things rather than people, and having narrow technical interests, generally choosing to specialize in engineering and physical sciences.

- **Diverger.** Persons with this as their preferred style draw on imaginative aptitude and the ability to view complex situations from many perspectives. A Diverger performs well in brainstorming sessions and tends to be interested in people. With broad cultural interests – often specializing in the arts – counselors, personnel managers, and sociologists tend to have this as their preferred style.

- **Assimilator.** Persons with this as their preferred style excel in the creation of theoretical models and inductive reasoning. Although concerned with the practical use of theories, they consider it more important that the theory be logically sound; and if the theory does not fit the "facts," then they must be reexamined. This learning style is more characteristic of persons in the theoretical sciences and mathematics than the applied sciences.

- **Accommodator.** The strength of the Accommodator style lies in doing things and getting fully involved in new experiences. Quite the opposite of the Assimilator, this person excels in situations calling for theory application to specific circumstances; but if a plan or theoretical explanation does not fit the situation, the Accommodator will discard it. Problems are approached in an intuitive, trial-and-error manner. The Accommodator is at ease with people and often found in action-oriented jobs in business, marketing, or sales.

A word of caution

Many researchers, David Kolb included, warn against the use of any self-reporting instruments for the categorization of individual styles.[2] Neat classifications have their attractions, but no instrument is absolutely reliable. It is important not to typecast people into one style. Most people operate with a combination of styles, depending on circumstances. However, we can make good use of test scores as indicators of preferred style.

Practical applications

If we want to find out how learners differ from each other, we usually rely on common sense, intuition, feedback from participants, and consultations with colleagues. However, learning-style data offers some interesting possibilities.

- Team-building tool

Instruments can be used as projective devices during trouble-shooting and team-building sessions. Instead of relying on the scores, use individual survey questions as discussion starters and to address interpersonal conflicts.

- Ice-breaker

To draw attention to individual differences, use a learning styles inventory as a warmup activity. Right from the start, the focus is on learning, on styles, and on ways each person can contribute to the group.

- Part of a needs analysis

Consider sending an instrument to potential participants and incorporate the results in the course design. Ask respondents also to indicate their preference for types of learning activities (rate your favorite classroom activities on a scale from one to five: lecture, discussions, individual projects, etc.).

- Aid to course planning

You can use individual or averaged group scores to custom-tailor certain learning activities for groups of like-minded participants. Or you can deliberately mismatch individuals with activities that will cause them to "stretch" their underdeveloped styles.

Our challenge

We can safely say that different people prefer to learn in different ways. Adult educators must design learning activities in which participants can develop a full range of learning styles.

The experiential learning cycle

David Kolb, a developmental psychologist, suggests we look at adult learning as an experiential process. According to Kolb, learning is a four-stage cycle.[3]

Concrete
experiences

Observations
and
reflections

Formation of abstract
concepts and
generalizations

Testing implications
of concepts in new
situations

To be fully effective, a learner must develop four interrelated abilities. The teacher's job is to provide conditions that enable learners to ...

- become fully involved in an experience
- observe and reflect on the experience from many perspectives
- create concepts to integrate these observations into logically sound theories
- use these theories to make decisions and solve problems

To illustrate Kolb's model, let's follow a part-time student enroled in a criminology course through the stages of a project.

• Concrete experience.

As her task, she arranged to spend "A Day in the Life" of a homeless person. During the experience, she kept a written journal, interviewed street people on tape, and captured her impressions with quick pencil sketches.

• Observation and reflection.

The next morning, she reviewed her notes with the help of reflective questions provided by the teacher. (What happened? Describe five specific events that illustrate the life of a street person. What was your biggest surprise? How did you feel when you went home – to your own bed?)

• Conceptualization and generalization.

She subsequently met with a support group comprised of fellow students with similar experiences. Using a debriefing sheet previously designed in class, they shared their experiences and began to make connections between their field

experience and theoretical materials. (How does your experience support or contradict your concepts of crime and poverty? Based on your experience, to what extent are the needs of your population understood and provided for by civic authorities?)

• Testing implications in a new situation.

On a subsequent field visit, she met with a social planner for the city to find out about services currently provided. Having learned about staffing and budget restraints, she met with her teacher with an idea for a new experience. She wanted to sound out several street people about the possibilities of forming a self-help group. The teacher pointed out relevant literature on the topic and suggested that the student meet with experienced street workers and members of a special policing unit in the downtown area.

And so a new concrete experience began ...

11

Observing group behavior

When working on group assignments, people tend to behave in one of three patterns. One type of behavior helps the group to accomplish its assigned task; another serves to create cooperation and support; the third is focused on individual needs.

If you plan to utilize small-group activities, reserve some time up front to discuss these behaviors. Ideally, schedule this session early in the program, before anyone has had much opportunity to display any of these behaviors. People are much more likely to consider your comments if the slate is still clean. Your group probably has a few behaviors to add to the list and may want to change some of the labels and descriptions.

They may also agree to your suggestion to have one or two members act as observers during the next group task. Ask them to use the observation sheet and, after a suitable interval, report back to the group on what behaviors are most prominent. Keep the focus on what can be learned from the information, and assist members to monitor their own behavior.

With the help of a vocabulary to identify helpful behaviors, groups soon exhibit more helpful than hindering ones. Feel free to duplicate the list of predictable behaviors for discussion and observation. As participants become more experienced in teamwork, they begin to balance task and support roles, reducing their need for self-serving behaviors. Specific feedback helps to identify problem areas early and promotes those behaviors that help the group to function well. Once the vocabulary is familiar, suggest that individuals experiment with unfamiliar behavior in order to expand their repertoire.

By focusing on behavior instead of personalities, people are more willing to own up to their share in the group's struggle. The Personal Action form below can be used to make self-monitoring an explicit part of the learning process.

Personal Action Plan

Part I

Today, in addition to my customary behavior, I plan to practice at least one of the task-oriented and one of the group-building behaviors.

My chosen task-oriented behavior is _____.

I plan to practice such actions as:

_____
_____.

My chosen group-building behavior is _____.

I plan to practice such actions as:

_____
_____.

To assist me in this undertaking, I have teamed up with
_____(insert partner's name).

Together we'll share our action plan at the outset, agree to keep an eye on each other during the morning, and spend some time afterwards to debrief.

Agreed _____

Date and time _____

Part II
to be completed after the debriefing

As a result of the feedback I have received from my partner, I intend to practice the following group behavior

... during the next session in class

_____
_____.

... when I meet with my group back home

_____
_____.

Adults prefer to partici-pate in planning and evaluating their learning.
– Daniel D. Pratt

Predictable group behaviors

An individual's behavior in a group can be viewed in terms of its function. A person saying or doing something that concerns the content and purpose of the discussion displays *task behavior*. Someone inviting a silent neighbor to speak up is engaging in *group-building behavior*. Actions aimed at satisfying personal instead of group needs are *self-oriented behaviors*.[1]

As your group becomes more experienced, you will find that behavior is increasingly focused on task and group-building functions. You can support this by soliciting feedback from observers, making appropriate comments, steering the discussion to the group process, and by encouraging individuals to monitor their own behavior.

Task-oriented behaviors

- *Initiating:* propose tasks or goals, define group problems, suggest a procedure or idea. Examples: "A good place for us to start would be to agree exactly what the problem is" or "I suggest we go around the group and find out what experience each of us has had with a similar problem."

- *Information or opinion-seeking:* request facts, ask for suggestions or ideas. Examples: "Dale, you work with this stuff all the time, what do you think we ought to do next?" or "Pam, you studied law – what are the rules on this?"

- *Information or opinion-giving:* offer facts, state beliefs, give suggestions or ideas. Examples: "There are two routes open to us ..." or "May I suggest we do a short brainstorming session to get our ideas on paper?"

- *Clarifying or elaborating:* interpret or restate ideas and suggestions, clear up confusion, indicate alternatives before the group, give examples. Examples: "So you are proposing that we present this agreement to the voters in a referendum. Is that right, Chris?" or "That's one way of going. How about an alternative. What if we ..."

- *Summarizing:* pull together related ideas, restate suggestions after the group has discussed them, offer a decision for the group to accept or reject. Example: "Let's just have a look at the ideas on the flip chart. It seems to me that two are impossible to achieve, but that the rest deserve further exploration. Shall we delete the first two from the list?" or "We now have to decide which plan to concentrate on, is it A or B?"

- *Consensus-seeking:* check with the group to see how much agreement has been reached, or can possibly be reached. Examples: "In spite of our differences, we seem to all agree on one thing ...; is that correct?" or "What would it take for each of us to agree to clause 4?"

Parking lot

During a meeting or workshop, a posted flipchart paper or electrostatic plastic sheet with the heading PARKING LOT serves as a temporary holding place for ideas that may be worthy of the group's exploration but, if attended to at that moment, would distract from the topic at hand. At regular intervals, draw attention to the listed items and deal with them appropriately. This is also way to diplomatically respond to participants who wander off topic.

Group-building behaviors

- *Encouraging:* be responsive to others, accept contributions of others, give others an opportunity for recognition. Examples: "Interesting question, Sandy" or "The sub-committee gave us such clear choices."

- *Expressing group feeling:* sense feeling, mood, relationships within the group and share personal feelings with others. Examples: "It seems to me we are overwhelmed by the amount of information we have to deal with" or "I like the way we're pulling together as a team."

- *Harmonizing:* attempt to reconcile differences and reduce tension by giving people a chance to explore their differences. Examples: "This has always been a contentious issue. What is it, I wonder, that both sides have in common?" or "We have been talking at each other for quite a while. How about we take turns to speak and before anyone can respond, we have to restate what the other has said."

- *Compromising:* offer a compromise, admit an error, discipline yourself to maintain group cohesion even when your own idea or status is involved in a conflict. Examples: "You are right, I have been stubborn on that point. I am prepared to ..." or "That was my mistake. How about we ..."

- *Gate-keeping:* keep the channels of communication open and make it easy for others to participate. Examples: "Devon, we haven't heard from you in a while. What do you think about ..." or "Gee, I have been doing most of the talking. I'd really like to hear what each of you think about the situation."

Self-oriented behaviors

- *Blocking:* interfering with the process by rejecting ideas, taking a negative stance on all suggestions, arguing unduly, being pessimistic, refusing to cooperate.

- *Deserting:* withdrawing in some way: being indifferent, aloof, excessively formal, daydreaming, doodling, whispering to others, wandering off the subject.

- *Bulldozing:* struggling for status, boasting, criticizing, deflating ego or status of others.

- *Recognition-seeking:* attempting to get attention by boasting, or claiming long experience or great accomplishments.

Content + process

When observing group activities, a distinction can be made between content and process. Content refers to what *the group is working on; process describes* how *it does so.*

Inside groups

Several researchers have developed theoretical models of the predictable stages in a group's life. I find such theories to be worthwhile reference points when observing and managing group activities. According to Will Schutz, individuals and groups want and express three needs: inclusion, control, and affection.[2] A learning group typically begins with the first, then moves through the second, and on to the third. However, these stages overlap and the cycle may reoccur several times before the course ends.

- Need for inclusion

How might these needs express themselves in the classroom? The beginning need for inclusion is triggered when the group first meets in the new setting. People wonder how they will fit in and what they have to do to be recognized and accepted. Very little academic or content work can be accomplished until these and related questions have been dealt with. Warmup activities and simple small-group tasks are ways you can assist participants to satisfy their initial need for inclusion. Through such activities, people begin to reveal themselves a little bit at a time, tackling increasingly risky tasks as their comfort level rises. Still, in every group, one or two people will be unable to meet their inclusion needs.

- Need for control

The second phase of group development touches on control issues. They become apparent, for instance, when you ask learners to share responsibility for the course and when the group struggles with deciding how decisions will be made. During this stage, each participant strives to establish a comfortable level of influence with the teacher and other members.

- Need for affection

The next issues members face are those of affection and closeness. Natural affinities in the group may affect who supports whom during discussions, and how project teams are formed. Compatible groups, says Schutz, have members who complement one another's needs. That's why some groups seem to click, while others stumble and struggle. By anticipating these needs, perhaps mentioning them as legitimate and natural occurrences, you can assist in the development of individual and group competence and cohesion.

12 Rallying learning circles

Ask the same question of several people. Don't stop after the first answer, even if it is correct. Otherwise, certain people will do all the talking and others will remain quiet.

– Peter Renner

This technique comes in handy when you want to unearth opinions and feelings about a topic. It makes for more evenly distributed participation and acknowledges everyone's contribution. Use it at the start of a discussion to see what everyone brings to the table. Use it equally well as part of a lecture to measure comprehension and to flush out points of contention. Circles are helpful to get people to share previous experiences, recall good/bad memories, and describe feelings associated with a topic.

In essence, learning circles are an improvement on the question so often directed at no one in particular, "What do you think about X?" Instead of a broad floodlight, this technique spotlights each participant. The quality of responses tends to improve and most learners take a greater interest in the proceedings if their input has been sought in a meaningful manner. Whenever you ask for input, however, be prepared to incorporate it in subsequent discussion.

Learning circles are best used to:
- gather quick statements about an issue from each participant
- focus the attention on the contribution of one person at a time
- demonstrate that all contributions are valued
- draw out reticent participators
- provide equal time and attention for each class member

Group size

This works best if there are fewer than twenty participants. In a larger class, two people could team up to prepare a joint response, or several circles could work independently. In such situations the outcome has to be summarized somehow (on flip-chart paper, or by an objective recorder) and brought before the whole group.

Time required

About thirty seconds per respondent.

Room setup

Ask participants to form a circle with their chairs. If that is not possible, ask people to situate themselves so they can see whoever is speaking at a given time.

How to proceed

1. Arrange seating.
If this is a new procedure, be clear with the instructions.

2. State a question.
Explain how you'd like participants to respond. The questions or issues may have been raised by students or the instructor.

3. Describe the process.
Explain that each person will take a turn to respond and that no comments are allowed during the initial round. Ask one person to start, then continue around the circle, until everyone has had an opportunity to respond. Begin the round with a different person each time you use this technique. Once the last person has responded, thank participants for their contributions, and summarize if you find that useful.

4. Model good listening behavior.
Use nonverbal encouragers to acknowledge and move along each speaker: nod, smile, make eye contact. If needed, keep the communications clear with clarifying and summarizing statements. If you can't fully understand what someone says, chances are others won't either. Clarify by saying something like, "I understand you to say that ... [summarize the speaker's main point] ... is that correct?"

Your listening and speaking behavior sets the norm for others. Avoid the temptation to evaluate or critique. Gently intervene if someone speaks out of turn or comments directly on another's contribution.

5. Ask for feedback.
How did we do? How did you like this activity? If we do it again, what changes would you recommend? Sometime after using a learning circle, ask participants about its usefulness. Be open to hear what's being said about the technique, your management, timing, and appropriateness. Listen for suggestions for improvement.

Variation: Small circles

This is similar to learning circles, but instead of working with the entire class, you shift to small groups doing their own work. Each small group reports to the large one through a recorder. This technique can be used at various points of a session: everyone has the chance to get involved, and the technique requires little practice to bring results.

Small circles are best used to:
- review material covered to this point
- concentrate learners' attention on a specific issue
- practice the use of peers' knowledge
- encourage learners to share their know-how
- develop group cooperation under time restraints

Group size

Use this whenever the class has more than twelve members. If there are fewer, use a learning circle.

Time required

Between eight and twenty minutes, depending on the complexity of the issue under consideration and the learners' familiarity with this approach.

Room setup

Enough space so that the class members can rearrange their chairs into small rounds. No writing materials are needed.

How to proceed

1. Form small groups.
State that the next task involves small-group work. Invite learners to form groups of about five to seven. Ask each group to shuffle so that they are equidistant from other circles.

2. Select recorders.
Request that groups select a recorder: it can be a volunteer or someone nominated by the group. Clarify the tasks for the recorder: jot down the group's comments and report to the whole class when asked to do so later. The recorder is definitely not the chairperson, but may briefly intervene if the group strays off the topic.

Don't assume that participants are competent in every instructional technique. The problem with some – brainstorming, for instance – is that they've been around for so long that we assume everyone knows what to do. It's a good idea to review the ground rules, and be ready to be a coach.

– Peter Renner

3. Appoint timekeepers.

Inexperienced groups will benefit from having a timekeeper. This participant takes on the additional job of letting the group know how much time is available at different stages of the discussion.

4. State the question.

Be very clear about the task you want the group to tackle. The technique works well with topics concerned with the learning process (How can we make best use of the discussion time?), as well as those addressing course content (What is your experience with ...?). Avoid simplistic questions and those that can be answered with a yes or no.

5. Set a time limit.

Write the task on the board for all to see and announce the available time in which to accomplish it. Such restraints add valuable structure to group activities. Should the work warrant an extension, you still have the option of adding time later.

6. Ensure understanding.

Too often groups get caught up in the excitement of the shuffling and socializing of group activities – until someone asks: what are we supposed to accomplish? Before sending the groups on their way, ensure everyone understands the task. One way to do this is to ask for one or two volunteers to restate the question. Another is to ask for clarification of the task from the group. Proceed only when the task is fully understood.

If you use time keepers, ask that they warn their group along the way ("Three minutes left") and towards the end ("You've got one minute left to complete the round"). For groups of six, you might start off with six minutes – one minute for each group member.

7. Brief the recorder.

This member, the only one who has to write, lists the contribution of each participant in the circle. A phrase or key point is enough for each response.

8. Propose a procedure.

New groups benefit from procedural guidelines at the outset. As groups mature and members become more familiar with your participatory mode, fewer directions are needed. You might say: "May I suggest you go clockwise around the group, beginning with the person

Occasionally, act stupid: "I may be a bit slow, could you explain ..." This will prompt the other person to think carefully and simplify the message. You'll also attract the group's attention and open the door to shared explorations.

– Dave Quinlivan-Hall

> A. Everyone contributes; no one may skip a turn.
> B. Only when a speaker signals the end of a turn can the next person speak.
> C. Don't criticize or evaluate another's comment.
> D. It's okay to piggy-back – that is, use someone's comment as a springboard for further remarks.

who sits closest to the door" or "Start this round off with the person who spoke last during the previous discussion." Remind the group that equal participation demands tight management of time.

Posting the small-circles rules provides an easy reference point.

9. Start and stop the discussion.

Check the time and get the groups underway. The preliminaries, even with a new group, won't take longer than about five minutes. When the time has expired (with extra time if that's what it takes to get the job done), ask participants to turn their attention from the small groups back to the large group.

10. Invite recorders to report.

Ask them to report in point form on their group's deliberation. You may have to prompt some and restrain others. Stay focused on the previously posted task. Thank recorders and groups for their contributions. Open up for discussion or continue with the rest of the session.

Variation: Talking stick

Gathering in a circle to speak and be heard is an ancient tradition; many regard the circle as the symbol for understanding of life's mysteries. This activity requires a small object—sometimes called a "talking stick"—to be passed around as invitation for each to speak in turn.

Introduce this activity when you sense that a moment of calm reflection and careful listening may be needed. This could be at the start of a course (to help participants settle down and express their hopes for the event), any time in the middle (to encourage whole-hearted reflection and expression), and near the end (to give voice to unfinished business, appreciations, disappointments, and parting thoughts). Explain that the rules are simple (speak honestly from the heart, be brief, and listen attentively[1]) and take your own seat as a member of the circle.

13

Brewing brainstorms

Brainstorming is well suited to release and channel a group's collective creative energy. It invites uninhibited participation and often results in surprising ideas and solutions to old problems. Although most people seem to know the term, the first time you use brainstorming with a group, a careful explanation of the procedure is worth the extra time.

Brainstorming is best used to:
- produce ideas about course content problems
- generate ideas arising from classroom process
- tap the collective creativity
- demonstrate the effect of synergy

Group size

This works well with about five to eight people. If your class is larger, two options are obvious: divide the large group into brainstorming groups of about six; or arrange one volunteer group in the middle of the room, with the remaining members as audience. In the second arrangement, leave an empty chair in the center group. Anyone from the audience can jump in and make a contribution at any time and then vacate the chair for someone else.

Time required

The activity continues until the group exhausts its initial idea pool, when no further ideas are forthcoming. It's hard to fix a time for this point to be reached, but five to fifteen minutes, plus time for evaluation and discussion, is the minimum requirement.

Room setup

Ask learners to shuffle their chairs so they face a mounted writing surface (chalk board, flip chart, or newsprint taped to a wall).

How to proceed

1. Arrange grouping and seating.

2. Post the target.
Examples: How can a manager avoid wasting time with telephone

calls? How can we have better participation during class discussions? Note that either/or-questions (Should we do X or Y?) aren't suitable, nor are those inviting simplistic or factual answers (What are the staffing requirements for the night shift?). Brainstorming is best suited to issues calling for creative, wide-ranging possibilities.

3. Clarify the rules.
Be sure everyone is clear on the rules. Post them.

4. Assign recorders.
Ask someone with clear and quick printing ability to stand in front of the group and record *all* contributions as they are made. Suggest the recorder alternate colors to distinguish one comment from another. Allow no editing – although abbrev. are permissible. A visual record often sparks further contributions.

5. Call time.
Intervene when there seem to be sufficient ideas on the board or the group runs out of steam. Unblock the flow by asking participants to think of opposites, upside-downs, what-ifs, variations, add-ons.

6. Review and evaluate.
One strategy is to assist the group(s) in identifying the three ideas that seem the most practical and three that are the most outrageous. Play around with these to capture their combined appeal. Although the strict brainstorming rules are suspended, the second one (any idea is valid) still applies. Subgroups can be assigned the task of expanding on ideas that show promise.

> - *Focus on quantity. Generate as many ideas as possible.*
> - *Any idea is valid. Piggy-back on what others have said.*
> - *Don't judge ideas. The crazier the better.*
> - *Keep responses simple. Short and snappy is best.*

How to get the lead out

Synergy: "the combined effect of group members that exceeds the sum of their individual efforts." (Oxford Dictionary).

The problem with any popular technique is that people can become numb to its potential. Here are a few ideas on brainstorming to play with.

- To limber up mentally, ask individuals to work alone for two minutes and prepare a list of possible ideas. This will provide each with something to contribute when the group gets started – or stuck.

- Similarly, teams of two could huddle and rapidly write down ideas on one sheet of paper. This huddling could occur at the outset or during a slump.

- Exchange recorders halfway through the proceedings, or when the group seems to run out of ideas. Any change in the group's makeup is likely to restart the flow.

- Try using two recorders working side-by-side to keep track of the ideas generated by a lively group. You could act as a traffic cop, directing words to one recorder,

then another, to maintain the flow of ideas.

- Use teams of two or three during the evaluation phase. Once the group identifies the ideas that are good candidates for "possible solutions," assign one to each subteam. Ask the small group to imagine obstacles and opportunities that would have to be dealt with to lead to an implementation.

Variations

Reverse brainstorming

Negative, or tear-down, brainstorming explores potential failures.[1] It follows the customary rules, with the trigger question phrased along the lines of "What could go wrong with this idea/proposal/decision?" or "What would make this problem worse?" The group needs to be briefed beforehand and debriefed afterwards. Taking a negative tack means looking behind the façade of an idea—to a place where some nay-saying and sceptical participants may be dwelling anyway. Reverse brainstorming may be especially useful when a proposed action plan is likely to encounter resistance.

Role-storming

This can be an interesting extension of regular brainstorming and may be of special interest to jaded participants who might be mumbling "not brainstorming again" under their breath. Invite participants to choose and temporarily assume the identity of another person or stakeholder. Instruct them to preface their contribution with "person X would say…," or, "As Y, I'd say …." By assuming someone else's identity—someone who is not a member of the group—participants may well feel emboldened to offer more off-the-wall ideas than they would normally. To energize the process, ask participants to switch roles once or several times during a brainstorming session. As a **variation**, ask just half the group to assume another identity.[2]

Idea dump

We rarely approach a problem from a neutral position, as our baggage of past experiences is weighted with preconceptions, judgements, and emotions. The purpose of an idea dump is to "unload" or, at least, "park" the most obvious blocks regarding the problem.[3] A cross between this and reverse brainstorming challenges participants to come up with reasons why the problem cannot be solved. Even if you do this just for a while and then resort to positive brainstorming, it should all be done in good fun.

Visualization

A technique borrowed from hypnotherapy uses mental images to bring about changes in attitudes and behavior. It uses that part of the brain that controls intuition, emotions, and nonlinear thoughts. Visualization can transform unconscious thoughts, bringing them to the surface and promoting action. For example, you could ask participants to sit comfortably in their chairs, close their eyes, and imagine a situation

---

Case study: how brainstorming was used to break the ice and generate ideas.

Brainstorming can be used in many ways for a number of goals. Here is an example in which it was used as both an icebreaker and idea-generator. The objective was to introduce a new administrative form to a group of government employees. For some this sounded like a dull topic; for all, it represented the threat of the unknown.

The trainer warmed the group to the topic by inviting them to brainstorm on the problems the new form was likely to present. After ten minutes even those who would otherwise have been silent realized they were in the thick of dealing with the issue. The trainer next handed out the new form and explained its features. The group then reviewed their flipchart listing of potential problem areas and, with a little coaching, was able to see how these were dealt with on the new form. This paved the way for the new form to be accepted with open minds.

where the problem has been solved or, alternatively, where a choice of solutions exist. Tell participants they may not know the specifics of these solutions, but that they exist. Ask them to look around themselves (in their visualization) and note the sounds, textures, smells, and so on. As we tend to respond more readily to visual rather than verbal stimuli, this image can help students to relax and, in turn, open them to possibilities they might otherwise not have imagined.

Guided imagination

This is a more elaborate visualization in which you take participants on a tour or journey. When they are sitting comfortably, eyes closed, ask them to imagine walking in a meadow or beach or forest (you pick one). As they walk along, feeling relaxed and enjoying the warmth of the sunny day, they come to a small cabin. As they approach, they see a door. They knock on the door and as the door opens, they meet a wise woman (man, child, creature—you pick). Ask them to put the brainstorming problem to that being. Allow a period of silence during which participants can listen for the answer and then ask them to slowly return to the room. Before anyone starts to talk, ask everyone to write down their "answer" and, if it's obscure or symbolic, to speculate on its meaning. Invite participants to share their responses briefly with the group.

Writing in circles

Begin the brainstorming as usual, by stating the problem clearly and posting it for all to see. Break the class into small groups and ask them to sit in circles. Ask one person to write two ideas on a blank sheet and pass the sheet to the next person who will add another idea or a variation on what's already there. That person passes the sheet along, and so on. Your facilitator task is to keep side conversations to a minimum and the process rolling along. Encourage everyone to put aside their mental restrictions and let their "inner critic" have a break. Continue until people seem to have run out of steam, then ask them to look over their lists and begin to sort and categorize (see sorting activities on page 73).

A **variation** involves using flip-chart sheets instead of writing paper to allow for the use of colored pens and easier sorting. Another **variation** is to post several sheets some distance apart and invite participants to wander from one to the next, adding ideas or piggybacking on ideas already recorded. As the facilitator, walk around and encourage the troops. Alert them not to repeat their contributions on different sheets, but to use what's already written as springboard and stimulation.

Every act of creation is first an act of destruction.

– Pablo Picasso

Topsy-turvy

After agreeing on the problem statement, ask people to partner up and take turns asking each such questions as the following:

• What would (your) life be like if the problem went away?

• Who do you think has the solution to the problem—and what might it look like?

• What if you turned the problem upside down, that is, look at an obstacle as an opportunity, failure as a success, hindering as helping?

• What would have to happen for the problem to go away (or be solved, transformed, reduced)?

• If you had it your way, what would be done—disregarding obstacles such as budgetary restraints, etc.?

The questioning process follows a set pattern: Person A quietly poses the first question and Person B responds. Person A repeats the same question two or three times, prompting Person B to dig a little deeper each time for a reply. Person A then shifts to the next question, repeating the circular process as before. Three different questions are enough for this part of the interview. As facilitator, circulate among the teams to monitor their progress; intervene only if they seem to stray off the assigned path. After about ten minutes ask the teams to switch roles. Person B now begins to put the first question to Person A, and so on. After about ten minutes, thank everyone and invite them to gather in a large half-circle around a board or flip chart. Open the conversation with such trigger questions as, "What did you learn during this activity?" or "What did you discover?"

How to process ideas

After exercises with rules like "the crazier the better" and "no criticism," participants may resist switching back to reality. The excitement of playing with ideas could make the return to serious business feel like a letdown, even invalidate the entire exercise, certainly look like a lot of work when energy is ebbing. People may be itching for a break, but ask them to hold on till the sorting phase has been launched. As the facilitator, you'll have to be especially alert and willing to infuse the group with fresh energy. To begin, get them to shift their chairs away from the "play area" to the side or back of the room, with filled flip charts in full view. Begin with something like "Now comes the hard (challenging, exciting, juicy) part. You've listed oodles of ideas, some crazy and others crazier, some silly perhaps, others seemingly unsuitable. But somewhere in there is the answer to your problem. It may not appear as such, but it is there! Your task is to sort through the many possibilities and extract the essence." Use one or more of the following tools to launch the sorting phase:

- Look for connections, affinities, possibilities. This approach works best when the idea list does not exceed two or three sheets of flip-chart paper. Using a set of colored pens, ideally colors that haven't been used in the original writing, apply a coding system that rates the ideas and begin to run through the list, top to bottom. To generate fresh energy, ask participants to gather around, away from their customary seats. Nudge them to look for ideas that seem to either fit the bill or otherwise display potential. Watch for ideas that hold promise if combined with others and connect them with circles and arrows. Transfer potential solutions to a fresh sheet of paper. Now it's time for a break.

- Create categories and arrange the ideas according to various criteria.

Super ideas	Have Potential	Toss!
They look as if they might work and could be tested right away.	Might do the trick, but require more details, authorization, investigation, etc. Worth keeping and having another look at.	Will not work for several reasons: too costly, too dangerous, may contravene regulations, etc.
•	•	•
•	•	•
•		•
		•

- Create filters—criteria for workability—and pass the most popular ideas through them.

List the "super" ideas here.	Can it be done in the time available?	Do we have the expertise?	Will management approve?	Do we have the money?	Other criteria...
Idea A	may need some testing	✓	✓		
Idea B	✓	✓		✓	
Idea C					✓
Idea D	✓		✓		

14

Directing role-plays

Role-playing involves experiential learning at its best. According to the *Concise Oxford Dictionary*, experience is the "actual observation of or practical acquaintance with facts or events." Experience can involve participants directly or vicariously; in role-playing there is no difference between the direct physical involvement or participation as an active observer. A well-managed role-play can be a powerful experience. We need only turn to reading and television to see how deeply felt vicarious experiences can be.[1]

By definition, role-playing involves one or more participants who act out a scenario, which is either scripted in advance or developed on the spot. Your task is that of casting director, stage manager, producer, and timekeeper. Participants become actors, audience, critics, and analysts. Even if you've never conducted a role-play, or remember previous ones with trepidation, I suggest you take advantage of this dynamic tool. Take a little leap of faith, then follow these step-by-step guidelines.

Role-play is best used to:
- insert a slice of life into the classroom
- connect theory with everyday practice
- practice unfamiliar skills in a safe setting
- learn to appreciate contradictory viewpoints

Group size

Depending on the complexity of the play, you need two or more players. All others are designated observers; they either watch or are assigned witnessing functions. There is no limit to the size of the audience, but for larger groups, pay special attention to visibility, staging, and follow-up discussion.

Time required

A role-play can take as little as ten, but no longer than thirty minutes to complete. Preparation time depends on the complexity of the scenario; the duration of post-play discussion hinges on the issues and their relevance to the participants.

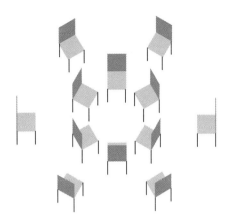

Seating arrangement for a fishbowl *or* group on group. *Divide the class in two groups, with one seated in a large circle to observe the workings of a smaller one in the center.*

Learning which involves the whole person of the learner, feelings as well as intellect, is the most lasting and pervasive.

– Carl Rogers

Room setup

Everyone must be able to see and hear the role-players. The play itself may require some setup to simulate the situation being played out. A variation on the fishbowl arrangement will work well.

How to proceed

Successful role-plays run through four distinct phases: setting the stage, conducting the role-play, debriefing the action, and concluding the events. Thoughtful attention to each phase goes a long way towards a successful role-play.

1. Phase one: set the stage.

Start by explaining why you want to use a role-play and describe its benefits and process. To illustrate different ways of handling this phase, here are three approaches taken from a workshop on developing team leadership skills.

- Start with a *discussion* of problem situations linked with the topic under discussion. Example: I asked the group to think of common errors the chair can make at the start of a meeting. The ensuing discussion yielded a ranked list of errors. I then suggested that we role-play the opening phase of a meeting. One person took the role of chair, with six others acting as members of the committee.

- Alternatively, begin with a *lecturette,* outlining the theory that underlies the practice. Example: I drew attention to a chart of common meeting mistakes and we discussed a manager's obligations during the opening phase of a meeting. I then proposed a role-play with one of the group in the chair and four others as participants. They then experimented with the alternative approaches we had just discussed.

- Another opening can be created by viewing a *training film* depicting a problematic situation. Example: In this group we stopped the tape at crucial points so that role-players could take over the meeting and experiment with alternatives to what they had seen. A similar effect could have been achieved with a written *case study* as stimulus.

2. Phase two: direct the action.

Be specific in your instructions, answer questions about the process, but stay away from predicting possible outcomes of the role-play. Act confidently to help alleviate any anxiety that arises at the sound of the words "role play." A pragmatic approach tends to ease apprehension. Underscore that role-playing is less about acting, and more about learning by simulation.

- Coach the players

Call for volunteers, or ask individuals you think will fit the part. There are usually enough people in any group willing to play; others take on the tasks of observers. Short written descriptions of characters and their scenario can be helpful; limit them to fifty words or less, just enough to sketch out the characters and their dilemma.

Elaborate scripts tend to restrain players' imaginations and will give you wooden performances instead of natural acting-out. Role-plays are meant to be a lively, lifelike enactment of some problematic circumstance.

- Brief the observers

Ask the nonplayers to find a spot from which they can best observe the play. Give them clear instructions on what to look for, what to write down, and what you hope to do with the collected data. For example, you can match observers with certain role-players and ask that they watch what that person says and does. Alternatively, observers can be assigned to report on player interaction – who says what to whom. The possibilities are plentiful: just make sure observers have a real function and don't see their role as busywork. Acting as observer offers valuable practice in observing, recording, and reporting. The fishbowl is a particularly useful room setup for such focused observations.

Six powerful interventions

1. You can kick-start a role-play with a role reversal, *where one player exchanges places with another. This can be particularly interesting in "us against them" situations where players stuck in one mode now have to see the world from the opposite viewpoint.*

2. Halt the role-play and conduct a short coaching session *with the player(s). You might ask, "How is the interview going for you?" or "Do you want to take a different approach? What would you like to do differently?" or "Let me make a suggestion: look at what we wrote on the flip chart earlier. Which of the alternative approaches might get you out of this jam? Please pick one, and just try it on for size." After such chats, players usually continue with new energy.*

3. Ask players to exaggerate the situation. *Instead of asking players to do it "the right way," instruct them to play the "wrong way" first, to overstate it until they get the feel for it. Example: In a workshop on interviewing techniques I said, "See if you can demonstrate an interviewer who is too preoccupied to really listen to the client." After a few minutes of that, I asked players to "become alert and apply as many active listening skills as may be appropriate."*

4. Intervene with an aside, *a technique frequently used in Shakespearean plays. When prompted, or at their own choosing, one player at a time may turn to the audience and share thoughts and emotions. One- or two-sentence asides can provide valuable clues to the observers and the other players without interrupting the flow of the play.*

5. Tell everyone that it is perfectly acceptable for a player to stop the action *at any time, to ask for directions, to say "I'm stuck," or to start over again. After all, role-playing is meant to be an opportunity to experiment!*

6. With a more experienced group, suggest the method of alter ego. *This involves seating a "coach" right behind one or more of the key players. As the play develops, such a coach assists by prompting the protagonist with key words or phrases. The player is free to pick up on the suggestion or pursue an independent course.*

Case #1: How to experiment with behaviors and achieve consensus on the "right way."

A group of trainers came together to experiment with ways to teach selling techniques to newly licensed real estate people. Aside from wanting to involve their learners more, these trainers also had a need for consensus on what to teach.

When they came to the topic of "cold calls," I suggested that two volunteers role-play a typical door-knocking situation. I briefed both to overplay, to do it wrong, but believable. After this hilarious opening, the group listed the flaws in the performance and generated "five rules for superior cold calling." Two fresh volunteers then replayed the scenario, this time by following the rules as much as they could. Their role-play took on a serious note and people later commented that it felt like the "real thing." Upon conclusion of the play, the rules list was edited and declared "correct" for future teaching sessions. Thus the role-play provided skills practice and consensus among a group of highly individualistic sales professionals.

Observer Record

- Your task is to concentrate on one participant *acting in the assigned role*. Sit so that you can face the person. Try to be unobtrusive.

- Note your observations on this sheet, and be prepared to report your findings at the end of the play.

- Quality will be more valuable than quantity. Record a few events in detail, so that you can report on who said what to whom, and what you saw happen because of that behavior.

1. Characterize the person's behavior *in the role*. Note a few specific behaviors and words to support your impression.

2. How did the person help or hinder the progress of the role-play?

3. If the person were to ask your advice on acting the part, what are your suggestions?

This is a sample only – adapt to suit your group's needs

- Begin the play
  For a while, stay out of the way and let the play proceed. There may be some initial hesitation until players get a feel for their role. If they get stuck, give them time to sort it out. If they become seriously stuck, make an intervention (see sidebar on page 66). Remember to jot down your own observations in preparation for the debriefing session.

- End the play
  After the play has taken its course, made a point, re-created a dilemma, or whatever you set out to achieve – call a stop. And how do you know when to stop and when to let it run for a little while longer? It may seem over, or the player may seem stuck, but with a little extra time or the right intervention, it could blossom into an unexpected surprise.

You must trust your intuition on this. If you sense a natural ending, but aren't quite sure what to do, step in, ask for a "time out," and consult the players. Ask if this is a good point to stop the play, or if a few more minutes would allow them to develop it further. Ask if they have gone as far as they can/wish/dare.

3. Phase three: debrief the events.

First, give each role-player an opportunity to report. Ask each person to describe the dilemma from their unique vantage point. This provides valuable inside information, and also helps players discharge any tension or discomfort they may have accumulated – especially important if a player had an unpopular part. Assist players to step out of their roles by suggesting they change seats and physically move away from their role.

Next, the observers report on what they saw and heard. This helps to develop their feedback skills. Ask them to comment separately on observed behaviors and their interpretation of them.

4. Phase four: wrap-up.

Assist participants to integrate role-play results with material previously discussed. Help them to generalize from the role-play to their real world. Ask "So what?" or, "What have you learned about ...?" Take the time now to thank the role-players for taking the risk, and perhaps make some light-hearted comments about what happened. Avoid identification of individuals with certain roles. Give feedback to the observers.

Ten tips for writing role-play scripts

1. Determine the purpose for the role-play and list the ability, awareness, or insight you hope participants will develop.

2. The value of a role-play depends on how successful you are in developing a scenario and role descriptions that suit the above objectives.

3. Outline the scenario. Decide on the name and nature of the simulated organization, and the number and type of roles. Sketch out the scenes of the role-play.

4. Use a plot line and props that are believable and consistent. Use realistic characters and events; for organizational scenarios, for example, use rules and procedures which might be used in the actual setting.

5. Provide relevant roles for participants. The best role-plays replicate situations with which they are familiar. Ask role-players to assume parts for which they have the necessary background. Adults like to see a job-related payoff in participating and acquiring skills.

6. Challenge participants. Ask them to generate alternatives as well as to choose among them. Train for the ability to propose options and criteria from which a decision will be made.

7. Check to see if the role-play fits the time available. Do participants have enough time to become familiar with the play, then analyze and generalize from it?

8. Give feedback. Emphasize positive features of each performance.

9. Test the role-play with a small group, possibly one that has had experience in experiential techniques. Analyze strengths and weaknesses and make necessary changes.

10. Solicit feedback from participants. Ask how relevant the role-play was in developing certain skills. Find out how realistic the scenario, the props, and instructions were.

FUNDAMENTALS

Body language

Apparently it is impossible for us not to communicate. Even when no words are exchanged, we communicate nonverbally, either through body movements, such as gestures, expressions, and stance; or by way of spatial relationships – the relative distance between people.

Albert Mehrabian reports on research into nonverbal behavior: the impact of facial expression is greatest (55%); next is the impact of the tone of voice (38%); and finally that of the words (7%).[2] Accordingly, if the facial expression or the tone of voice are inconsistent with the words, they will dominate and determine the impact of the total message.

The anthropologist Edward T. Hall coined the term "proxemics": the study of how we communicate through the use of space.[3] It deals with how far we stand from each other, how we arrange desk and visitor chairs, and how we respond to others coming into our space. Hall describes four distinct zones that North Americans unconsciously use as they interact: intimate distance, 0 to 18 inches; personal distance, 1/2 to 4 feet; social distance, 4 to 12 feet; and public distance, 20 feet and more. These spaces are largest in front of a person and smaller at the sides and back.

15

Teaching by demonstration

Most of us would rather avoid trying a new behavior than risk being seen as a fool. Encourage participants to try out new skills by reducing the stigma of failure. Emphasize the benefits of learning over instant achievement and perfect results. Ask what can be learned from trying that new skill.

– based on the teachings of Lao Tzu.

When it comes to teaching hands-on skills, the most reliable strategy involves a demonstration by the teacher, followed by supervised practice. Julia Child, television's *grande dame* of French cookery, is an outstanding demonstration teacher. Her shows come across as chatty and informal, but when carefully analyzed, they reveal meticulous planning and canny execution. Through hundreds of broadcasts, she has avoided "the deadly predictable sameness that shortens attention spans."[1] An equally impressive teacher is John Cleese – of *Fawlty Towers* and *A Fish called Wanda* fame – whose management training films are both entertaining and educational. Watching these two masters provides several teaching principles.

Describe the desired outcome

You need well-defined objectives that spell out what participants can expect to learn during the session. For instance, at the start of a show, Julia Child outlines her goals and displays the finished dish; viewers know exactly what she is aiming for.

Begin your own demonstration with a statement of objectives to describe the desired outcome in terms of *observable behavior*. State, for instance, that learners will able to "put the bridle on a horse" (riding course), "prune an established vine" (gardening course), or "prepare a Hollandaise sauce" (cooking course).

Since there are usually more wrong than right ways to perform a task, tell learners also the *acceptable standard* by which performances will be measured. Using our three examples, this could mean that "the bridle has to be fitted according to Pony Club rules," that the vines be "cut so that fruit spurs are spaced six inches apart with two buds on each new cane," and that the sauce must be "prepared in under two minutes, without curdling." Now teacher and learner have a clear depiction of what is expected.

Hands-on practice

Kazuaki Tanahashi—poet, translator, and peace worker—also teaches East Asian calligraphy and Zen painting. In his retreat classes, he applies demonstration-practice techniques in unique ways. He first explains and demonstrates a procedure, such as drawing a Chinese pictogram. He then asks students to draw their own by copying from templates. During the practice time, he observes from the side-lines, without walking from student to student, so as not to intimidate with his presence. Next, participants bring their brushes and blank paper and sit at his table. Kaz steps behind them, holds their brush hand, and guides it through the motions. Having thus experienced a master's touch first-hand, students return to their table to continue practicing. Throughout, Kaz maintains a quiet atmosphere—continually encouraging students and frequently making light of his own shortcomings.

Create a context

One trainer calls this the "zoom principle"[2] – giving the broad picture before going into details. John Cleese's training videos typically start with the whole story, explain why the job has to be done, how it fits into the whole picture, and only then teach the detailed steps. In the riding-class example, the teacher might show pictures of incorrect and well-fitted bridles and, through questioning, prompt students to name the differences.

Identify the steps

Detailed steps, presented in a handout or wall chart, are ideal learning aids. They make it possible for participants to follow the demonstration and to check their own practice later. Such a published sequence also helps the teacher to avoid the "do as I say, not as I do" trap that can snare even the most seasoned practitioner.

Pace the sequence

Several techniques are available to spark interest and prepare the group for what is to come. The gardening teacher in our example could use the following techniques.

- Go *from the general to the specific* by asking participants to speculate on the reasons for regular pruning. This could then be followed by a demonstration of specific techniques.

- Start with the *first step first*, showing the untouched vine and ways to prune. Alternatively, she could demonstrate the *last step first*, beginning with a fully-pruned vine and, working backwards, show the cut-off shoots that resulted from the pruning.

- Ask learners to *experiment* before finding out the right way. For example, she could ask them to place twist-ties on unpruned vines to mark possible cuts. After a brief discussion, followed by the teacher's demonstration, learners would examine their markers and revise their intended cuts.

- Tell learners to validate their markers against correct ones shown on an *illustrated checklist*. They could also be asked to team up and check each other's handiwork. Only when confident, and with the teacher's go-ahead, would they finally put their pruning shears to work.

Personalize the demonstration

Ensure each participant has an unobstructed view of the demonstration. Clarify how questions will be handled: as you go; after the demonstration; when asked for by you; or as posted on a flip chart or in a handout. Address people by name and maintain frequent eye contact. Synchronize your demonstration with the listed steps. Offer relevant background information as you proceed, but avoid getting sidetracked. Involve participants by inviting them to inspect the materials, hold tools, or manipulate equipment.

Another way to personalize is to establish a link to participants' lives outside the classroom. "Teachable moments" are created whenever instruction matches the immediate needs of learners.

Devise opportunities for practice

Whenever feasible, give participants an opportunity to practice the new skill. Even if that's not possible for all, at least have selected volunteers practice on behalf of the group. This way, others can observe, follow the steps on a checklist, and join in a discussion afterwards. Alternatively, arrange for small practice groups, with members taking turns performing the operation. Expensive, dangerous, or complicated practice may have to be simulated. Much of pilot training is done in simulators and the twist-ties in the vine pruning is an everyday example of simulated practice.

Act as coach and arrange for performance feedback

Supervise the practice and try to observe each participant at work. Learners can also team up and supervise each other, following a checklist or diagram and practicing until they are confident.

Feedback is most effective if given immediately after a certain action and if it specifically describes a behavior. Its value is enhanced if given in a helpful manner and perceived by the learner as aiding in skill acquisition. Provide participants with various measures of progress, and reward even approximations of the correct behavior.

Nudge learners through one-on-one commentary, questioning, and assisting. Assist participants in helping each other to learn. Simple feedback tools (see sample on page 83) and coaching guidelines will enhance cooperation. Ultimately, participants must be able to assess their own mastery of the demonstrated task.

Teachers need to bring themselves to school— use their lives, knowledge, and explorations as elements within the curriculum.

– Maxine Greene, *Releasing the imagination: essay on education, the arts, and social change.*

Performance Feedback

Use this form to provide feedback during a practice session.

Name:

Task:

Date:

Place:

Coach:

Sequence of skills to be learned	Rating	Helpful comments
1. _____	1 2 3	_____
2. _____	1 2 3	_____
3. _____	1 2 3	_____
4. _____	1 2 3	_____
5. _____	1 2 3	_____

Key to ratings
1 = competent
2 = needs some more practice
3 = unsuccessful, needs further coaching

Facilitate transfer of learning

The real value of most skills training, and the justification for most adult-education efforts, lies in real-life application. This last stage in the demonstration-practice cycle must help learners to integrate newly acquired skills where they matter most. This could be on the job, at home, during leisure pursuits, or wherever the needs exist that brought people to your class in the first place. Several techniques are available:

- Build upon the new skill during subsequent practice sessions.

- Ask learners to reflect on how they can use the new skill outside the class. Have them contract with a partner to discuss its application in person or over the phone.

- Assign homework tasks that involve the use of the new skill, or invite participants to design their own.

- Suggest participants put their goals on paper and place it in a self-addressed envelope. Promise to mail it two months later as a reminder and reinforcer.

- Make time in a future session for reports on participants' use of the new skill.

Behavioral instruction

Robert Gagné describes conditions that make for effective instruction.[3] Sequence is not as important as the inclusion of as many components as possible. Here are his nine points with my commentary.

1. Gain and control attention.

Advertising people have a knack for this, as do entertainers and successful public speakers. They use gestures, examples, statistics, and dramatic statements of benefits and consequences to draw attention to themselves and their message.

2. Inform the learners of the expected outcome.

Most of us appreciate knowing where we are going, what's in it for us, and why we should make the effort. Tell participants what they can expect to gain from listening, participating, experimenting, and studying.

3. Stimulate recall of relevant prerequisites.

Connect new material with old, unfamiliar with commonplace. Examples: "Remember the last time you tried to get your partner to listen to you, but ended up frustrated?" or "Our previous discussion raised some points we didn't get to. I've written them on this flip chart so we can deal with them today."

4. Present new material.

Now that you have "primed the pump," continue the flow of learning by presenting new information, demonstrating a skill, or facilitating a discussion.

5. Offer guidance for learning.

Do whatever it takes to help participants learn. This book is filled with techniques, including small-group activities, individual projects, questioning, role-plays, and case studies.

6. Provide feedback.

Inform the learners yourself, expose them to appropriate models, or create situations that will yield the data, so that participants can gauge their progress.

7. Appraise performance.

Before moving to the new set of materials and experiences, learners should have a chance to measure themselves against some external standard. Techniques that can help them include models, tests, trials, experiments, reflection, and evaluation by self, peers, and experts.

8. Make transfer possible.

Adults don't learn for the teacher's sake, but for many reasons of their own – perhaps to upgrade their job performance, raise their academic standing, develop their hobby skills, improve their functioning as a parent, or enrich their enjoyment of life in general. Practice sessions in class and individual projects and assignments can help facilitate transfer.

9. Ensure retention.

To take hold, new attitudes, knowledge and skills need to be used and reinforced. Try ways of applying new data to familiar problems, draw connections between new and old, use methods that demand recall and retention.

Generating participation

There will always be some people who naturally participate and others who sit back and remain relatively silent. Both present a challenge: how to slow down the keen ones without offending and how to bring out the quiet ones without pressuring. Speedy Memo and Spend-a-Penny are two structured activities to insert whenever you wish to increase the degree of participation. Starting on page 88 you'll find many more ways to invite group members to participate actively.

Speedy Memo

This is a quick way to sort out any number of unspoken elements in a group. With only a minor interruption of the proceedings, it serves to clarify a fair measure of what's going on in the room. Everyone has a say and only minutes are required to gather and process the information.

Speedy Memo is best used to:
- obtain quick feedback on opinions, facts, and feelings
- bring personal comments to light – in confidence
- create an opportunity to find out learners' hidden needs
- pause for a midstream assessment
- conduct an informal opinion poll

Group size

This can be used with groups of any size. To save time during processing of responses, large groups may be broken into subgroups of five to seven to collect and announce their data.

Time required

Less than it would take for a coffee break, when some of these things would be discussed anyway – without the benefit of being analyzed or used.

Room setup

The existing one. Even in large lecture situations, subgroups can be formed by people briefly turning to those sitting behind them.

How to proceed

1. Describe the process.

Ask participants to briefly pause and listen to an explanation of the Speedy Memo process. Explain what it is you want to know. Examples: What was the highlight of today's session? What part of the lecture warrants further exploration? How do you feel about the way this role-play is going – what should we do in the remaining ten minutes?

Of course, you'd only ask one question at a time, or, as in the last example, raise two related items. Write the question on the board to be absolutely clear.

2. Do it.

Ask each person to get a small piece of paper – something torn from a notebook or the corner of a handout will do.

Invite participants to respond with one or two words. They should be as concise as they possibly can. Suggest using a noun, an adjective, a verb or an exclamation: at most, one telegram-style sentence.

Quickly collect the papers, mix them up, and ask one or two people to read them out loud. Now everyone knows what others are thinking and feeling.

3. Process the new data.

Respond to the message. This may be something you can do, or, more likely, something others can help with. If appropriate, engage the class in discussion on how to deal with the information.

Spend-a-Penny

Although simple, this can be a very effective technique to get everyone to participate in class activities. It can be quickly inserted at any time without detracting from the content of the session.

Spend-a-Penny is best used to:
- encourage even the most timid learner to participate
- slow down frequent contributors without cutting them off
- demonstrate that everyone has equal rights and responsibilities
- shift the focus from content to process
- add a playful element – with a very functional purpose

Group size

This can be done with groups of any size.

Time required

Just enough to explain the rules and distribute tokens. From there, the class continues to work on the task at hand.

Case #1: How did I do?

Once I was sure that my presentation had bombed: participants had left in a sombre mood, no one had lingered behind. I was sure I had created more confusion than clarity. The next morning, before doing anything else, we used a Speedy Memo asking for a one-word description of my lecture. The responses surprised and humbled me: I was told that yes, my presentation had been incomplete, but, more importantly, thought-provoking. People recalled leaving the room in a pensive mood, not because of a job poorly done, but because I had got them thinking about the subject in a profound way. The fact that I showed such concern for their moods made quite an impression and furthered our development as a group, learners and teacher alike.

Materials needed

Three pennies (coins, poker chips, or any symbolic token) per person.

Room setup

Participants stay where they are.

How to proceed

1. Explain the purpose of the exercise.

By being brief you'll hardly lose the flow of what's been going on. Introduce this as a way to encourage and equalize participation. It is probably best to avoid singling out individual behavior you wish to remedy, but I have been known to say something like, "two or three people have been doing all the participating," or "the participation on this topic has been a bit lopsided this morning and I'd like to hear what the rest of you have to say."

2. Explain the activity.

Tell everyone to stay where they are. Distribute tokens, or simply ask participants to produce three coins.

3. Explain the rules.

Pennies can be spent during the ensuing session in the following manner: Every time a person speaks up, it costs a penny, which is placed in front of the speaker. Once all three are spent, the participant has used up his or her opportunities to participate and must remain quiet. This way everyone has equal opportunities.

4. Get on with it.

Engage participants in an activity that offers active participation, such as a discussion, demonstration, question-and-answer session, or case study. You may need to remind them of the basic rules, but people usually get into the swing of things.

5. Invite discussion on the activity.

Some time after using Spend-a-Penny, ask the group to comment on its usefulness and future use. This should not be a critique of the exercise, but an assessment of its effect on the level of involvement. Ask the group to think of ways everyone can ensure a more balanced participation. "Pennies" might become a code word for the group. If, for instance, a discussion becomes too one-sided, anyone could invoke the "equal-penny rule" as a reminder to let everyone have an equal share in the proceedings.

Case #2: Computing priorities

In the midst of a day-long workshop, I needed help in deciding where to go next. Our agenda still listed several points as important, yet we were running out of time. Several options lay before me. I could, for instance, exercise my teacher's prerogative and choose the items to cover. Or I could ask the group and spend precious time on a selection process. A show of hands with quick tallies next to the remaining items might have been the way to go, but because of the sensitive nature of the issues, anonymity was called for. A Speedy Memo soon yielded the top two items on the group's priority list.

How to slow down the fast ones

Spend-a-Penny is an effective way of handling the expert in the class who always has something to say and may prevent others from making a contribution. I have found that such frequent contributors, rather than being put off, respond positively. For some, it was a relief to sit back and let the others speak.

How to encourage the quiet ones

Those who usually sit back in relative silence find this an easy way to make contributions. Some have said with amazement that spending their pennies represented a change in their usual behavior: They got caught up in the play and found it easy to speak up. Not having to compete and being assured an equal voice can be quite liberating.

How to let "nothing" happen

Parker Palmer reminds us of the value of silence. He occasionally asks participants not to speak more than twice over the period of an hour. The pauses and slowed pace tend to deepen the quality of the ensuing conversation. "We need to abandon the notion that 'nothing is happening' when it is silent," writes Palmer, "to see how much new clarity a silence often brings."[1]

Thirty-three more ways to generate participation

Appreciative inquiry. This technique is based on the premise that an organization inquiring into problems will keep finding problems, but an organization attempting to appreciate what is best in itself will discover more and more that is good.[2] As an illustration, let's assume that you want to involve participants in the management of the course.[3] Introduce the activity by asking them to see themselves as codesigners and colearners of a course component (e.g., how projects are assigned, grades determined, class time is used). Explain that you'll do everything possible to realize their wishes.

- *Discover what is*. Students interview each other and report back in story form. Their aim is to discover what learning situations have been positive for the interviewee. The following questions are helpful at this stage: What has contributed most to our learning? What is working? What energizes us? What do we do well?
- *Dream what might be*. Engage the class in the creation of shared images of what might be possible in the future. Help them to envision and describe an ideal learning community: What is important for us to move ahead? What kinds of values inform our deliberations? What might "even better" look, sound, and feel like?
- *Design what should be*. In small groups or the large class (this depends on their experience with this kind of work), guide them in designing the setting and structure they dream of. Trigger questions might include the following: How would we organize ourselves to create such a course? What steps do we need to take? Where should we start?
- *Deliver what will be*. This stage begins the implementing of the desired structure, which will continue throughout the course. It includes monitoring, quality control, and fine tuning. The following questions may be helpful: What progress have we made? What have we learned

so far? What obstacles have we encountered? Who else has expertise in this area? What do we need to learn in order to move forward?[4]

Ask the neighbor. Sometimes all that's needed to clear up a point of content or procedure, or to sort out muddled thinking, is to have a short conversation with another person who's familiar with the situation. This activity simply encourages what many people will do naturally, albeit in whispered tones or by surreptitious message systems: talk to their neighbor. You may sense a need for such consultation by puzzled looks, increased whispers, or general unrest. Introduce the activity by giving clear instructions: "Please turn to your nearest neighbor. Take about [give time] to see what questions have arisen, try to answer them between yourselves, and prepare to clearly state anything that remains unresolved." As the facilitator, keep an eye on the time, monitor the discussion without interfering, and eventually call everyone back to attend to unresolved issues. A **variation** on this activity is to assign a specific topic—perhaps connected to a lecture, text, or dynamics in the room.

Brainstorming. Try any of the variations, starting on page 68.

Buzz groups. Explained in detail (page 34), they involve small groups of three to five students working for a short time on a specific task, followed by a debriefing and reporting process.

Checking in. This is an informal assessment to determine how the course is progressing from the participants' point of view. It can be done at any time: the end of a day during a weekend workshop, halfway through a semester-long course, or during the last get-together on any event. Write the trigger questions on the board or—probably better for subsequent tabulation and your own record-keeping—distribute them as a handout. Look for examples in *Assessing the course* (page 155).

Circular response.[5] Do this anytime to kick-start a discussion (before, during, or after a lecture), in response to a text, or to draw on peoples' opinions and experience generally. Instead of a free-for-all discussion, which tends to favor the vocal ones and inhibit the reluctant ones, circular response makes for a nice change. Begin by asking participants to pull their chairs in a circle; about fifteen is the maximum. If your class is larger, form two circles, or don't use this activity. Write the topic on the board (for instance, "The importance of student participation in an adult education course" or "The problems with advance readings"). Explain the process as follows: "I'd be interested to hear what you think about this topic, whether based on your experience, your belief, or on your understanding of the literature. Let's have a structured conversation, with equal air time for everyone. We'll start with one person, who may speak for two minutes. When the timekeeper calls time, the current speaker will pass the floor to the person sitting to the left. The

Adults learn best when they are curious, challenged, or desiring of competence.

– Daniel D. Pratt

new speaker begins by paraphrasing what the previous person has said and then adds her own comments. This way, one person's ideas are linked to another's." Ensure that people are clear on paraphrasing and that a timekeeper is ready. Don't get entangled in lengthy deliberations on the pros and cons of this activity, simply ask participants to give it a try. As facilitator, your role is to guard the rules and to coach people as they are becoming accustomed to the activity.

Code of conduct. Participants first reflect individually and then contribute publicly to writing a set of rules by which they wish the course to be governed. You could liken this to a country's constitution, with frequent amendments and healthy court challenges, designed to help people live together in a democratic society. Revisit the rules once or twice during the course and refer to them whenever there's a conflict or infraction, or when it's time to review group process.

Collage. This requires a bit of preparation and may, at first, seem difficult for some participants. Students are asked to create a display, which could depict an idea, a personal development, or an imagined scenario. I've used it in a life-writing course (where participants explored aspects of their personal journeies and depicted them as a collage) and at the culmination of a career planning workshop (where students traced their paths up to the time of the workshop and then projected their imagined progresses in time to come). Materials needed are old magazines (ask people to bring them), containing lots of pictures and headlines, as well as scissors, glue sticks, and poster boards (or recycled cardboard boxes cut to sheet-size). Begin with a brief explanation of the process, ask for quiet or minimal conversation, and invite everyone to spread out to begin. Some will take to the task with ease, others may need some assistance to get going.

Continuums. This activity explores the range of opinions around a topic or issue. Begin by establishing the opposite extremes of the debate. Designate a physical space across the classroom—indicating high, low, and middle—and ask participants to position themselves physically along the continuum. Ask them to look around and see who their neighbors are. Ask what surprises, if any, occur to them. Invite volunteers to briefly describe the reason for choosing their spot along the continuum. Ask people standing near each other to form small groups and provide questions to stimulate interaction: What would require you to shift your position? How did you get to this particular place on the line? Would you prefer to be in another spot—and where might that be? Why not try that out! What do you have in common with the person next to you?

Critical incidents. These are miniature case studies which may be in writing or simply explained by the instructor along the lines of "this

One important indicator of good teaching is the readiness to take risks, particularly the risk of departing from the previously written "script" of an educational encounter to build on those "teachable" moments of energy and drama that arise unexpectedly in a class every so often.

– Stephen Brookfield, *The skillful teacher.*

recently happened in a nursing home ..." or "I recall a situation during my apprenticeship ..." or "when the first on-line courses were offered we found ...." It all depends on your group and the course content. The point is to bring in a real-life incident to link theory and practice. You might ask participants to think about the case and call out reactions, or huddle with their neighbor(s) in duos or triads and come up with a collective response.

Debate. A proposition, or motion, is posted and the group is divided into two (or more) subgroups, each charged with the task of arguing for or against the motion. Traditionally there are two sides, pros and cons, but you might want to alter this and have multiple views represented. Also consider asking people to switch roles and argue from the opposite viewpoint. This activity can be inserted spontaneously, especially with controversial topics, or be preceded by a reading assignment or similar preparation. For details, turn to *Inviting experts* on page 103.

Gallery. When using flip charts to record and sort the flow of words, the walls are soon covered with a jumble of details. This may be a desirable indicator of active participation, but can also contribute to information overload. In using the gallery technique, call a "time out" and ask everyone to meander from poster to poster. Invite participants to pay attention to certain aspects of the posted material, such as themes, blind spots, fresh openings, questions, opportunities, insights, and so on. You can also assign these tasks to specific individuals or viewing teams with a request that they be prepared to make brief reports on their findings. Moving around quietly—just as one would at an art exhibit—makes for a nice change of pace.

Gift giving. Students typically focus more attention on the teacher than on their classmates. To offset this, nudge participants to become aware of each other's contributions. This activity opens up new channels through personal observation and anonymous feedback. After the class has been together for a few sessions, introduce the activity by asking everyone to write their name on a half-page of paper. Collect and randomly distribute the sheets and explain the assignment by saying something like: "Please spend a quiet moment to think about the person whose name is on your sheet. Don't look at them right now. Reflect on their contribution in class, their apparent expertise and life experience, their contribution to your own and others' learning, and so forth. Even if you haven't taken much notice of this person—take the time now to consider their presence here. After a few moments of thought, write down a sentence, beginning with *I'd like to give you this gift.* Then add, *Your presence in this class ...,* or, *I've noticed you helping ...,* or , *I appreciate the way you ...."* Tell participants they will all get to read the descriptions of themselves, but the authors will remain anonymous. Once everyone is done writing, collect the sheets and distribute them to their intended recipients.

Guided imagination. Take participants on an imaginary walk to tap their subconscious memory and imagination. For a detailed description, turn to page 71.

Ice breakers. Many of the activities in the chapter on *Using icebreakers and energizers* (page 15) can be adapted for use to give everyone a chance to participate and engage with the course material.

Ideal learning setting. This is similar to the *Memorable teachers* activity on page 24. Ask the group to break into pairs and interview each other about their ideal learning situation, formal or informal.[6] Invite them to describe the process, persons, or place they would like most to have as their setting for learning. Ask them to think back on times when things went really well for them, and to extrapolate and project from there. Partners take turns explaining and listening. You could follow up with a whole-group discussion. As a **variation**, ask the partners to write each other's ideal situation on a card and then exchange cards. Most likely, this will create another round of conversation as partners correct, amend, and edit the written version. Once they agree on the content, ask them to either post the cards or send them to you as e-mails, which you can organize for the class. This activity can be a useful needs analysis and discussion starter at the beginning of a course or workshop.

Learning circle. A structured activity where participants sit in a circle and take turns speaking either on a stated issue or relate something from their personal experience. For details, see *Rallying learning circles* (page 63); also *Whip-around* (page 96) and *Circular response* (page 89).

Magic wand. Ask participants to imagine they have unlimited power (or substitute "three wishes" or "being king/queen/CEO for a day"). This can be used to analyze what's going on in the course and how participants would like it to proceed. Or it can be adapted to any course topic when you'd like students to look at things in creative ways. Ask trigger questions, such as: What would you do? Who would you like to be? How would you change the situation? What laws would you pass? How would you rearrange the world?

Meditation. This is simply a way to help participants prepare to work and center themselves. I've done it at the beginning of a course or session, after a break as people get settled, or after a heated discussion or emotional event in class. In a quiet tone, ask participants to seat themselves comfortably, place their feet firmly on the ground, sit upright, and either close their eyes or allow their eyes to go slightly out of focus. Continue by saying something like: "Our minds can be busy with

In most places where people meet, silence is a threatening experience. It makes us self-conscious and awkward; it feels like some kind of failure. So the teacher who uses silence must understand that a silent space seems inhospitable at first to people who measure progress by noise. Silence must be introduced cautiously.

– Parker J. Palmer, *To know as we are known.*

many distractions, some inside this room, others outside. You have many things on your plate and that makes it hard sometimes to concentrate. Before we tackle the next part of the course agenda [name it here], allow yourself the luxury of a quiet moment. Feel yourself supported by the chair ... your feet connecting to the ground ... your head gently pulled upwards as if by a balloon on a string.... Now notice your breath, just notice, whether it is slow or fast, shallow or deep, silent or audible.... Note where the air enters your nostrils.... Notice your chest expanding, and your belly move ... calmly, not judging ... your body does what it does, by itself ... it is neither right nor wrong, it just is and it just does.... Note the temperature of the air as it enters ... follow the breath through your nose, your mouth, into your chest, and into your lungs.... Notice and give it a simple descriptive label ... as in slow, calm, hectic, rushed, cool, humid, fresh.... Note whatever word comes to mind, not judging, merely describing.... Note and label the quality of the breath ... do this for a minute.... Now notice your breath on the exhale.... Note its temperature, its texture as you expel the air, through which nostril, if it has a sound, a feel, a sensation.... All the while, thoughts will come and go through your mind.... Some call it monkey-mind, as in thoughts jumping from branch to branch, appearing and disappearing, some staying around, others disappearing to be replaced by others.... As thoughts come into your mind, note them as well—but let them be, don't follow them, just for now.... Merely note, and label ... as in "the car" or "the office" or "pick up kids" or "phone client" or "why are we doing this?".... Just notice and return to your breath, following it again, in and out, in and out.... And now, open your eyes wider, let the light come in, expand your awareness to this room, the people around you, the furniture and décor.... Return refreshed and grounded." If you are unfamiliar with giving such instructions, copy this page and read the text in a calm, slow voice. Allow about 10 seconds between sentences (indicated by "..."). The total meditation as described here takes about six to eight minutes.

Missing pieces. This quick needs analysis requires little time, yet offers useful data. Ask participants to tear off a slip of paper and jot down three things/aspects/questions/skills they would like to learn/try out/have explained immediately. Collect the slips and ask two volunteers to tabulate and feed back the outcome. Respond appropriately. Alternatively, you can take the slips away, sort by some criteria (e.g., can do/cannot do; nice to know/must know; will cover in session X/not part of our mandate/outline/contract), and bring them back to class along with your response.

Needs assessment. Do this at any point in a course to find out what participants say they need to learn. Do it by asking, "What do you

What a person already knows/believes is the single most important variable in determining what he/she will learn.

– Daniel D. Pratt

think—we could do X now or go directly to Y," or through a simple pencil-and-paper response. Some people find it easy to respond off the cuff, while others need think-time. Try alternating discussion and written responses. For a sample survey form, turn to pages 21 and 29.

Observers. Working in small groups or as a member of the class as a whole, participants may benefit from the observations of an "outsider." Ask for volunteers to act as observer and brief them on what to look for, keep notes, and report back to the group(s). This sort of input can be of particular value as groups learn to use brainstorming, role-playing, group discussion, or similar tasks that rely on cooperation and concerted efforts. See the chapters on *Directing role-plays* (page 74) and *Working in groups* (page 34) for more on using observers.

Peer teaching. Participants come to a course with different skill levels. There's always someone who knows a better way, a quicker method, a safer approach, a more interesting angle on any given task or topic. Peer teaching taps these talents. Recipients benefit by experiencing a different teaching style and gain a new appreciation for their colleagues. Peer teaching frees you up to observe, listen, and assist in unfamiliar ways. Safety may be an issue to watch if instruction involves dangerous tools, equipment, and procedures.

Poster session. This activity is similar to *Presentation* below, except that the material is displayed on large sheets and posted on a wall. Alternatively, posters can be mounted outside the classroom, in public places such as a hallway or cafeteria where others can get a glimpse of your group's work. Posters should stand alone; that is, function as educational tools without further explanation. They can, however, be staffed at certain times so that visitors can engage course participants in conversation.

Presentations. Similar to *Peer teaching* (above), this activity asks students to be teachers. Assign presentations requiring advance preparation to individuals or teams, or spontaneously insert them into the proceedings. They can serve as summaries, discussion starters, or skills assessments. They can be used to respond to a lecture, video, or text. Encourage presenters to get away from the lecture mode by stipulating that a presentation use no more than a certain percentage of lecturing; involve hands-on practice by the class; or use props, visual aids, or physical activity.

Question and answer. It's such an obvious activity that we sometimes forget to use it. In the midst of new and confusing material, all a learner wants sometimes is to have an opportunity to ask for clarification, ask a question, raise an objection. Simply call a halt to the proceedings from time to time and make room for a free exchange of

In the beginner's mind there are many possibilities, but in the expert's mind there are few.

– Shunryu Suzuki, *Zen mind, beginner's mind.*

questions. Depending on class size, time available, and participant sophistication, this can be accomplished by fielding questions verbally or by asking that questions be written on a slip of paper for collection. If you do the latter just prior to a break, you'll have time to look through the questions, arrange them by themes or topics, and get ready to tackle them. The drawback to this approach is that you'll miss out on your own break (not a good idea if you want to preserve your energy), so consider asking a couple of volunteers to do the sorting. This will yield the additional bonus of letting everyone know that the answer-part of the activity is not your responsibility alone.

Reading aloud. It's story time ... gather around ... once upon a time.... Remember the pleasure of being read to? This unexpected "time-out" looks like a break but is more a shift in voice. A few paragraphs from an expert author, read aloud at just the right moment, can make a greater impression than a paraphrased reference in a lecture or on a handout. Have the book or articles handy, or at least the full citation, so that those interested can follow up on their own. These readings are an opportunity to expand the scope of the class by introducing divergent and unexpected voices. In past workshops I've brought in a teacher's personal journal on mental depression, a travel writer's observation on being lost, an artist's description of being seen as weird, and a dying person's words on what really matters. For a different approach, ask members of the class to be the readers—a good way to offer the shyer members a moment's safe exposure.

Role-storming. In this variation on role-playing participants assume another's identity. Can be lots of fun. For more, go to page 70.

Storytelling. An informal variation on *Reading aloud* (above). This is a time-out from formal course work to share tales from the school of lived experience. You might want to go first, then invite others to speak. For example, "Tell us more about that incident you mentioned earlier."

Tracking questions. Ask participants to set aside a space in their notes to write down questions as the course progresses. Explain that just writing a question down can help to reveal an answer. If certain questions remain unanswered, ask students to raise them in class or informally in conversation with others. Mention that you plan frequent stops for questions and answers.

Visualization. This is described in *Brewing brainstorms* (page 68). Use it if you'd like participants to look beyond their everyday viewpoint and imagine a world without a particular problem, say, or with one they hadn't ever thought of.

Voting with your feet. A way to get participants off their seats and in contact with others to share views or interests. Especially useful with contrasting or polarizing models, ideas, or lists. Ask everyone to first look over the choices and then step up to the one they like the most, are most curious about, wish to argue for or against, or whatever other criteria you consider important. **Variation**: I have used this with survey results (pertaining to learning styles, communication styles, and leadership styles). Once everyone had scored their survey and determined their preferred or dominant style, I asked them to place themselves physically on a large grid previously marked with masking tape on the training room floor. This became our starting point for a lively exchange on the characteristics and applications of the style under discussion.

Whip-around. This is a "taking-the-pulse" activity, a way to quickly hear from everyone. To get started, walk around the room and, as you near a person, address them by name and ask, "What do you think [insert name] about [insert issue]?" Or toss a crunched-up piece of paper (or a soft tennis-size ball), to someone, address them by name, and ask the question. After replying, that person tosses the ball to another participant, addressing them by name and putting the question. Aim for a playful, breezy quality to this activity. To stimulate a deeper conversation, use *Circular response* (page 89).

F U N D A M E N T A L S

Facilitating adult learning

Carl Rogers proposes guidelines for the facilitation of learning which have become my creed.[7] Accordingly, I ...

... consider myself largely responsible for setting the initial mood or climate of a program.

... try to elicit and clarify the specific goals of individuals as well as the more general purposes of the group.

... rely on each participant's desire to implement those goals as the motivational force behind significant learning.

... organize and provide access to the widest possible range of resources for learning.

... regard myself as a flexible resource to be utilized by the group.

... aim to become a participant learner, a member of the group, expressing my views as an individual.

... take the initiative in sharing myself with the group – my feelings as well as thoughts – in ways which the others can take or leave.

... strive, frequently surprising and always humbling as it may be, to accept my own limitations as a facilitator of others' learning.

Studying cases

Case studies typically describe a sequence of events and challenge participants to come up with an analysis and recommendations. Working alone or in small teams, learners are asked to deal with one or more questions, from simple to complex. For instance: What happened here? Define the problem. How can the problem be resolved? What impact might the proposed solution have?

If the only tool you have is a hammer, every problem will look like a nail.

– Abraham Maslow

Case studies are traditionally presented in writing, but could also arise out of a training film which is stopped in mid-action. Potentially, case studies offer exciting opportunities to link theory and practice. To do that well, they have to be believable and challenging.

Why not write your own case studies? You are eminently qualified: you know the participants, their backgrounds, their practical experience, and you are familiar with the terminology and jargon of their field. You also have pretty clear expectations of how a case might contribute to everyone's learning efforts. All you need, it seems, are some tips on writing cases that capture the reader's imagination.[1]

Write in the form of a story

From children's fairy tales, teenage comics and adventure books, to adult novels, films, and television series, we are fascinated by well-told stories. A good case study must have a story-telling quality to it.

Give the characters real names

Instead of referring to the protagonists as Boss, Supervisor A, Irate Customer, Secretary, Department Head, Lab Technician, or even Dr. Brown or Sue White, be more adventurous. Give them interesting names: D'Arcy, Karline, Jean-Marie, Sebastian, Wolfgang. Or play with words: Fred B. Friendly, Jura Paine, Thorfie Thorfinson, Zyzzy Zazu.

Put words in the mouths of characters

When Red Riding Hood arrives at Grandma's house, she doesn't cry "Wolf" immediately; she puts Grandma through the interview. We all know that she's addressing a wolf in drag, but the dialogue adds much-loved suspense. So instead of writing that the manager asked her staff for details on the incident, report the interaction in realistic words. It might be something like: "Rollo, I just read the complaints log for last night. What a mess! What happened?"

Use realistic details

Use authentic terminology, everyday jargon, and convincing details to make the case study believable. In a case involving hotel operations, when receptionists worry that they may have to "walk" a guest, they mean that because of overbooking a guest will have to be sent to another hotel and given complimentary accommodation and transportation. When they calculate the number of registered guests, they speak of a "house count"; "walk-ins" are guests who came without prior reservation; and the general manager is the "GM."

Be descriptive

Appeal to readers' senses; make it easy for them to imagine what it was like: describe sounds, textures, and movements. Let's apply this to a line from a case study on emergency procedures. "At the time of the accident, the reception area was very busy."

A more vivid description does a much better job of conveying the drama of the case. "The digital clock showed 6:32. Kelly was alone at the desk while Chris was downstairs having dinner. The airport bus had just left, dropping off all kinds of people. Through the glass doors, the doorman could be seen helping four people out of their taxi. Kelly reached for the phone to ask Chris to come back early. Suddenly she heard a thundering bang, followed by a sharp cracking sound, and the noise of breaking glass. And then – a loud scream. She dropped everything and ran over to see what had happened."

Make the flow easy to follow

Present the events as they occurred. The previous paragraph describes the chronology of the incident from the staff's point of view. It sets the scene, then describes specific events and Kelly's action. Avoid the use of flashbacks.

We all know what will transform education is not another theory, another book, or another formula, but educators who are willing to seek a transformed way of being in the world.

– Parker J. Palmer,
   The courage to teach.

Be complete and mysterious

Unless you specify that learners find supplementary information, the case study should contain all that's needed to proceed with the analysis. Information should be contained in the case description itself, or be provided in accompanying materials. The accident case above is accompanied by a copy of the hotel's emergency procedures manual. Depending on the experience level of the participants, a case study leaves room for interpretation and speculation.

Provide lead questions

Conclude the case study with questions or assignments that clarify the objective of the exercise. In our accident example, they are asked to meet in groups of three and assume the representative roles of management, union, and safety committee. They are then given two starting questions: How were the emergency procedures followed? How could our response capability be improved?

F U N D A M E N T A L S

Portfolio assessment

Portfolios have long been used by artists, designers, and photographers to demonstrate their work to clients.[2] In the context of adult education and training, portfolio assessment goes beyond conventional tests and examinations, asking students to demonstrate completion of specified objectives and requirements in a variety of ways. In vocational training, a portfolio might include work samples, designs, drawings, and written specifications to demonstrate certain skills. Traditional crafts have a long history of practical examinations culminating in a piece of work (master piece) as tangible evidence.

Academic achievements can be similarly evidenced through essays, journals, learning logs, and presentations. As it is not teacher-driven, the portfolio process involves students directly in their own assessment. They are asked to manage and monitor their learning, document their progress and achievements over time, and articulate their achievement levels. "A good assessment model supports students' desire to learn, rather than imposing a set of demands and expectations on them, which will blight their intrinsic motivation" writes Scott Willis.[3] Portfolio assessment is not easy—for students,

teacher, or administrators. Grading and reliability are obvious obstacles and lack of standardization in the way portfolios are produced can be problematic. Some teachers may feel unqualified to judge or grade subjective evidence. However, a desire to help adults learn to measure their own relative strengths, and the willingness to risk honest conversations about acceptable performance, will be richly rewarded.

For conventional testing, see chapter 25 starting on page 129.

Reading together

Initially developed to help so-called poor comprehenders in high school literacy programs, the concept of "reciprocal teaching" can be adapted to adult education settings to help remedy the problem of assigned texts not being read. Having been students and teachers ourselves, we know how difficult it is to get through a stack of readings. I recall living through many professional workshops and three graduate programs, each with endless lists of reading assignments. Sometimes I read and read, only to not "get it." Other times I forgot, or simply didn't have enough time. In class I developed all sorts of coping behaviors: from ducking behind others, to faking it, to admitting non-compliance. When thrown into discussion-of-the-readings groups I often confessed my ignorance, but always felt bad for letting others down. There has to be a better way!

Reciprocal teaching offers a fresh approach. The teacher prepares students by linking the readings to the material being studied and by offering tips on how to approach the reading. By definition, reciprocal teaching is a process whereby teacher and students engage in discussion with the purpose of achieving a joint understanding.[1] The teacher is a facilitator who guides the discussion, clarifies content from time to time, and provides *scaffolding* (see sidebar on page 101). The students employ such techniques as predicting, summarizing, and question-generating. When engaged in **predicting**, students guess or imagine what the author is about to say in the text. Looking for clues in the introductory or summary statements, sidebars, headings, they tap into their background knowledge and begin to connect new knowledge with what they already know. When **summarizing**, they identify (circle,,underline, write up) what to them are the most important pieces of information in the text. They might summarize sentences, paragraphs, or the passage as a whole. (Initially, students might work at the sentence and paragraph levels and, as their confidence and competence develop, advance to the paragraph and passage levels.) This activity helps identify misunderstandings and missing pieces in learners' comprehension of the text, which might give rise to opportunities for discussion, tutoring in critical thinking skills, and exchange of ideas among learners. The third strategy, **question generating**, arises from summarizing and moves learners into higher-level comprehension activities. At this level, they question material by drawing on their own experience or other knowledge bases.

Research

A series of studies designed to determine the effectiveness of reciprocal teaching in public school settings found that students functioned more independently of the teachers and improved the quality of their summaries over time. Students' ability to write summaries, predict the kinds of questions teachers and tests would ask, and detect incongruities in the text improved. Teachers observed fewer behavior problems in reciprocal teaching groups than in control groups.[2]

Variations

How to RAP

The next time you assign advance reading, offer students a technique to go with it.[3] Tell them about the acronym RAP, which has three parts: 1) read the item. 2) ask yourself, "What are the main idea and details here?" and 3) put the main idea and details into your own words. You might ask students to jot their response to the third question on paper and bring it along to class. Let them know that the discussion will be grounded in these advance summaries.

Reading proactively

This is a good way to look at a number of books with a group of people. Assemble and distribute the books and ask participants to exchange books with their neighbors so that everyone has a book that is new to them. You can also do this with a single title for everyone—what a way to crack the course text! Lead them through the steps by giving the following instructions:[4]

1. Hold the book, turn it over, leaf through it the way you might at a book store. Look at the blurbs on the covers. See if you can find information about the author's qualifications and background.

2. Open the book and look at the front matter—the dedication, introduction, foreword, and maybe the author's or publisher's orientation to the text.

3. Read through the table of contents and, if available, scan the chapter descriptions.

Temporary structures

Scaffolding is a fresh name for good teacher behavior. It helps students build knowledge and skills in a systematic manner. A scaffold is literally a safe structure around a building under construction. In this context the students are the builders—and you are the site supervisor, safety inspector, architect, and supplier of materials. You organize unfamiliar material and processes. You encourage and motivate by linking their current understandings to what lies ahead—in manageable steps and increments. You "scaffold" the pieces they don't know (yet), by providing them with temporary structures until they build their own.

4. Put the book down and write three questions on a piece of paper—things you'd want to ask the author or publisher, things you've become curious about.

5. Look for answers to your first question: look in the index or table of contents, browse through the chapters, and so on. Do the same with the remaining questions.

When everyone has completed the steps, engage them in a discussion of the usefulness of this approach. (If you use this activity with the prescribed course text, the various questions will offer wonderful ways to proceed.)

FUNDAMENTALS

Autobiographical learning

In 1926, Eduard Lindeman wrote that the "resource of highest value ... is the learner's experience ... it is [their] living textbook."[5] Since then, generations of educators have been influenced by Malcolm Knowles's call to utilize adult learners' life experience and create activities that help them to analyze and build on their experience.[6] Today, students are encouraged to use autobiographical and narrative learning in case studies, critical incidents, role-playing, and simulations. In addition, personal journals, learning logs, and life-writing activities assist them in the excavation of such personally significant questions as: Who am I? How did I get here? and What is my purpose?[7]

Autobiographical learning occurs when we engage in deep reflection on and critical examinations of our lived experiences. As Irene Karpiak explains, "Autobiography involves not only recounting memories and expressions but also finding their larger meaning, and to the extent that the activity expands the individual's knowledge of self and the world, it constitutes learning."[8] Reflecting on her use of autobiographical writing with adult students, Karpiak finds that it leads to learning and growth as it enables them to bring a sense of order to life, highlight moments of decision, bring closure to painful events, and gain insight into their own development.[9]

For more, see chapter 24 starting on page 125.

19

Inviting experts

There are points in any course when it makes sense to employ an outside expert to contribute timely information and valuable experience. But what's the best way to integrate guests into the program? Customarily, teachers make all arrangements and then hope that the guest brings content expertise *and* teaching ability. Course participants have little say in these arrangements and in the end may derive little benefit from the expert's input. A waste of time and talent? It doesn't have to be.

I suggest you involve the participants from initial planning to final event. Instead of bringing strangers together and praying they'll connect, take a pro-active approach and organize a debate format. It will reduce the pressure on the guest to cope with a strange environment and at the same time involve the whole group. Now everyone has a stake in making this event a success.

After all, you know your students and you probably have strong ideas of the guest's role in the overall course plan. This debate format leaves you in control of quality while taking full advantage of the expert's know-how. As the interviewer and moderator, you will be able to prompt the guest with questions, demonstrate interviewing techniques, and act as traffic control during the questions and answers.

Occasionally a guest is chosen to present a formal lecture or speech. In this situation, your function will be limited to introducing the speaker, possibly to moderating the question period, and to expressing appreciations at the end.

Expert presentation is best used to:
- involve participants in every phase of a guest presentation
- work with novice guest speakers
- ensure that the guest's presentation fits into the course agenda
- ensure fruitful interaction between guest and class

Class size

As long as everyone can see and hear the guest, there's no limit to the class size. If you are counting on interaction between speaker and participants, then the group has to be small enough to allow that. If yours is a very large group (over twenty, say), you can use small buzz groups as a way of bringing audience and guest together.

Time required

Long enough for the guest to deliver the information and for your class to have the chance to raise issues, ask questions, or debate points made by the guest.

Room setup

Arrange the furniture in some way so that you and the guest face each other *and* the audience. You can easily add a chair or two to accommodate more than one guest.

How to proceed

1. Select potential guests.

If possible, involve your participants in the choosing. Be clear what function the guest is to fill to enhance the group's learning experience.

2. Meet with the guest.

Do this face-to-face if possible. Otherwise discuss things by phone or correspondence. I suggest you negotiate directly with one person to ensure you know who is coming. After all, you are trying to fit this expert into your course and you are acting on behalf of all participants to ensure you get the best. The potential guest, too, deserves a fair chance to make an informed decision. If possible, give the class a choice of speakers. Involving the participants in this phase will enhance the guest's contribution and class participation.

3. Arrange logistics.

Once you have the right guest or guests, confirm the details of date, start and finish time, pay, parking, security, and telephone contacts. Sort out who is responsible for audio-visual aids, duplication, and other support materials.

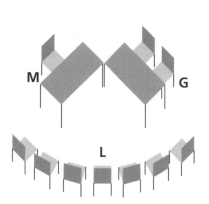

M = Moderator
G = Guest(s)
L = Learners

4. Work out a teaching plan.

Go over the details of the event and agree on a schedule of who does what and when. Discuss timing for start, breaks and finish, and when and how participants will get involved. Clarify your own role: explain that you'll be sitting with the guest at the front of the class, that you'll be acting as interviewer only to keep the discussion on topic, as moderator only during the question-and-answer session. Determine if any preparation or prior reading is required.

5. Prepare participants.

The guest session begins long before the expert arrives. If participants were involved in the initial decision, tell them why you are asking this guest to come and what can be expected. Prepare the class by brainstorming questions, assigning and discussing preparatory readings – anything you can do to "prime the pump." Explain the teaching plan for the session; describe what's expected of each participant. Ask for volunteers to introduce and thank the guest.

6. Manage the event.

When the day arrives, arrange furniture (get help from the participants), introduce the panelists, act as interviewer to get the guest going and on topic, and eventually be the moderator to direct the interactions. Try not to dominate the discussion; instead, do everything possible to bring out the best in your guest *and* boost learning opportunities for everyone involved.

Variations

Class members as expert panelists

Right from the start of a course, assign participants the job of paying special attention to given course material in order to develop a special expertise. Later on, arrange panel discussions among these "experts." Example: in a philosophy course, participants took on the roles of dinner guests at Plato's *Symposium* and argued an issue as they imagined their characters might have. In another case, management students discussed the issue of quality control in hotel services from the perspective of manager, desk clerk, and frequent guest. In both situations, the audience initially observed the discussion, then interacted by quizzing the experts on points that had been raised by the staged discussion. The instructor acted as moderator, continually bringing it back to the objectives for the session and away from personalities and preoccupations with acted roles.

> *Trusting the other is to let go; it includes an element of risk and a leap into the unknown, which takes courage.*
>
> – Milton Mayeroff,
>   *On caring.*

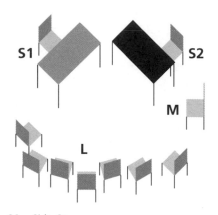

S1 = Side One
S2 = Side Two
M = Moderator
L = Learners

Arguing different sides of a controversy

This is a variation on the panel debate. It works well when your topic involves strongly held views on controversial issues. During the debate, equal time is given to each side of the argument. Use this technique in an impromptu way as an issue arises, or plan – even rehearse – it as part of your agenda. The room setup is similar to that for an expert debate. To heighten the drama, seat the opponents face-to-face with only a table to separate them. The moderator, either the teacher or an experienced participant, sits off to the side or between the arguing parties.

Example: In a course on environmental issues, we frequently ran into situations where people held strong personal views. Although the group agreed on most fundamental issues, when it came to matters concerned with individual versus public rights, tempers flared. A debate format allowed the airing of opposing viewpoints and gave each side a chance to hear and learn from the other. Coupled with the variation below, this technique frequently led to new insights and softening of rigid postures.

Hearing opposing views

After the first round of debate, ask the opposing sides to switch positions with each other and continue the discussion. This gives each person an appreciation of the other's position.

20

Learning outside the classroom

Occasionally a dose of reality is needed to put classroom activities into context. You can do this by discussing a case study, viewing a film, reading relevant articles, or by bringing in expert guest lecturers. Alternately, you can send participants out for interviews and first-hand observations. They can go as a group under your guidance, or individually, having made their own arrangements. Aside from logistical responsibilities, your main task is to ensure that every bit of learning is first extracted and then connected to the rest of the course of study.

A field trip is best used to:
- provide a first-hand view of a process, procedure, event, or location that cannot be brought to the classroom in a better way
- establish connections between classroom instruction and real-life practice
- collect impressions and information for classroom analysis and discussion

Group size

If you plan to go as a group, keep the party to under ten participants for every guide. In larger groups, people tend to form smaller ones, where they end up with their own conversations, trying to make some sense of what's going on around them. If your group is larger, break it into subgroups. Assign a guide to each group, or if that is not possible, begin the tour with an assembly in a place where everyone can hear the speaker, then send participants in small groups, with a printed guide or observation sheet. Agree on a time for all to reconvene and conduct a question-and-answer session to tie up loose ends.

Time required

First, allow time to make the arrangements. Leave enough time to explain the goal of the visit to the class and to put the visit into a context: here's why we are going; this is what I'd like you to look for; here's what you are expected to bring back. Finally you need to count on travel time from one place to another. To eliminate loss of class time, persuade participants to travel on their own time, using their own transportation.

Learning is more meaningful and lasting when it is immediately applied to real problems or situations.

– Daniel D. Pratt

How to proceed

1. Make the arrangements.

Do this well in advance and confirm them in writing. Visit the site yourself. Discuss the planned sequence of events and walk over the proposed route. Confirm the name and title of the person who will be your host; find out who might be the alternate in case of unavoidable substitution.

2. Get to know your host.

Unless you will provide the expert guidance during the visit, get together with the person who will perform this function. Treat the guide as a guest speaker: you need to work together to make the visit educational, rather than social. Try to get to know the guide; describe your participants, their backgrounds and their expectations. Explain what your learners already know and where, in the overall scheme, this visit fits in.

3. Prepare the participants.

Brief the class by telling them about the site you plan to visit, why you are going there, and who will be there to meet them. The class as a whole can make a list of questions about the site.

4. Confirm directions, time, and place.

Make sure everyone knows where to go on the date of the visits, as well as other information: emergency telephone contact, rides, material to bring, dress.

5. Follow up.

After the visit (or during your next class meeting), discuss the trip, give additional information and relate it to the course.

Send a note of thanks to your host; there is always next season's group to think of.

Variation : Individual field project

Instead of taking the whole class on a guided tour, participants go on their own or in teams of two. Such a scheme is especially useful if the location and times for visits fall outside normal class hours. Carefully planned and integrated, projects provide personalized learning opportunities through observation, reflection, and reporting.

Learning occurs within a specific situation and is profoundly influenced by that situation.

– Daniel D. Pratt

How to proceed

1. Establish a list of potential hosts.

Arrange for a list of potential hosts and leave it to each participant to arrange the details. If you state your criteria for what makes a suitable project site, students can find alternate placements to those on the list.

2. Prepare students for the project.

If this is a mandatory component of the course, participants need to be clear on what's expected. Discussions, handouts, and role-plays can help to prepare them to make contacts and to derive the greatest benefit from the project. A letter of introduction and observation forms can be made available as additional support. If a grade will be assigned, evaluation criteria must be agreed upon prior to the visit.

3. Debrief and integrate the project.

As with any experiential learning event, the debriefing is crucial. You can assist participants to identify key learning points by teaching them to recall details, reflect on events, and draw personal conclusions, making valuable connections between the abstract and the concrete.

Case #1: Anatomy of a field trip

Once a year I offer a continuing education course on wines and spirits. Halfway through the course, when participants have theoretical knowledge of the wine-making process, we visit a winery.

Participants are involved in the planning decisions, but it is up to me to make initial contacts, visit the site beforehand, meet the wine maker, outline the course, describe participants' backgrounds, and explain our objectives. During my initial visit, I'm able to gather information on the operation and get to know our host. Arrangements are confirmed in writing. When the class meets just prior to the visit, we develop a list of questions students are curious about. Everyone makes their own travel arrangements, but maps, names, and phone numbers are exchanged to avoid lost sheep.

Once at the site, we begin in a meeting room where introductions are made and the day's plan is sketched out. Our host, the company's wine maker, then explains the production process by way of a flow chart. The subsequent tour more or less follows this outline, and we scramble through laboratory and loading docks, past refrigerated tanks and noisy bottling lines. Eventually, everyone reassembles for a tasting session and we are joined by the marketing manager. We use this time for questions and answers and after a brief stop in the winery's retail store, we depart.

Soon after the visit, a letter of thanks is signed by the participants and sent to our hosts. We also discuss points raised by the visit and the tasting. Occasionally, observed practices differ from those discussed in class or read in a book. Such details make for interesting discussions and serve to integrate theory and practice.

Case #2: Anatomy of an individual field project

We have used individual projects in several settings where groups would not be allowed. The hotel business is a good example. Managers don't want to see a horde of students traipse through lobby, restaurants, and guest rooms, yet they are hospitable and keen to show their properties off to newcomers. Individual projects have worked well with students in junior college programs, night classes, and people enrolled in distance education courses.

Students are asked to select their own hotel operation, to contact the owner or manager, and to arrange for a minimum of four hours "working" behind the front desk. They are given study guides that outline the learning goals and the reporting procedure. They also receive a letter from the course coordinator, explaining the project and expressing appreciation for any assistance. Beyond that, students proceed on their own.

Results have been positive. Participants have brought back reports that show how much they have learned; some came away with part-time job offers, others with the realization that this kind of work, after all, was not for them. In many instances course material was verified; in others, it was questioned by more confident students. Instructors and managers report that projects keep them on their toes and that students value their new industry contacts and the opportunity to make "cold calls" for interviews. They also returned with information and anecdotes that would contribute to everyone's classroom experience.

21

Assigning projects

Determine learners' prior educational experience. People's expectations are influenced by previous learning, especially childhood experiences. Some may need to learn how to learn, including how to take increased responsibility for their own learning.

– Peter Renner

Give me a fish and I can eat today; teach me to fish and I can provide for the rest of my life. Or so goes the saying. If you believe in developing self-directed learning skills, then delegate certain tasks to the participants. Such tasks are typically done outside class time, by individuals or teams, and may involve library research and assigned readings, in addition to writing and/or presentation components.

Adults have little tolerance for busywork and appreciate assignments that have high relevance to their personal needs, stretch their individual learning style, and constitute a legitimate course ingredient.

Individual assignments are best used to:
- create self-teaching opportunities that recognize individual differences
- develop the skills necessary to search for data and analyze it critically
- reduce the teacher's function as primary information source
- complement information provided by the teacher and usual references
- develop supplementary reading lists

Time needed

Although the assignments are done outside class time, you need to create ways (and time) to integrate the material into the classroom activities.

How to proceed

1. Define topics.

2. Provide guidance.
Assist with access to information. Put participants in touch with specific literature pertaining to both content and process of the research. Make referrals with resource personnel, such as librarians, information officers, and faculty members.

3. Set a completion date and discuss consequences for late completion.

4. Plan how to make best use of the material being collected.
This can be done in a variety of ways, including annotated reading lists, abstracts of journal articles, executive summaries, book reports, and bulletin boards. Depending on your circumstances, information can be shared through oral report, electronic mail, visual display, or a number of print formats.

5. Ensure a good fit between the students' material and your own.
Clarify discrepancies, draw attention to contradictory and supportive data, correct misleading interpretations.

Watching for news

Current information is available in newspapers, trade magazines, professional journals, and the electronic media. Designate members to keep track of one medium each and report on items of relevance. Incorporate that information into the ongoing course discussion.

Selecting a textbook

Give a sample chapter from several texts being considered to small evaluation teams, which will report to the whole class on the pros and cons of the text.

You might want to provide them with guidelines for their assessment: reading level appropriate to the group; clarity of explanations; style of writing; quality of illustrations; bibliography; index; plus other criteria suitable to your setting.

Really using a textbook

Assign just a section of a text to be read prior to a given class. Provide written questions that help focus attention on the most important points. Draw attention also to supporting and peripheral issues. With the basics already covered through the readings, a foundation has been established for further discussions and teacher input. As is to be expected with assigned readings, some people will be better prepared than others. But that is their choice. The advantages of this approach – the sharing of responsibility for learning – tend to outweigh any shortcomings.

F U N D A M E N T A L S

Learning from experience

Give participants every opportunity to transfer insights from experiential learning into their everyday behavior. Kurt Lewin provides the theoretical foundation for a three-phase model.[1] Use it as a planning checklist: the more consideration you give to each, the higher the chances for individual discoveries.

- Phase one: experience the action: the learner experiences an action by trying out a set of behaviors, a strategy or procedure.

- Phase two: observe the consequences: the learner experiences the result of the actions by receiving feedback and through reflection on the experience.

- Phase three: develop an action theory: the learner is prompted to organize the new information into an action theory – a statement that describes what actions are needed to achieve a desired consequence in a given situation. "If I behave in such and such a way, then this and that will happen."

To some, the use of library facilities and data bases is an everyday undertaking; to others it's downright scary. One way to anticipate and build on these differences involves assignments with differing complexity. This allows participants to select a task at their comfort level without having to make a public admission (or a cover-up) of their lack of experience.

The first aims at developing the skills of analysis, summary, and application of relevant data. The second assignment involves familiarization with the tools of library research, including computerized data bases, catalogues, abstracts, and indexes. Participants are handed the following outline.

• **Assignment one: executive summary**

An executive summary recapitulates a body of information and provides a thumbnail synopsis of one or more sources. Your task is to investigate and summarize a topic of special interest to you. The topic must fit into the course agenda and provide valuable information to your classmates.

Your choice of presentation methods will be influenced by the nature of your topic and by the class timetable. Please discuss this with me.

To get you started, here's a list of possible topics.

1. How do seating arrangements influence power structure?

2. What leadership behaviors are most effective in task-oriented groups?

3. Summarize the essentials of Robert's Rules of Order and identify their pros and cons.

4. Select two or three publications from our list and search and summarize recent articles on small-group behavior.

• **Assignment two: annotated bibliography**

This type of bibliography identifies publications pertaining to our topic. In your annotation give a two- or three-sentence summary and critical evaluation of the content. Ideally, an annotated bibliography gives the reader a quick overview of what's available; gives details on title, author, publisher, and date; and provides a succinct content summary.

Several people have agreed to prepare bibliographies on related topics. Please complete yours by (date) so that we can collate them into one document.

Please use the following format.

William Strunk, Jr (and F.R. White, editor). The elements of style. *New York: Macmillan, 1972. (78 pages)*

A classic distinguished by brevity, clarity, and good sense. The most concise book on the fundamentals of composition.

Peter Elbow. Writing with power. *New York: Oxford University Press, 1981. (384 pages)*

A practical handbook with down-to-earth advice for beginning and seasoned writers. Not about getting power over the reader, but over yourself and the writing process. (Includes a twelve-item bibliography on publishing, and an index.)

Henriette Klauser. Writing on both sides of the brain. *San Francisco: Harper Row, 1986. (139 pages)*

How to use right-brain techniques to release your expressive powers. Good stuff on ordering ideas, overcoming procrastination, whole-brain spelling, and using visualization for creative purposes. Good ideas on overcoming writer's block while staring at your word-processor monitor.

Show articles in journals and chapters from edited collections as follows.

Jules Henri Poincare. "Mathematical creation," in The creative process, *ed. Brewster Ghiselin. New York: New American Library, 1952, p.38.*

22

Using journals

Learning journals, also called logs or diaries, are simple tools that can help to integrate learning from inside and outside the classroom. They further create a confidential connection between teacher and learner, or among small groups of participants. They are also excellent tools for teaching the skills of observing and reflecting.

Journals are best used to:
- assist participants in making connections between course material and personal lives and work
- draw participants' attention to personal learning opportunities that might otherwise be overlooked
- provide participants with a structure to keep track of multiple experiences during a course or workshop
- collect material that can be used during debriefing and evaluation sessions

Group size

Since this is an individual exercise, the size of the participant group puts no limitation on this tool. However, the optional sharing of the information requires the intimacy of small groups.

Time required

Most of the recording is done on the participants' own time. But it can be very useful, especially with novice diarists, to dedicate five-minute periods during class time for individual entries.

Materials needed

Ask participants to set aside either a small notebook or a section of their binder. Unless people explicitly wish to make their journal entries public, confidentiality must be guaranteed.

How to proceed

1. Introduce the idea.

Explain how a journal permits the recording of personal impressions, experiences, and questions over a given time span. Even a one-day workshop can yield much valuable data which, if unrecorded, would be lost to conscious memory.

If you plan to use a journal in conjunction with classroom activities, explain how easily we can become overwhelmed with information and miss out on meaningful connections and applications. A journal provides a possible remedy.

If the journal is to be used in conjunction with field work, internships, or independent learning projects, phrase the explanation accordingly See the sidebar for innovative uses of journals.

2. Emphasize privacy.

Underscore the private nature of these entries, but add that you would appreciate it if people would share their entries with the class, particular individuals, or yourself, either at certain times during the course or at the end.

3. Explain the process.

Give an example of what might go into the journal and how to record events. Offer examples, verbally or in written form. (See the written sample provided below.)

Find out who has had previous practice with educational journals and invite old hands to briefly describe their experience. Be prepared to balance such descriptions. You might ask everyone to suspend their judgment for a while.

4. Provide a structure for systematic recording.

At certain points of the course allow time for participants to pause, reflect, and record. With inexperienced journal-keepers, provide key questions to guide them through the exercise.

5. Arrange for ways to exchange information (optional).

Invite individuals to share whatever they wish, either with a partner or in small groups of not more than three. Sharing selected data does several things: it reduces isolation, validates individual experiences, and provides new ways of viewing common experiences. Following the small-group sessions, issues of interest to the whole class could be aired – with confidentiality preserved by such preambles as "Our group raised the concern that ..." or "We were surprised to discover that...."

By arrangement, you may ask to read each journal at regular intervals. This will give you the opportunity to gain insights and feedback you

Adults don't just bring experience with them; they are their experience. Therefore, to reject or ignore that experience is to reject or ignore an integral and important part of the person.

– Daniel D. Pratt

wouldn't otherwise have access to. You are also given an opportunity to respond to individual concerns on a one-to-one basis. If the situation seems appropriate, you can later raise important issues in class while still honoring individual confidentiality.

6. Suggest ways of writing

As your group becomes more and more experienced with journal-writing, you can offer directions and suggest certain themes and topics to focus on. This still leaves room for unstructured, personal commentaries.

For short-term courses or special projects, journals can be used on a one-time basis only. Of the examples provided on the next pages, **A** asks the student to reflect on the emotions surrounding plans for a job placement. Examples **B** and **C** require more complex reflections: first on individual behavior, then on a group process, and finally on possible action.

Variations

Combine and adapt various types to suit your students. Journals and logs are not just trendy embellishments—they are legitimate learning tools. They can assist learners in making connections between new and existing knowledge; they can demonstrate what students have learned; they can support independent thinking; and they can encourage deep rather than surface learning.[1]

Stephen Brookfield offers three conditions that must be met if students are to take journal-writing seriously. "(1) They must be given some specific guidelines on what a journal should look like, (2) they must be convinced that it's in their own best interest to keep a journal, and (3) their effort must in some way be publicly acknowledged and rewarded."[2]

Clinical journal

Used in conjunction with on-the-job experiences in nursing, they provide a vehicle for student-instructor communication, especially in situations where students are dispersed over several job sites. Students may be asked to send their journal entries via e-mail by a certain time and day.

Team journal

Use a team journal to promote interaction between team members on project-related issues and to introduce students to different perspectives on the project. Students can take turns recording shared and individual experiences, reactions and observations, and responses to each other's entries.

We had the experience but missed the meaning.

– T.S. Eliot, *Four quartets.*

Critical incident journal

This could pertain to classroom experiences over a specific period of time, such as a weekend or semester. Participants record events that involve decision making, conflict resolution, and problem solving. The journal provides a structure to record ways the group deals with problematic situations. Follow-up consultations with the facilitator and group-wide discussion of the incidents prove rich sources for teaching and learning.

Structured journal

This variation uses questions to provide uniformity (which is helpful in terms of student responsibility and teacher feedback), without impinging on individual creativity. Here is an example from nursing training:[3]

- *Pre-experience:* Describe how you prepared for the practicum. If you were working towards a research-related objective, read an appropriate article before the experience, relate your journal entry to it, and cite the article using APA format. Note your thoughts, feelings, concerns as you prepare for the experience.

- *Post-experience:* Identify three learning objectives that apply to the clinical experience. Note the extent to which each was met. If a research-related objective is involved, describe how the research findings pertain to this training site or target population.

- *Personal reactions:* How successful was the experience for you? What made you feel uncomfortable? How did you respond? Given a similar situation, what might you do differently? What are you taking away from this experience?

Electronic journal

These are frequently used in distance education but can just as easily complement classes that meet face-to-face. Using e-mail and chat rooms, participants engage in reflective dialog with each other and the teacher. A drawback can be student discomfort with the technology; a benefit is the deepening of relationships, especially for isolated students.

Reading response log

The teacher provides prompts to help participants relate assigned readings to their personal experience and understanding. For example: "As you read, write your personal response in your reading log. Describe your feelings, thoughts, reactions, and questions about situations, ideas, actions, characters, settings, symbols, plots, themes, and any

What if autobiography could actually be viewed as accomplishing educational goals that serve the learners with respect to enlarging their understanding of themselves and of the world around them? What if it could help individuals to know themselves, to appreciate their own accomplishments and to reach a level of integration concerning their life experiences?

– Irene Karpiak

other elements in the text. You can't be wrong in your responses, so take risks and be honest. Write about what you like and dislike, what seems confusing or unusual to you. Tell what you think something means. Relate personal experiences that connect with the plot, characters, or setting. Let me hear your voice. These starters are simply suggestions for you to use. Remember your response journal is a place to record your reactions and questions, not a place to simply summarize what you've read."[4]

Maintaining a journal during a field project

Students on work assignments benefit from regular communication with their instructor. Both parties need to monitor how things are working out. Where face-to-face meetings are difficult to arrange, a written log or journal may be the answer.

From the outset, the student must be encouraged to express any concern or question – about the placement, the on-site sponsor, the relevance of assignments, or any other matter. Assure participants that no one but the instructor will read the entries without their permission. You'll be astonished at how honest students can be.

For best results, provide learners with a recording system. It supports self-exploration and helps to develop observation and reporting skills. In the example

below, the students had discussed the giving and receiving of feedback and participated in a role-play about feedback. Their log for the following two weeks asked them to observe and describe performance-related comments directed at them.

The following questions are designed to stimulate recall and focus reflection:

- How did you do in your placement today? Please provide a brief description of the tasks, the site, and the people you worked with.

- How do you feel about this latest work assignment?

- If you received any feedback about your work, address the following questions. Who gave the feedback? What were the circumstances? How did you feel at the time? What did you say/do upon receiving feedback? Illustrate your answers with specific examples.

- Describe what you would do differently the next time you receive feedback on your performance.

- If you had occasion to provide feedback to another person, describe the circumstances: What did you say, to whom, about what? Describe the other person's reaction. How did you feel when all was said and done?

- Describe what you have learned about receiving and giving feedback. Be as specific as you can.

- Describe what you would do differently the next time you offer feedback to a coworker.

Example A

Date:_____ Topic:_____

What happened:

Today Peter mentioned that we were required to visit a hotel and arrange for a four-hour practicum. We are supposed to do it at a place where we would like to work some day. He said he wouldn't make the arrangements for us, but gave us a letter of introduction. The rest is up to each of us.

How I feel/felt about it:

I am not sure if I like this: going to a strange place to ask such a favour makes me nervous. What if they are too busy? What sort of place would I like to visit? Maybe this would be a good exercise for me to see if I really like the hotel business. Peter says that the people are usually very friendly.

Action plan:

I will look at the list of hotels Peter gave us and pick two that appeal to me. I'll go to each sometime before the next class, just to have a look around. From these impressions, I'll pick the place I like best. Then I might be ready to make that phone call.

With headings provided by the instructor

Example B

Completing the Learning Loop

Date: _____ Topic: _____

1. What questions do you have as a result of todays' learning experience? Jot down two or three.

2. From these questions, what key concepts can you extract? List at least two for each question.

3. How can you go about finding answers to these questions? For each question, select at least one specific approach you can take.

Example C

Evaluating - Reflecting - Planning

Date: _____ My role: _____

I learned these three things about the way task groups operate.
• _____
• _____
• _____

If I were to assess my own behavior during the task, I'd say that ...
_____
_____
_____

If I could make one change about my participation in the group, I would ...
_____
_____
_____

If I do change my behavior, here's how I'll know that I have been successful.
_____
_____
_____

So the point of my keeping a notebook has never been, nor is it now, to have an accurate factual record of what I have been doing or thinking.... How it felt to me: that is getting closer to the truth about a notebook.

– Joan Didion, *On keeping a notebook.*

Three case studies

Case #1: Chronicling a placement experience

At Boston College, undergraduates were assigned one of thirty-five different placements, from tutoring refugees to working in a residential setting with abused children.[5] For many students, this was their first serious challenge of previously established opinions, values, and priorities. Their course work asked them to examine the failures of institutions and the effect these have on the lives of individuals. By using journals, students found an outlet for troubling questions and their own feelings. Their instructor stressed the need to be sensitive to the confidential nature of journal entries. But once a level of trust had been established she was able to use the journal materials (anonymously) during class discussions and suggest alternate ways of viewing the problems confronting the students.

Case #2: Recording experiences thematically

In the community involvement program at Macalester College, St. Paul, Minnesota, students were encouraged to organize journals thematically in a loose-leaf binder.[6] Some themes reflected the writer's personal life (such as dreams, fears, and relationships); others addressed aspects of relationships with

institutions, their current job, or the educational program. Within each theme, students were encouraged to create sub-categories pertaining to work, practicum, or academic life. "Be ritualistic," their instructor recommended. "Set aside a time every day for reflection and writing. Be analytical. Allot 20 percent of writing time for describing the problem and 80 for possible solutions. Be optimistic. Even a placement that falls apart offers a rich source of learning."

Case #3: Journals as professional conversations

At McGill University in Montreal, two-way journals are used to document an ongoing dialogue between mentor and trainee during professional training in education, dietetics, and nursing.[7] The writing is used deliberately as an instructional device, in which instructors, as expert practitioners, give direction and feedback to interns. This professional conversation provides opportunities for trainees to raise questions regarding their placement. In their written responses, "instructors assist the integration of learning and the framing of mechanisms for deriving meaning from the practicum experience and theory and skill classes."

Students are told about the importance of intentional reflection and the merits of writing as part of their professional development. They are assured that this kind of writing is neither academic nor objective, and are encouraged to express their emotional responses. Such personal writing serves, among other purposes, to vent "problems, frustrations and high points of the day." They are told to record their reflections frequently and as soon as possible after the event. Using loose-leaf binders allows the instructor to read and respond, while the learner continues to write the journal on pages that can be inserted when the binder is returned. For the most positive response, journals are made a practicum requirement, but are not graded in any way.

With large classes and intensive schedules, students and instructors benefit from this written conversation. Students have private access to their teacher and can set the agenda for that encounter. Instructors learn more about each learner, can stimulate thinking through probing questions, and receive valuable feedback on the placement experience. Most importantly, "these professional conversations provide learners with explicit modeling of the productive use of reflecting; they have a window on the reflection and decision-making processes of the expert practitioner."

23

Processing feedback

Personal feedback gives information about behavior, performance, and conduct. If done well, feedback helps participants recognize potential problems and correct them. It can improve performance and interpersonal communications. Occasions to exchange feedback arise frequently in a learning group; following are some examples:.

- When you ask small groups to report. Example: "How did you do as a group?"

- When you ask for comments on the progress of the course. Example: "Tell me, how do you like the way we are spending class time?"

- When students comment on teacher behavior. Example: "Your instructions confused me and there was no time to ask for clarification."

- When participants speak to each other. Example: "Kiran, when you got up and started to write things on the flip chart, it really helped us to get focused."

- When you comment on a particular group behavior. Example: "I'm impressed with the quality of work the groups are producing."

- When you offer feedback to an individual after a specific behavior. Examples: "Thank you Sandy, for bringing us back to the agenda – the discussion was drifting off topic" or "Evan, you have answered almost every question I have posed: could you sit back for a little while and let others have a go?"

Guidelines

Here are some guidelines that make the process simple and educational. They address both the giving and the receiving of feedback information.

• **Give and receive with care.**

Above all else, giving and receiving feedback is an act of caring. It is an exchange of gifts. Ideally, the sender's intentions are simple: Please listen to what I've noticed about you. You may find it useful information, or you may not. It's just my perception and you don't have to do anything about it.

The receiver, to make best use of the feedback, accepts it: Thank you for taking the trouble to share your observations and to share them with me. I'll take what you tell me as information, as your view of my behavior. I may or may not agree with you and I am under no obligation to behave differently.

• **Ask to be invited.**

Most people are more receptive to potentially sensitive information if they have either requested it ("Tell me what you saw me do") or when someone has first asked them ("May I give you some feedback about ...?").

• **Concentrate on behavior.**

Behavioral feedback is about what can be observed, not about hunches, inferences, second-guesses, or judgments. Example: "You are very quiet tonight," instead of "You aren't interested in what we are doing?"

• **Make it easy to receive.**

Describe the behavior on a continuum of "more or less," rather than as "either/or." Example: "Daily journal entries are a good idea; your writing has become much more detailed since you began four weeks ago," instead of "We are half-way through the course and your entries are still without focus."

• **Don't delay.**

Feedback carries more weight if given soon after the observation. The person can then relate it to the specific situation and internalize the information more meaningfully.

• **Small doses, please.**

Give just enough information for the other to digest. Overloading someone with information dramatically reduces the effect. Dumping large amounts of information may give instant relief to the sender, but it makes it very difficult for the receiver to process.

• **Feedback comes in different disguises.**

Feedback doesn't always come in the spoken form. It can be communicated through gestures, eye contact, body stance, and relative distance to others. However, these messages may be misinterpreted. Quite often, nonverbal messages make a stronger impact than spoken ones. Ensure that your expression and body language is congruent with your verbal message.

How to better hear the feedback you are given

1. Concentrate on listening.

You don't need to do anything with the feedback. Simply look at the person giving you the feedback and listen carefully. Try to hear the words, see the gestures, and remember to keep breathing.

There is a story of Buddha, sitting under a tree, meditating. A man approaches him, full of rage. Buddha looks at the anger as a gift, but instead of taking it as expected, he thanks the man and regrets that he won't be able to accept his present.

2. Don't feel you have to respond immediately.

Most of us have difficulty hearing both positive and negative things about ourselves. To cover our discomfort, we guard ourselves with quick responses. Unfortunately, valuable opportunities for growth are lost and both sender and receiver lose out. The receiver is prevented from hearing the full message and the sender may think twice before offering feedback again. Avoid the following defenses.

- diverting: "I think that most people ..."

- explaining: "That's because ..."

- rejecting: "Yes, but ..."

- discounting: "Gee, that wasn't anything special ..."

- intellectualizing: "From a post-structuralist viewpoint ..."

- attacking: "Who are you to make such comments ..."

- whining: "If only I had advance warning, I'd ..."

3. Make sure you understand.

However much both parties may try, not every feedback message arrives neatly packaged and clearly understood. Giving and receiving involves a conscious effort on the part of both people involved. If you don't understand, say so, but let the other person know which part of the feedback message is unclear to you ("You are saying that my contributions irritate you. But I'm not sure how. Could you give me an example?"). Now both are engaged in working towards an understanding of the issue.

Occasionally, a third person – the teacher or another participant – may step in to ask for clarification ("Did I miss something here? I don't think you heard what that group is asking for."). The thing to do now is check with the parties involved and find out how satisfied they are with the exchange.

4. Say when enough is enough.

Should people get carried away and end up overwhelming someone with suggestions, advice, or criticism, it is the recipient's prerogative to say so. If things seem to be getting out of hand, the teacher must intervene ("Sean, that may be enough feedback for you right now – what do you say?").

How to approach a difficult behavior

Every so often, people behave in ways that irritate and interfere. Confronting this calls for a clear focus on behavior – not the person. Joseph Raelin offers a three-part memory aid, known as "when/I/because."[1]

- **Part one:** The "when" is followed by the naming of the specific behavior. For example: "When you read your newspaper during the group discussion...." Note that the behavior is described objectively and that no blame or value judgement is attached.

- **Part two:** The "I" statement follows with a description of the feeling you experience as a result of the behavior. "When you read your newspaper during the group discussion, I felt let down." Note how the feedback provider is taking ownership for the feeling, rather than holding the other responsible. Citing feelings in this manner personalizes the feedback and adds meaning to the exchange.

- **Part three:** The "because" part of the statement informs the recipient of the effect of the behavior. "When you read your newspaper during the group discussion, I felt let down because you didn't share any of your expertise. Also, by tuning out you made the task more difficult for your group." Hearing the consequences stated in a clear manner will make it easier for the recipient to listen and respond nondefensively. The path is paved for both partners to engage in problem-solving.

24 *Learning autobiographically*

by Irene E. Karpiak[1]

Up until recently, writing a life story was reserved for the elderly undertaking a life review or for those in the public eye. Now autobiography is being used as an instructional method to foster literacy, to stimulate creative writing, and to promote personal learning. When adult learners undertake autobiographical writing, they embark on a process of exploration that can further self-knowledge and understanding as well as enlarge their view of themselves and the world around them.

In autobiography the writer transforms his or her life into a written text. This exercise differs from journals and diaries and other kinds of personal writing in that it involves considering one's life in its entirety over time. The autobiographer looks back, re-collects the scattered memories of his or her life, and reflects on the pattern of this life, on the meaning of certain events and experiences, and on the possible larger story that might be revealed.

The consequence of writing may include heightened understanding of the writer's life and of the many factors that shaped it, appreciation of the actions of others, a sense of the roles the writer may have unwittingly played, consciousness of aspects that have been up until now unconscious, and a determination of what they want to do and how they want to live in the years ahead.[3]

The purpose that autobiography can serve for student/author

In personal learning

In the course of their writing, students may turn to early childhood and educational experiences that influenced their view of themselves as learners. Through this process they may ascertain that their present attitudes and values concerning education have roots in certain early school experiences. Some may use the opportunity to look back on points of decision or on defining moments in their life that brought new challenges, prospects and often growth. Others may examine different eras—childhood, adolescence, leaving home, marriage—and consider how related experiences have shaped their life. Still others may highlight moments of pain and loss and begin the process of confronting the past and taking steps toward healing and resolution.

Those who do not have the power over the story that dominates their lives, power to recall it, rethink it, joke about it, and change it at times change, truly are powerless, because they cannot think new thoughts.

– Salman Rushdie[4]

In career and professional learning

In addition to more personal purposes served by writing, some writers may focus on their professional growth. Some look back and uncover the basis of decisions they made concerning their choice of profession or career. Some may look at how their present career has been part of a longer story and discover a pattern of motives, values, skills, talents, and learning. For others it can be an opportunity to articulate a commitment to their field and can help define what is so meaningful to them about this work (or alternatively, what changes need to be made).

For connecting to the content

Some students find that the act of writing their story and bringing it into the current picture helps them understand and appreciate the concepts and theories in the course content. Reflecting on their personal experience can enable them to see how the course material fits into their life.

The purposes that autobiography can serve for instructors

Instructors who assign autobiographical projects to students are often taken aback by the strength and style of this kind of personal writing. It is often so different from formally written assignments —so much more creative, evocative, and powerful.

In addition, autobiography provides instructors with a window—an "inside" view—into the lives of learners, reminding them that this is a classroom not only of students, but also of individuals with unique and diverse personal histories. Knowing about students' backgrounds helps instructors to become more mindful of these differences among their students. It can help them become more sensitive to learners and to the possible ways in which the new knowledge being presented in the course may clash with their previous knowledge and experience.

And should instructors be motivated to write their own story—as a learner, or teacher, or developing individual—the same opportunities offered to the students would be available to them. They, too, could possibly uncover the basis for their career choices, theoretical orientation, or teaching philosophy and style.

Autobiography can promote learning when authors are encouraged to
- avoid simple recording of events in a chronological manner
- search for metaphors and patterns in their story
- take a step away and critically reflect on their experiences
- discover the meaning and significance of their experiences.

How to introduce autobiography to students

The following guidelines may be useful for initiating autobiographical writing. Students are generally asked to submit an outline of the chapters for review before proceeding.

- A publisher has given you the option of writing five chapters of your life story.
- Prepare an outline that includes the chapter titles; consider a title for your story.
- Write two pages for each chapter.
- Try to move beyond a simple chronology of events.
- Pay attention to any metaphor, thread, or pattern that emerges from the events of your life.

The instructor, as the audience of the life story, bears a responsibility to provide the sort of feedback and response that communicates understanding and appreciation of the story, as well as to offer support for future learning and growth.

Variations

James Birren[6] suggests providing a list of questions for students to consider before they proceed.

- What audience will they aim at?
- What themes will they explore?
- How will they arrange and relate the life incidents?
- What guiding metaphor will they use?
- What message do they want to convey?

Pierre Dominicé[7] asks students to begin by preparing oral "educational biographies" that focus on their life experiences as learners or as teachers. A written narrative follows the oral version. The reading audience is the other students, with whom the stories are later shared, discussed, and even analyzed.

Catherine Hobbs[8], professor of composition, provides a set of criteria intended to help students revise their papers, as well as to help instructors read and respond to student autobiographies:

- Focus-Purpose: What is the center of gravity of this piece of writing? Does it explore a matter of personal significance or follow a simple chronology?
- Development; How does use of description, detail, anecdotes, settings, and dialogue support this piece?
- Outcome: Does the piece deliver on the promise made at the start? What questions are left?
- Organization: Is it effective for the focus, reader, and situation? Do the parts fit?

Telling our own stories is a way to impose form upon our often chaotic experiences and, in the process, to develop our own voice, Listening to our own stories is a way for us to nourish, encourage, and sustain ourselves, to enter into a caring relationship with all the parts of our self.

– Joanne E. Cooper[5]

- Style: Does the language of personal experience support the focus and purpose?
- Conventions: Does the piece adhere to standards of writing?

Valerie Jansick[9] offers a variety of activities for the development of interpretive skills. Adapt her ideas by asking your students to use photographs, mementos, collages, family letters, and haiku poetry as triggers for writing brief autobiographical accounts.

Two examples of student autobiographical writing

David, shortly after returning from serving in the Gulf War, reminisces about his childhood in rural America.

I grew up like Tom Sawyer. The river was not the Mississippi, but the Tennessee. Still, my childhood had the color and texture of rural southern wonder. There were horses, cattle, endless rides, forested hikes, and lazy days on the river. There are no better smells than freshly tilled earth and the lather of a horse mingled with the smell of saddle leather.

Roberta compares her life to a novel, still unfinished.

… my life is the making of a story I couldn't have predicted and one [that] careful planning hadn't phased, couldn't touch. I like the idea of being an unfinished novel, an untold story in the process of the telling. My task in life is reading the book as I'm in the midst of the writing, replete with experiences, changing meanings, and a cast of real people.

It is fitting to end with Roberta's comparison of her life story to a novel that is still being written. She is living the story, and she is also the one reading it and the one creating and changing its meanings. The difference between a novel and an autobiography is that the latter is never finished. As students write their story, compressing and organizing scattered fragments of their life into five chapters, they come to know themselves … even as life continues and they continue to change.

Darkness within darkness,
The gateway to all
understanding.
…

Just realize where you
come from:
This is the essence of wisdom.

– Lao tzu[10]

25

Designing tests and quizzes

In his autobiography, Malcolm Knowles ranks "learning about meaningful evaluation" as one of the eight episodes that changed his life.[1] On the road to this discovery, he had to shed the belief that evaluation had to be quantitative, limited to the type of pencil-and-paper tests most of us know and dread. He learned to use many of the qualitative approaches mentioned in these pages, including interviewing, observer feedback, journals, case studies, and self-assessments.

Meaningful evaluation helps participants gain insights into how and what they are learning. According to Stephen Brookfield, "the only educational justification for evaluation is to assist learning."[2] Therefore, evaluation activities must be integrated into every learning activity, regardless of whether the course intent is the acquisition of information, the development of skills, or the exploration of feelings and attitudes.

More than before-and-after testing

Written tests still have a place, but they must be used in a new way. In the traditional scenario, an instructor might begin the day with these remarks: "Before starting the course, please complete the pretest so that we know your entry knowledge. It'll help us assess your progress later." At the end of the day, participants complete another test that attempts to measure their progress and "satisfy the course requirements."[3]

By contrast, in a course that integrates evaluation with other learning activities, the day starts out differently: "Let's begin with a self-assessment of your knowledge, skills, and attitudes. This will help you think about the work that lies ahead." At the end of the course, a concluding test is introduced in a similar light: "As I mentioned this morning and throughout the day, our last activity is another self-assessment. It'll help you to review what we have covered and identify what you've learned." Finally, participants are reminded that they'll be contacted again in the near future for a similar test – this one to reinforce what's been learned and to determine how useful the new learning is.

Which do you consider were the most alike, Caesar or Pompeii, or vice versa? (Be brief.)

– This and the following test questions appear in *1066 And All That*, a satire upon textbook history and our confused recollection of it.

Note that the evaluation design still uses written tests, but it is now solidly based on these adult learning principles: learning is amplified if participants know what they will learn; it is further enhanced by immediate reinforcement (through the end-of-day test) and over the long term (through the follow-up survey).[4]

Benefits of written tests

Learners and teacher benefit from carefully thought-out evaluation activities.

To the learner they provide:
- realistic short-term goals
- motivation to study notes, texts, and handouts
- increased retention of learned material
- direct feedback on progress
- objective evidence of accomplishment

Teachers and course planners derive:
- ways to assess the appropriateness of instructional objectives
- evaluation of teaching techniques and materials
- feedback on teaching effectiveness
- support and reward for everyone's efforts

Ideally, tests should reflect clearly defined instructional objectives. Techniques of writing instructional objectives and designing tests are beyond the scope of this book, but the following summaries and checklists will prepare you for further exploration.

Types of tests

The tests with everyday application are called objective tests, since the correct answer can be objectively determined. *Selection-type* tests require the learner to choose one or more of the given responses; examples include multiple-choice, true-false, and matching-items types. *Supply-type* tests ask the learner to provide a correct response; examples include short-answer and essay questions.

• Multiple-choice items

Each starts with a *stem* and is followed by four or five *alternatives*. Example:

> Which province lies between Alaska and Washington?
> a. Alberta
> b. British Columbia
> c. Yukon
> d. Oregon

Experienced test designers follow certain ground rules in the construction of multiple-choice tests.[5] Use this checklist to see how well your test items measure up:

☐ Each item measures only important learning outcome.

☐ The stem is stated in simple, clear language.

☐ Most of the wording is in the stem, rather than the alternatives.

☐ The stem is stated in positive form, wherever possible.

☐ Negative wording is emphasized whenever it is used in the stem.

☐ The intended answer is correct or clearly best.

☐ All alternatives are grammatically consistent with the stem.

☐ The item contains no verbal clues to enable learners to select the correct answer or to eliminate an incorrect alternative.

☐ The length of correct answers is varied to eliminate length as a clue.

☐ "All of the above" is not used as an alternative.

☐ "None of the above" is used with extreme caution.

☐ The position of the correct answer is varied in random order.

☐ Each item is independent of other items in the test.

Have you the faintest recollection of
(1) Ethelbreth?
(2) Athelthral?
(3) Thruthelthrolth?

- **True-false items**

  Here the learner is required to judge a declarative statement as either true or false. Alternatives to true-false may be yes/no, agree/disagree, right/wrong, fact/opinion, and the like. Examples:

<u>True</u> False	The rivers Mosel and Rhein join near the city of Koblenz.
<u>Agree</u> Disagree	The kestrel is also known as the sparrow hawk.
Fact <u>Opinion</u>	White wine should be drunk with seafood.

  You can also combine multiple-choice and true-false items.

  Grape varieties permitted under Bordeaux Appellation Contrôlée rules include:

A. Pinot Noir	T <u>F</u>
B. Cabernet Franc	<u>T</u> F
C. Chardonnay	T <u>F</u>
D. Merlot	<u>T</u> F
E. Semillon	<u>T</u> F

In addition, learners may be asked to judge the statement as true or false, and then provide a true statement. They may be further asked to explain their choice in a short statement. The problem with true-false items is that they are very difficult to construct; they must be either undeniably true or clearly false. There is also a danger of discrimination against learners capable of perceiving possible exceptions to even the most obvious true or false answer.

Use this checklist to help keep each of your true-false items honest:[6]

☐ The statement includes only one central significant idea.

☐ The statement is worded as unquestioningly true or false.

☐ The statement is short and uses a simple language structure.

☐ The statement contains no double negatives.

☐ Statement of opinions are attributed to a source.

☐ Overall, negative statements are used sparingly.

Estimate the average age of
(1) The Ancient Britons.
(2) Ealdormen.
(3) Old King Cole.

• **Matching items**

The matching item is a modification of the multiple-choice format, consisting of two lists – a series of stems, called *premises*, and several *responses*. For instance, lists may contain parts of a diagram and names of the parts, problems and solutions, countries and capitals. The learner must match the items on one list with those on the other. Here is an example from an equestrian test.

Directions: Column A contains a list of basic tack; Column B a list of variation on basic tack. On the line at the left of each tack item, put the letter of the item in Column B that best fits the item. Each response in Column B may be used once, more than once, or not at all.

Column A	Column B
(D) 1. Bridle	A. Bridoon
(E) 2. Saddle	B. Chin harness
(C) 3. Rein	C. Martingale
(A) 4. Double bridle	D. Snaffle
	E. Sweat flap

In a matching-items test, all responses must appear as plausible alternatives for each premise. If that is not possible, resort to separate multiple-choice items.

• Short-answer items

These consist of a question or an incomplete statement to which the learner is asked to supply a response. Among the many variations, three are most straightforward: direct question, fill-in-the blank, and association.

Direct question:

In what part of North America does the ruby-throated hummingbird live? _____ *(the East)*

Fill-in-the-blank:

Unlike most birds, cardinals mate for _____. *(life)*

Which came first, A.D. or B.C.? (Be careful.)

Association or identification:

After each (male) bird listed below, write the dominant color.

1. Baltimore oriole   _____ *(orange)*

2. Steller's jay   _____ *(blue)*

3. Northern cardinal   _____ *(red)*

4. Northern mockingbird   _____ *(gray)*

Let this checklist help you construct and evaluate short-answer items:[7]

☐ The length of the statement is kept uniformly short.

☐ For each statement, only a single, brief answer is possible.

☐ The blank is at the end of the statement.

☐ The learner is not required to supply such words as "the" and "an."

• Essay question

This test item consists of a question, topic, or brief statement to which the learner must supply an extended response. According to one authority, essay questions have many uses, including the measurement of a person's ability to make comparisons, apply principles, organize and summarize information, communicate ideas, conduct a critical study, make judgments, draw inferences, be persuasive, use logical reasoning, and demonstrate in-depth knowledge of a topic.[8] The following are examples of essay-type questions:

- Describe the principles of ... (summarizing)
- What additional data are needed to ... (inferring)
- Propose a solution ... (creating)

To the teacher, essay questions offer the advantage of quick construction and the disadvantage of the time it takes to evaluate each. Subjectivity in scoring presents a further complication. In fact, some studies report that independent grading of the same essay by several teachers can result in marks from excellent to failing and that the same teachers grading the same essay at different times gave significantly different grades.[9] The quality of handwriting and composition can also have a negative influence on the one who grades.

Whether you have to assign a grade or are free to do without them, your learners are entitled to careful comments. To that end, evaluation should always be *educative*. That is, feedback should assist learners in three ways: to become more adept and critically reflective about the task; to gain insights into their habitual learning processes and enable them to decide whether to maintain or alter them; and to nurture their self-confidence as learners.[10] Aim for these goals every time you evaluate an essay question. Instead of a cursory check mark for a right answer, or a routine "well done!", say what you find good about the essay, assess how the learner has demonstrated (or failed to show) proficiency in the material under study, acknowledge any progress from previous work, and indicate areas for further growth.

This last checklist will assist you in writing and scoring essay questions:[11]

Preparation

☐ Participants have had prior practice (not graded) in understanding and responding to essay questions.

☐ The participants are clear on the scoring method and know to what extent organization of the material, handwriting, grammar, etc. are taken into account.

Test design

☐ The directions are specific and to the point. The learner knows exactly what's expected.

☐ The vocabulary and jargon are consistent with the learner's experience.

☐ The time it takes to answer each essay question is about twice as long as it takes the teacher to write the answer. (Adjust this, depending on participants' familiarity with the subject matter and the process of testing.)

☐ The test contains more than one essay question and offers a choice of questions to be answered. This increases participants' chances to be successful.

☐ The value for each question (or part thereof) is given on the test paper.

Evaluation

☐ Learners' names are concealed or coded to reduce personal biases.

☐ Questions are evaluated one at a time, on all tests. This tends to increase reliability in scoring.

☐ Each learner receives personalized comments in line with the goals outlined above.

Write not more than two lines on The Career of Napoleon Buonaparte, or The Acquisition of our Indian Empire, or The Prime Ministers of England.
N.B. Do not on any account attempt to write on both sides of the paper at once.

26

Projecting overhead

Next to a chalk or white board, the overhead projector is the most widely available visual device. You can make transparencies quite easily, either by writing and drawing directly onto the acetate or with transfers, using an ordinary duplicating machine. This chapter provides some straightforward instruction on how to make transparencies, how to operate the machine, and where to place it in a room.

Advantages of the overhead projector

- The machine can be operated from the front of the room while the presenter faces the audience.

- The time spent on each item is completely under the presenter's control. The lamp can be switched on or off to project the image at certain times. A transparency can be brought back at a later time for review and to stimulate recall and discussion.

- Room lights remain on, so that learners can take notes.

- Since the transparencies are right-side-up as you look over the projector, you rarely need to lose eye contact with your audience.

- Instead of individual transparency sheets, you can use a roll of transparency sheeting, making the machine into a continuous bulletin board. If needed, you can wind back to review previous writing. Later, the roll can either be stored for review or cleaned for reuse.

- The sequence of a presentation is easily modified by the deletion or insertion of transparencies.

How to prepare transparencies

You can write directly on transparency sheets or use a duplicating machine to transfer an image from a sheet of paper onto a transparency. With the direct method, use special marking pens; they are available in many colors, some water-based (erasable) others alcohol-based (permanent). With the machine method, use a clean original and copy in either black and white or full color. If you have access to cardboard frames, mount the transparency and use the frame to record your notes and reminders.

Basic transparency design

1. Check the size.

The usable surface of a standard transparency frame is 7-1/2" x 9-1/2", so your prepared copy must not exceed these dimensions. If you omit the cardboard frame, your usable light surface becomes 8" x 10" in size.

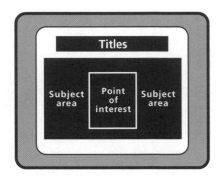

2. Keep it simple.

Too much detail creates confusion; after all, the image is meant to support your verbal presentation, not take its place.

Use no more than six words per line and six or fewer lines per image. Select only key words and phrases. Don't try to summarize an entire presentation on one transparency.

3. Apply layout rules.

Double-space all lines. Use simple, bold lettering types, at least 1/4" high. Plain type is best. Horizontal is considered the best format, although vertical is acceptable.

4. Avoid typewritten material.

It does not project well, even if it is large type. Some laser printers may do a better job, as long as you follow this rule: if you can read the original at a distance of ten feet, the transparency should project well.

5. Make transparencies into handouts.

Transparencies can be photocopied and become handout material for people who missed a session.

6. Special effects.

Unusual effects, such as silhouettes and cutouts, are easily prepared. Two superimposition methods are possible: one involves stacking transparencies layer upon layer, thus illustrating complex models and processes as you talk about them. The other method involves projecting an image onto a writing surface, such as a white board, and adding the details by writing on that surface.

Operational dos and don'ts

- DON'T show more information than is necessary at one time. If you show too much, viewers will get ahead of you or their minds will wander; either way, they won't pay attention to you.

- DO use the revelation technique. Place a sheet of heavy paper under the transparency. By moving the sheet down, you reveal the image line-by-line and thus control the viewers' attention.

- DON'T turn the lamp on before you have positioned a transparency. The bright white field on the screen is annoying to look at – yet everyone will.

- DO line up the image and when it's needed, turn on the lamp. When it is no longer needed, turn the lamp off. Switch whenever you want to tear your audience away from the lit image. You may be talking about a new bit of information, but if the old transparency is still on, you can count on people still looking at it. Light fascinates.

- DON'T turn off the room lights. At most, turn down the lights immediately over the projector. Otherwise, natural and electric lights can stay on to allow note-taking and minimize disruption of the proceedings.

- DO use overlays to provide a sense of progression. Up to four transparencies can be placed upon each other in succession with the light shining through. This is particularly effective for flow charts, graphs, and complex models. Start with a simple image, and as you describe additional features, build it up one sheet at a time.

- DON'T wave your hands or other objects over the transparency. The shadow, multiplied many times, will show on the screen and become another irritation.

- DO indicate an item on the transparency by placing a pencil or other pointed object that won't roll away. Like an arrow, it'll focus viewers' attention. Remember to remove the pointer when it has served its purpose.

Room setup

You'll rarely have the ideal physical setting, so check the room beforehand and arrange the furniture to suit your needs. The following diagrams illustrate some setup possibilities, but you'll have to improvise on the spot.

This could be any classroom. Sometimes the screen is mounted so that it sits in the middle of the front wall, right behind the presenter's desk, often obscuring the chalk board when pulled down.

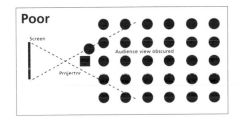

But don't let that deter you. Come early, inspect the setup and see if you can get a portable screen and put it off to the side. Following are a few ideas for good arrangements.

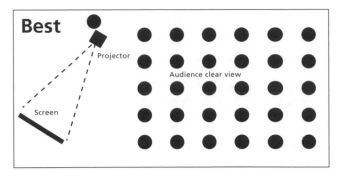

When using an overhead projector, arrange the room so that the audience's view of the screen is not obstructed.

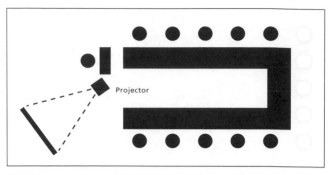

U-table arrangement. Suitable for thirty people or fewer. This arrangement is ideal for group discussion and interaction.

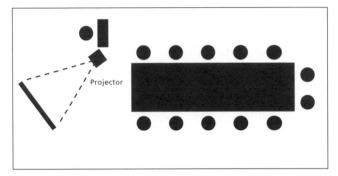

Centre table arrangement. Suitable for under twenty people. This setup promotes discussion and is best for long meetings.

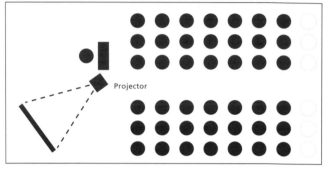

Auditorium/theater arrangement. (Single projector) Suitable for any size audience, but most efficient for large groups.

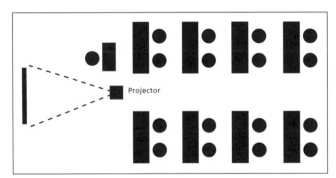

Classroom arrangement. This is a standard arrangement suitable for any size group.

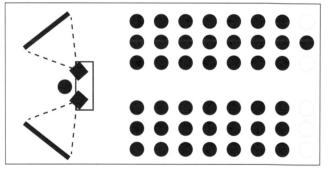

Auditorium/theater arrangement. (Dual projectors) As above, this arrangement works well with large groups. Two projectors and screens give the presenter more latitude in her or his presentation.

These diagrams were provided by the 3M Company

The practice of andragogy

Malcolm Knowles uses the term "andra-gogy" to describe his theory and prac-tice of adult education (in contrast to "pedagogy," which is concerned with the education of children).[1] Knowles advocates a learner-oriented approach to teaching based on the following assumptions.

- Adults are motivated to learn as they experience needs and interests that learning will satisfy; therefore, these are the appropriate starting points for organizing adult learning activities.

- Adults' orientation to learning is life-centered; therefore, the appropriate units for organizing adult learning are life situations, not subjects.

- Adults bring with them the richest resource for their own learning; there-fore, the core methodology of adult education is the analysis of experience.

- Adults have a deep need to be self-directed; therefore, the teacher's role is to engage in a process of mutual inquiry with them rather than to trans-mit knowledge and then evaluate con-formity to it.

27 Presenting with PowerPoint

by Kathryne Roden[1]

PowerPoint is simply a series of sequenced slides that can be easily prepared in advance on your computer, and then projected onto a screen for everyone to see during a presentation. The presentation can be amended or new slides added at any time. Incorporating video clips is even a possibility and can be developed with an infinite variety of color, graphics, and sound. A well designed PowerPoint presentation is visually captivating, extremely versatile, and allows the prepared facilitator to focus more on the learning process and less on managing the teaching materials. Additionally, the presentation can be accessed on an instructor's web-site or through an on-line resource library, for future reference or by someone who may have missed the initial presentation. This availability can reduce or eliminate in–class note-taking and the entire presentation may be downloaded and a hard copy run off for further use.

Probably the major disadvantage of PowerPoint presentations is their overuse, both in frequency and length of presentation. They can be overly complex or 'slick', where the technical gimmickry and dazzle, are more captivating and enduring than the quality and usefulness of the material and content. This, in fact, can create barriers between the presenter and the audience if the presenter relies less on active participation with the students and more on the format of the presentation. Too many PowerPoint presentations can dull the senses, reduce critical thinking, and place students or participants in a deceptively passive role unless the instructor determines otherwise. Overusing any learning tool or method is likely to produce boredom and disinterest, and PowerPoint is no exception.

How to begin

The first step in developing a PowerPoint presentation is to prepare an outline utilizing the *Outline* link located just to the left of the slide link. With each slide displayed on the outline, the main idea and supporting points can be developed. Use the outline format to develop the storyboard with the slides by planning the location of the text and the location of the graphics. The main idea generally is stated within the *heading* of each slide and the supporting points will be included in the *body* of the slide.

Once the outline is completed, you are ready to develop the design for each slide. Find the slide design by going to *Format*. It is recommended that you keep the design simple so the blueprint does not overshadow the content of the presentation. This selection can be changed at any time throughout the preparation or even after you have completed the creation of the PowerPoint; however, it generally is best to do it at the beginning of the presentation because a change in the slide design alters the slide layout.

Next, choose the *slide layout* by going to *Format* and selecting *slide layout*. The layout formats are quite varied. The layout is formatted for headings and the body for each slide. Headings increase readability and help focus attention for each slide. When selecting the layout for each slide in the PowerPoint presentation it is vital to consider the body of each page. The body of each slide is important because it determines the format of the slides. The format for each page helps guide the eye. It also allows you to determine the type of material presented.

Other considerations

The choice of **font** contributes to the effective presentation—it can also distract. As a basic rule, use the same font throughout. The font size is best determined in relation to the size of the group and the room, but generally 24 points or larger is recommended. Keep in mind that not all computers have the same fonts. If the computer used to create the presentations on is different from the one used during the presentation, it is critical that the fonts on both computers are compatible.

Capital letters should be used only when grammatically appropriate and for emphasis, titles and headings. Using both upper and lower case letters generally provides the best readability.

The ***Word Art*** function allows words to be colored and altered along a non-linear axis. While it can add a creative element to a display, it can easily distract from the main topic. Use it guardedly.

Color can successfully highlight key phrases and draw attention to important concepts. Do not overdo it. It may also be used to evoke certain tones or emotions, such as green as relaxing, red and yellow for urgency, blue to either relax or convey seriousness depending on the hue, and black for power and authority. Refer to the color wheel to avoid combining opposite colors.

The **amount of text** on each slide is an important consideration. Of course, the number of words per slide varies with the font, the font size, the material being covered, the types of transitions, and the purpose of the slide. Slides with fewer words allow for greater comprehension of the material. It is better to have more slides with fewer words than to crowd too much material onto one slide.

A POWERPOINT PRESENTATION WITH ALL CAPITAL LETTERS IS VERY DIFFICULT TO READ SO USE THEM SPARINGLY.

Use spell-check. Spelling and grammatical errors are distracting and reduce the credibility of the overall presentation.

Text expressions can be included in the presentation with any of the slides. Using a variety of transitions is possible, but a faster one tends to retain audience attention better. One of the best special effects is *Appear*. Avoid such special effects as *spinning* and *boomerang*.

Transitions. Some presenters use a *dimmed* approach with transitions. In a group of text introduced one piece at a time, the previously introduced text is dimmed once the new text arrives on the screen. This can be effective but ensure that the dimmed text is darker than the newly introduced text to create a clear demarcation between newly introduced lines and previous text.

Graphics may be added to any slide, but they should only be used to advance the purpose of the slide; go for quality rather than quantity. Selection of the graphics may include charts and graphs, as well as artwork or photography from the Internet or material that you scan to your computer.

Incorporating other media

Use of multimedia can provide opportunity to sustain interest, enhance material presentation, facilitate retention, and appeal to a wide variety of learning styles. Most importantly, a multimedia presentation creates more opportunity for an active and engaging connection between the subject and the students.

DVD capabilities in personal computers and the companion use of Smart Board enable the use of film clips of movie scenes to illustrate a point or convey specific attitudes and emotions. Similarly, sound clips and sound bites can be inserted at appropriate junctures within the lecture in order to add affect and maintain interest. However, sound bites should be used sparingly.

Is a projector available for the presentation, or do you need to bring one? Is it a PowerPoint projector, a Smart Board projector, or some other type? Will technical assistance be available?

Audio clips are interesting to include throughout PowerPoint, assuming your computer has sound capabilities. Like the occasional sound bite, this can be an entertaining method to redirect attention back to the presentation when done correctly. Effective use of audio clips might include clips of interviews or dramatic readings of quotes, poems or speeches. Using clips in these ways can add additional interest to the presentation and bring focus to the lecture.

Limit each PowerPoint slide to one multimedia file. More than one movie or sound clip per slide can be confusing and even difficult to track. Discussion as well as descriptive text located above or below the multimedia can announce the purpose of the movie, to reinforce the purpose or objective of the presentation.

Be aware that use of multimedia can take up much file space. If the clips are lengthy, consider using a separate DVD or CD player.

Incorporated these film clips into the PowerPoint by including a slide in the presentation that introduces the multimedia selection. After viewing the multimedia choices, the PowerPoint may then be continued. Even if alternate forms for presenting the film or audio is used, the inclusion of the multimedia selection in the body of the PowerPoint choice is useful.

Setting up the display system

Having the PowerPoint software allows for the creation of slides but delivering a presentation before a group requires a viewing projector and connecting cables. The system should always be tested beforehand to ensure compatibility and correct connections. Technical glitches are common if the operator is not bringing or using her own equipment, which often results in a great deal of frustration, wasted time, and distraction.

The media for transferring the PowerPoint is limited by the host computers and various transfer media options, which include floppy disks, Zip disks, CD-ROM, DVD, and flash drives. Consider the limitations of the system when transferring a PowerPoint file from one computer to for the presentation. If the computer has Internet capability at the location of the presentation, you can email the file to yourself for the actual presentation or use it as a back-up.

Presentation

Good delivery is also essential to an effective presentation. The facilitator needs to maintain eye contact with the audience and this is only possible by a thorough knowledge and understanding of the material, as well as preparation. It is critical to refer to the objectives on the PowerPoint without reading from the PowerPoint slides. In addition, avoid standing in front of the screen, moving ahead of your slides, and presenting slides out of order.

Summary

Active participation with the students can alter some of these established strategies under certain circumstances. Moreover, effective PowerPoint presentations will evolve as new uses of art forms and media are discovered and are utilized to enhance the presentation. Therefore, use these guidelines as a starting point. Above all, enjoy using the capabilities of PowerPoint by actively engaging the students in the presentation.

28

Flipping charts[1]

The next best thing to a large white board is newsprint. Sheets can be mounted and turned over on an easel just like a writing pad, or posted directly on the wall. A combination usually works best. You might start writing on the easel and then, so the information remains visible, tear pages off and post them on a nearby wall. You thus create a visible record of the discussion, and it's easy to refer back to previously made points. Be selective in what you post, since displays can distract. Leave up only what helps to focus the discussion.

Paper

Flip-chart paper, also called newsprint, comes in loose sheets or in large pads. Some pads are mounted by being clamped to the easel, others by using holes along the top to fit metal rings or screws at the top of the easel. Make sure your paper fits the easel you'll be using.

Some types of paper have a grainy surface and are unmarked; other products are smooth and marked with lines one inch apart. Purists insist on un-lined paper, but if your writing has a tendency to wander and get smaller towards the edge of the paper, lines are a blessing.

Tearing sheets off a pad may look easy, but it can be tricky. A colleague suggests practicing the "matador tear": stand facing the easel, hold the sheet at the bottom left corner (if you are right-handed) and, stepping back slightly, pull away and up, cutting the sheet off at the top, along the metal clamp or the glued binding. Some pads come with a perforation that runs just below the top of the pad. Even they need practice.

If you don't want to tear off the full page, flip it over. That is why they are called flip charts. Depending on your height and reach, an elegant flipping style improves with practice. It's all part of feeling and looking confident.

Easels

Insist on an easel with a stiff (metal) backing that gives you a firm writing surface. If at all possible, work with two easels: one for the main points of the topic, the other for lists, asides, brainstorming, or keeping track of miscellaneous points. Even better are several flip charts, placed side by side across the front of the room. They make it possible to record a continuous flow of ideas as your presentation unfolds. Experiment also with easels placed in different corners of the room. Move from one to the other, redirecting attention to different angles of a topic and shifting the participants' interest around the room. Or use one or two charts for the main record and others for small-group activities involving written results.

Blank walls

If you shun the use of easels, consider working with wall-posted sheets. Begin by placing a band of tape about two inches above where you plan to post the flip chart paper. This gives you a ready supply of tape where you need it. Keep this line of tape supplied during slow times in the meeting or at break times.

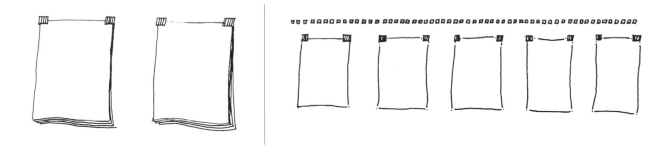

Do all this on a blank, well-lit wall. First remove all pictures and nails: keep a screwdriver and pliers in your briefcase for this purpose. Tape the sheets in five or six sections eight sheets deep; more than eight sheets tends to pull them all down. By overlapping the tape as shown above, it looks neat and well prepared. One sheet is easily removed without bringing the other sheets down. Hang sheets high enough for all to see and for you to work comfortably.

Tape

Applied carefully and removed soon after use, masking tape does not damage the walls. Seek out smooth surfaces, since walls covered with paper or textiles won't work as well. Half- to three-quarter-inch masking tape is convenient and has the sticking power – although some brands have more than others. If you use easels, cut (or neatly tear) two- to three-inch-long pieces of tape and attach them lightly to the easel legs. There they wait until you tear off a sheet and need tape to attach it to the wall.

Pens

Water-based, flat-tipped ("chisel-tip") pens work best. They do not give off the odors that make your head ache, and water-based ink on your clothes will often wash out. They also don't bleed through the sheets, whereas others can leave embarrassing marks on the wall. The chisel rather than the pointed tip makes a broad line that is easier to see. Water-based pens are available scented, a different aroma for each color. Why not?

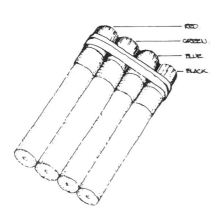

To reduce fumbling with pens and caps, make yourself a handy four-color dispenser by wrapping some masking tape around the tops as illustrated. One pen can be removed while the other three and all four caps stay taped together.

When not writing, recap and put down the pen. Holding on to pens and caps easily leads to fidgeting, which can be distracting to participants. You can also end up with messy pen marks all over your hands and clothes.

When pens run low on ink, colors fade and you hear squeaky noises when writing. The natural reaction is to put down the tired pen and reach for a fresh one. But chances are you'll pick it up again later and have to go through the rejection process all over. So, discard old pens right away.

Colors

Pens supplied with rented flip charts in hotels, schools, and training rooms usually come in one color: basic black. Come prepared with your own set and use them for the following purposes:

- Contrast: use strong colors and avoid pastels. Black and shades of green, brown, and blue are the working colors, with red reserved for emphasis. The pastels may be used effectively for underlining and circling. I'm not sure why yellow is included in the commercial packs: it is very hard to see from any distance.

- Alternate: when generating lists (during brainstorming, for instance), switch from one color to the other to distinguish one idea from the other.

- Organize: systematically use one color to label each sheet, one for topic headings, one for major points, a fourth for minor ones.

- Highlight: use circles, ovals, squares, rectangles, lines, double lines, waves, arrows, and bullets to draw attention to items on the sheet. Use symbols sparingly for maximum impact; add them as you go or to emphasize points during subsequent reviews.

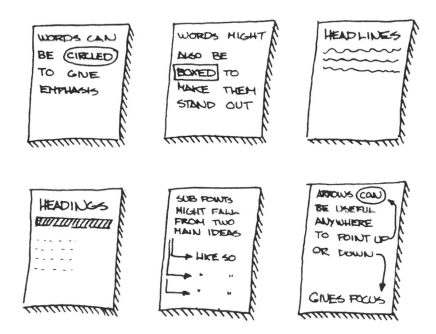

Recording techniques

If your style is anything like mine, you know that you can talk faster than you can write and that most handwritten notations are difficult to read. Experiment with the following guidelines:

- Resist the temptation to write down everything: abbreviate and condense! The idea is to capsulate an idea and record its essence.

- Print in block letters over one inch tall, even larger so that even the most distant participants can read your writing. Check occasionally to see that everyone can read it.

- Limit the entries per sheet to between eight and twelve lines; the number will depend on the size of lettering and amount of underlining and highlighting.

- Anything below table height probably can't be seen from deep in the room. To compensate for this, either leave the bottom section of the sheet blank or switch to the wall-writing technique, which allows for height adjustments.

- Write in headlines. Listen to a paragraph of words and write one line to capture the essence. Separate key thoughts from supporting ones. As participants see their words in writing, they begin to present information in recordable form – thus increasing productivity and satisfaction.

- Develop an index of abbreviations appropriate to your group and topic. My colleague David Quinlivan-Hall suggests these examples from working with business groups.

+/-	plus/minus, more or less
id	identify
diff	different
w/o	without
w	with
sp	spelling
ie	that is
eg	for example
PM	participative management
EI	employee involvement
TQM	total quality management
DMR	desired meeting results
COMP	competition
MGR	manager
EE	employee

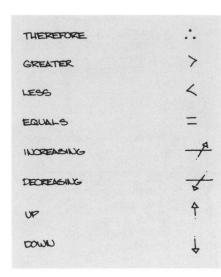

THEREFORE	∴
GREATER	>
LESS	<
EQUALS	=
INCREASING	
DECREASING	
UP	↑
DOWN	↓

He also recommends symbols and diagrams which can speed up the recording function as long as your group is clear on their meaning.

Where to stand

- Don't talk to the flip chart. Write, then turn around and continue the interaction.

- Do pace your recording. When done writing, step aside and give participants a few moments to read, reflect, comment, or take notes.

- Don't block the view. If people can't see well, move the easel around or suggest participants relocate to where they can see. By the way, such an invitation offers those with hearing and seeing difficulties a gracious opening to change seats.

- Do walk around the room and look at your own handiwork from the participants' angle. If necessary, adjust your recording style and technique.

Prepared sheets

- Some charts, models, lists, and diagrams benefit from advance preparation and artistic touches. If meant for repeated use, they can be laminated for a clean appearance time after time.

- Mistakes are easily repaired. Minor ones can be fixed with white-out liquid (there's a special one for pen and ink). Larger errors can be pasted over with a piece of newsprint attached with transparent tape.

- Transport prepared sheets rolled up, in a cardboard mailing tube or, for that smart look, in a shoulder-strapped tube. People will think you are an artist – and so they should.

- Reveal the prepared posters when the time comes. Putting them up too early will divert attention from your lead-in discussion. Leaving them up too long may clutter the room and distract participants. Some posters are needed for reference and should stay posted throughout the session.

Spirituality in adult education

Spirituality has been given little attention in mainstream adult education—it is difficult to define and frequently confused with religion. For many of us, our adult spirituality is clearly informed by how we were socialized both religiously and culturally. Yet, spirituality is not the same as religion. Religion is an organized community of faith that has written codes of regulatory behavior, whereas spirituality is more about one's personal belief and experience of a higher power or higher purpose.[3] Most recent discussions in adult and higher education specifically focus on the role of spirituality in teaching and learning. Attending to spirituality in learning doesn't necessarily mean that one needs to discuss it directly in classes or learning activities, although there may be occasions for drawing it into course content. John Dirkx suggests that our interest is not so much to teach spirituality, but rather to nurture the soul, "to recognize what is already inherent within our relationships and experiences, to acknowledge its presence with the teaching and learning environment, to respect its sacred message."[4] In a similar vein, Parker Palmer discusses the importance of attending to paradox, sacredness, and graced moments in teaching and learning, in developing a spirituality of education.[5] Spirituality is one of the ways people construct knowledge and meaning. It works in concert with the affective, the rational or cognitive, and the unconscious and symbolic domains. To ignore it, particularly in how it relates to teaching for personal and social transformation, is to ignore an important aspect of human experience and avenue of learning and meaning-making.

29

Showing videos

Training films can be entertaining and provide visual stimulation. But their real value lies in supporting and expanding your instructional activities. Such use involves extra work, not less. To use films as legitimate partners in the facilitation of learning calls for thoughtful selection, prescreening, integration, and follow-through.

Use films to:
- present alternative means of transmitting information (film may require few reading skills)
- make visible things that are too small to see with the naked eye or too large or difficult to view in person
- provide a close-up of processes and experiences, bring experts to the classroom, demonstrate complex procedures and equipment, visit out-of-the-way locations
- take advantage of frame-by-frame analysis and discussion by stopping the films at any time; films can also be shown or viewed again, either by the whole group or at individual learner's convenience

Three cautions

Outdated films quickly lose their appeal.
If the language is dated, the lapels too wide, the hairstyle too fluffy, training films lose their impact on the viewers. Preview them in their entirety to assess suitability. If in doubt, don't show.

By themselves, films are mere one-way communications.
And they assume everyone follows at the same speed and level of comprehension. Since learning styles differ from viewer to viewer, some may be bored and others overwhelmed. Create preparation and follow-up to alleviate these limitations.

Films must have a clear purpose.
Why are you showing this film or tape? How does it contribute to learning? If it is for entertainment only, say so; if it is to teach, make sure learners are ready and willing. Don't use films to fill time.

Feature films as teaching tools
Aside from designated training films, regular feature films, television sitcoms, and cartoons can help bring the world into the classroom. They tend to have good production values, carry star recognition, and are easily available as rentals and from a home library. The possibilities are endless. Examples from my own practice include silly vignettes from Faulty Towers *in customer service training; touching moments from* Dead Poets Society *in a train-the-trainer workshop; bittersweet scenes from* Enlightenment Guaranteed *with managers in a cross-cultural seminar; and the whole of* Groundhog Day *with a group exploring the concept of cause and effect in human interaction. A word of caution: commercial films are made for a different audience and may offend members of your group with their use of language and/or actions. Careful prescreening and selection of specific scenes is advised!*

How to make the best use of films

1. Plan ahead.

- Find out what's available. Check with various sources, including the resource center of the public or college library, in-house inventory, trade and professional associations, foreign trade commissions, and government agencies. Don't trust the descriptions given by lenders and distributors. Their job is to make the product enticing and to sell or rent it.

- Determine the usefulness of the film to your particular situation. Only you can assess whether it contains the right message, is appropriate to the maturity of your group, and uses suitable examples, situations, and language. Poor acting, even dated hairstyles and lapels, will interfere with an otherwise well-written film: viewers get easily turned off and will miss the content. A poorly acted or dated film will reflect negatively on your judgment and expertise. The production quality also influences an audience's acceptance; raised on slick television and film programs, few people will tolerate poorly produced training films.

- Check whether this audience is already familiar with the film. Some people may already have seen it. Do this in advance and find out what they thought of the film. It may be possible to show it again *if* you can ensure that your context is distinct from the previous one. The techniques explained below can also help to make this quite a different viewing experience. If in doubt, don't show a repeat film.

2. Preview the film.

- If you can't preview a film, talk to someone you trust who has seen it and can provide an objective description. If only parts of the film suit your instructional goals, consider blocking those parts (by keeping track of the meter reading) and show only these segments. (Make sure the preview equipment and the one you will use in class have matching meters.)

- Determine rental costs and sources of funding. Get this sorted out in advance to avoid being stuck with the rental fee afterwards.

- Book the film in advance and obtain a written confirmation. Determine whether it requires delivery, pickup, and return. Ensure its arrival some time before you actually need it. This will give you time to trace its whereabouts should there be a foul-up.

> *When using comedy make sure that all humor arises out of the teaching points themselves so that every time the audience laughs, they're taking a point. And if they remember the joke, they've remembered the training point.*
>
> – John Cleese

- Book and inspect the projection equipment. Familiarize yourself with its operation. Check all cable connections and do a quick trial run. Whom do you call for assistance if there's a technical problem?

- Inspect the room arrangement for its suitability for viewing. Overhead lights may cause an on-screen glare, so experiment with the lighting or positioning of the monitor. Video-playback does not require blackout: it only enhances napping and makes note-taking difficult. You may be able to switch off some of the lights or relocate the monitor to somewhere other than the front of the room. You can even dramatize the film's contribution by placing the screen at the side or back of the room and asking the group to temporarily change position.

3. Prepare participants.

- Relate the film to the course content. Explain its setting and peculiarities if any, and quiz students on relevant background information. Get students to start thinking about the film in advance. Refer to vocabulary and concepts the film will use. Foreshadow the action by such comments as "The film depicts three incidents in which ..." or "Once you have seen the example in the film...." By setting up the film and bridging it with already familiar materials, you can ensure a smooth flow from in-class discussions and readings to the film and back again.

- Tell viewers what they can expect to see and learn from this film. You can lend extra depth to it by preparing and going over a handout which states the objectives, concepts, and special terminology of the film. Describe how it fits into the overall content of the course and what the learners are expected to take away from it.

- Instruct participants to look for specific problem areas illustrated in the film. For example, when viewing a management training film, one group could be asked to look specifically at nonverbal communication, while another group observes areas that relate to team building.

- Be clear if you expect learners to take notes. You may also ask them to jot down questions that arise as the action unfolds. Tell them what types of activities you have planned after the film: a discussion, a question-and-answer session, opportunity for practice, etc.

4. Show the film.

- Avoid fumbling with mechanical details. Rehearse if necessary. You may want to stop at certain points to raise a point, elicit questions, or receive reactions regarding its content and presentation.

- Remain in the room during the entire showing – even if you have seen the film before. If you leave the room, what are you saying about the importance of the film? If you talk or cause distraction during the showing, can you expect others to give their full attention? Your behavior portrays your attitude towards the material being shown and can influence your audience's acceptance of the film.

5. Integrate the film with other activities.

- Plan to make the film's message a legitimate part of the course content. Opportunities present themselves prior to the showing, at important points during the film when you can stop the action, or at the end. If the film is controversial or has aroused strong emotions, effective questions might be "What is your reaction to that scene?" or "How do you feel about the situation you have just witnessed?" If the material is complex and apt to cause confusion, consider breaking the film into chunks interspersed with brief summaries and discussions. Identify the key concepts thus far or ask specific questions pertaining to the material.

- Be prepared to summarize key scenes, elicit lists of major points, or offer connections to previously studied material. Ask if anyone wrote down questions or wants to ask about specific issues raised by the film. Use whatever response is given to expand into a discussion that involves more than just one or two participants. If you prepared a previewing handout, use the discussion questions mentioned there to get things rolling. Ask learners to refer to specific instances in the film. Encourage them to argue with points raised in the film.

6. Follow up.

- Keep a record of the course name, the audience profile, and the film's acceptance. Note when in the proceedings you showed the film, how you introduced it, what activities followed, plus other comments to help you make good use of the film the next time around (or avoid ever using it again).

- Refer back to the film on subsequent occasions: "How did the trainer in the video approach this situation?" or "What were the three exceptions to the rule which we saw illustrated in the film?"

I find television very educating. Every time somebody turns on the set, I go into the other room and read a book.

– Groucho Marx

Eight ways to integrate films

Experiment! Assign any of the following roles to individuals or small groups of three to six people. Tasks can be assigned before or after viewing. Allot between five and thirty minutes of class time.

• **Frame questions.**

A straightforward technique is to discuss the film with the aim of generating a list of questions the film raised. Questions may be posed by small groups and responded to by individuals, other groups, or the class as a whole.

• **Specify learning.**

Another easy way to put the group to work is to ask them to zero in on one or two important ideas that are introduced in the film. The group is challenged to think in terms of "what have we learned?"

• **Respond to specific questions.**

Have small groups focus on specific questions raised by the film. The questions may be posted on newsprint or distributed as a handout in advance of the session. You may give each small group one or two questions of a special sort, or all small groups may work on the same question(s). Depending on the available time, the process may be repeated.

• **Brainstorm.**

The film may introduce a problem which can be worked on in a brainstorming session. A group of six to twelve people, plus a recorder to capture the ideas, works well. You might serve as a recorder, or the recorder might be drawn from the group, depending on the number of groups at work.

• **Critique assigned readings.**

Provide a relevant article or handout and ask for it to be discussed in relation to the film. Steer the participants away from a discussion of cinematic qualities and ask them to concentrate on the film's content.

• **Function as viewing teams.**

Assign small groups specific viewer roles and ask them to comment on the film from their respective vantage points. For example, different subgroups are assigned one or all of the following roles.

Questioners: "The film raises these questions for us."

Clarifiers: "The film contradicted the text's contention that ..." or "There was some confusion regarding...."

Dissenters: "We didn't like ..." or "We don't agree with...."

Assenters: "We respond positively to ..." or "We agree with...."

Appliers: "We can see the following applications...."

• **Assess personal effectiveness.**

Invite participants to assess their own behavior in relation to the examples depicted in the film. For instance, for a film on team-building techniques, they could be asked to identify and discuss their own difficulties with the task of delegation. Or for a film on discrimination, they could share personal experiences with the situations depicted in the film. Both will involve self-disclosure on the part of participants and will require an atmosphere of trust.

30

Assessing the course

We learn by trial and error, not by trial and rightness. If we did things correctly every time, we would never have to change directions – we'd just continue the current course and end up with more of the same.

– Roger von Oech, *A whack on the side of the head.*

There are many ways to gauge the success of a course. Customarily, some sort of standard evaluation form is handed out near the end, asking, among other things, that participants "rate the refreshment service on a scale of 1 to 5." Such indexes hardly yield information of value to course designer and teacher. Another problem with routine evaluations is their timing; you won't get thoughtful responses amid the rush of end-of-course activities.

Choose your timing carefully

To obtain meaningful opinions and suggestions, set time aside and make this a legitimate course component. Asking for feedback after the first day, a major activity, halfway through, or just before the end will bring interesting information to light and permit corrective action before it's too late.

Explain the importance of feedback

Tell participants why you are asking and what you plan to do with the information. Solicit their careful attention and invite candid responses. Share the collected information with the group and process it. In a multi-session course, I have asked for written feedback on Day One and brought the comments – summarized on newsprint – back to start Day Two. This took only about twenty minutes, but demonstrated how much I valued the input and made it obvious that I was prepared to respond to the issues.

Give it a fresh name

Instead of calling this an evaluation – which suggests judging or grading – think of less loaded labels for this activity. Feedback, check-up, taking stock, feeling the pulse, assessment, opinionnaire, or inventory might do.

Invite participants to design the evaluation

Whenever possible, involve participants in the design of the feedback process. If a form is to be used, ask for help in its design. To make best use of class time, you could start with a collection of forms and ask groups to contribute questions that should be on them. Make sure your own questions are added as well. If you have the time and if the atmosphere is right for it, invite groups to come up with creative ways of giving feedback; they may end up using collages, slide shows, "award" ceremonies, skits, or scrapbooks as very effective feedback mechanisms.

Keep good records

In addition to the participants' comments, record your personal remarks about the group, the course, the ups and downs. When the time comes for a repeat performance, you can make good use of these notes in your planning. Let them also be a measure of your own development: you'll notice you are getting better!

Examples

Here are a few forms to get you started. Use them as they are or change them to suit your needs. Strive for a balance of questions to bring out critical as well as supportive comments.

If it's worth teaching, it's worth finding out whether the instruction was successful. If it wasn't entirely successful, it's worth finding out how to improve it.

– Robert Mager, Making instruction work.

Daily Questionnaire

What do you consider today's most valuable experience?

Why is that?

What aspect of today's activities could have been strengthened ?

How could that be done?

What other comments do you have?

Your name _____

optional

This is the most versatile of all. It can be filled out at various stages of the course. It concentrates on high and low points and asks the respondent to give reasons for each issue.

Our First Session Together
Please finish the sentences below.

When I first walked into the room ...

Now that the session is over I wish ...

My first impression of the instructor was ...

The get-acquainted activity was ...

I found the small-group activities ...

About the proposed course outline I think ...

I'd also like you to know that ...

The first session together in a new group can be overwhelming for many participants. This form asks them to look back, report their feelings and impressions, and identify the highlights. Teachers can use the same form. Follow-up discussions can bring information to light that would otherwise be missed.

FUNDAMENTALS

Domains of learning

Robert Gagné holds that learning is not one process, but consists of domains, depending on what is to be learned.[1] When planning educational activities, be aware of the domain you are dealing with.

- *The cognitive domain deals with the recall or recognition of knowledge and the development of intellectual abilities and skills.*

- *The affective domain describes changes in attitude and values, and the development of appreciations and adequate adjustment.*

- *The psychomotor domain has to do with the development of manipulative skills, involving tools, machinery, procedures, and techniques.*

Halfway Through

We are at the halfway mark of your workshop and this seems a good point to stop and see how we are doing. I am particularly interested in your views of the way each session is structured, my own performance, and your sense of the usefulness of it all.

Please complete the following sentences.

1. The structure of the sessions ...

_____

_____

and I wish we ...

_____

_____

2. About your performance, I'd like to say that ...

_____

_____

and I wish you ...

_____

_____

3. I wish we did more ...

_____

_____

4. I wish we did less ...

_____

_____

5. With only three more sessions remaining, I suggest we ...

_____

_____

6. To sum up my feelings about the workshop, I'd say ...

_____

_____

_____
                                               signed

This is another variation using the unfinished sentence technique to obtain quite personal information about the course and its direction.

Teaching holds a mirror to the soul. If I am willing to look in that mirror and not run from what I see, I have a chance to gain self-knowledge–and knowing myself is as crucial to good teaching as knowing my students and my subject.

– Parker J. Palmer, *The courage to teach.*

Self-Evaluation Checklist

	hardly	on and off	quite a lot
I was interested in this unit	☐	☐	☐

What helped or hindered?

_____

	hardly	on and off	quite a lot
I learned about group process	☐	☐	☐

Mostly about

_____

	hardly	on and off	quite a lot
I participated	☐	☐	☐

How

_____

	hardly	on and off	quite a lot
I contributed task functions	☐	☐	☐

Which

_____

	hardly	on and off	quite a lot
I helped build group spirit	☐	☐	☐

How _____

Based on this brief assessment, I have these three goals for the remainder of the course.

1._____
_____ .

2._____
_____ .

3._____
_____ .

*This questionnaire was developed for a training event on group leadership and partici-
pation skills. Respondents were asked to rate themselves on the quality of their interaction with others. The collected data was discussed with the group. It brought out some
common difficulties pertaining to course content and was used to redesign parts of the
theory session that followed. Since this form was used with a group of coworkers, a
symbol was used for identification to encourage candid responses. Participants quite
naturally "owned" their comments during the ensuing discussion. Subsequent forms
asked for names instead of codes.*

After the Discussion

Please respond to these questions and be prepared to share your observations during the 4 o'clock debriefing session.

What role(s) did you assume most of the time. Name one or two.

Comment on the effect your contribution might have had on the group's progress.

What is your personal reaction to the way your group worked together?

What problems did you observe in your small group?

What could the instructor do to alleviate the problems you have observed?

What could you do to increase productivity?

What could you do to help build cohesiveness?

_____

signed

This questionnaire was designed to assess a section of a workshop on group dynamics. Participants were asked to do two things: reflect on their contribution to the group task and comment on the course design. The form worked because of the mutual respect between learners and facilitator.

Glossary

Where are the references?

A full list of the works cited is available at www.peter-renner.com/glossary.html. By keeping this list on-line, we'll be able to make frequent updates and to provide you with direct access to relevant Web sites.

What do the symbols mean?

See explanations at the bottom of each page.

A

accelerated learning (AL) Also known as superlearning, AL is based on "a philosophy of learning and of life that seeks to deemphasize and rehumanize the learning process and make it a ... whole-person experience" (Meier, 2000: xxii). A number of movements have influenced AL, including *natural learning, the theory of *multiple intelligences, *learning style research, *collaborative learning, and the decline in *behaviorism as the dominant educational philosophy. ᐈ Imel (2002).

acceptance Behavior by a teacher that displays a "warm regard for [another's] unconditional self-worth ... respect and liking [for another] as a separate person" (Rogers, 1961:34).

accountability Educational philosophy and practice are frequently driven by concerns for efficiency, politics, and cost-effectiveness. Accountability requires teachers to produce measurable evidence regarding the quality of their work, usually in terms of students' progress. *Behavioral objectives and *competency-based education are closely linked concepts.

active listening A careful *attending to what another person says, paying attention to ways the other's words are being modified by nonverbal and paralinguistic cues (Egan, 1975:69). In so doing, a teacher shows that she wants to know about the experience and behavior of the student, tries to see the world from the student's frame of reference. ⇨ congruity, empathic understanding.

adult development Several theories attempt to predict the phases in a person's life. See the summary by Romero (1990:3), which outlines Erikson's eight-stage psycho-social development theory (1943), Havighurst's notion of developmental tasks (1972), Perry's nine developmental positions (1970), Kohlberg's cognitive-developmental stage theory (1971), and Loevinger's milestones of ego development (1976). Also of interest: Levinson on male development (1978), Belenky on women's ways of knowing (1986), and Bridges on transitions in adult life (1980). ᐈ Lewis & Caffarella (1990:77) for an annotated bibliography.

adult education, adult learning Claiming status as a distinct profession with a unique knowledge base, adult education advances the idea that teaching adults is different from teaching children (Merriam, 2001). Such a definition is not without its critics: Draper (1998), for instance, calls it a "false dichotomy," as differences are of a qualitative nature; Vaske (2001) points out that no single theory explains how adults' and children's learning differ. ᐈ Kerka (2002) on key assumptions, opinions, and research that shape the debate. ⇨ andragogy, pedagogy.

affect *n.* Used in reference to emotion, feeling, mood, as in *affective dimension, *affective domain, *affective education.

affective dimensions of learning Pertains to elements of attention, emotion, and valuing.

affective domain Individual behaviors grouped according to the principle of internalization (Anderson & Krathwohl, 2001) as follows. 1. *Receiving,* being aware or sensitive to the existence of certain ideas, material, or phenomena, and being willing to tolerate them. 2. *Responding,* being committed in some small way to the ideas, materials, and phenomena involved by actively responding to them. 3. *Valuing,* being willing to be perceived by others as valuing certain ideas, materials, and phenomena. 4. *Organizing,* relating the value to those already held and bring it into harmonious and internally consistent philosophy. 5. *Characterizing,* acting consistently in accordance with the internalized values. ⇨ taxonomy of learning.

affective education Pertains to the development of interpersonal and intrapersonal skills and attitudes.

andragogy Term coined by *Knowles to distinguish the education of adults from *pedagogy, the education of children. Based on the belief in adult learners' ability, need, and desire to take responsibility for their own learning. Andragogy has been posited as a learning theory, teaching method, and philosophical statement and is not without controversy. ᐈ Pratt (1993) for a critical retrospective; Tisdell (1998) for a feminist critique; St. Clair (2002) for a summary of the continuing debate. ⇨ humanistic psychology.

APA style Academic journals, dissertations, and conference proceedings in education adhere to the formatting rules of the American Psychological Association (APA). ᐈ Amato (1995) for a bare-bones introduction to this complex matter.

appreciative inquiry (AI) Engages people and organizations in discovering what gives life to human systems when they are most effective and constructive and using that knowledge to envision and create the preferred future. Instead of beginning with problems to be solved, AI uses a social *constructivist view that reality is socially created, and people can choose to focus on life-giving, generative aspects rather than deficit-based perspectives (Cooperrider, 2000). ⌒ Kerka (2003c) for a summary and annotated reading list.

apprenticeship Traditionally a contractual arrangement where a person works for another in order to learn a trade, craft, or art, often for little or no wage. The term is also used for informal arrangements where an expert agrees to train one or more people, typically to learn certain skills. ⇨ cognitive apprenticeship. ⌒ Wonacott (2000) for a summary.

approximating, approximation Learner's attempt to reach a prescribed standard of expertise. For instance, while tackling certain *psychomotor skills, trainees first may observe the correct procedure, then practice until they arrive at a satisfactory level of performance. Or, in a question-and-answer exchange, the teacher guides students towards the "better" answer with a series of questions that build on students' prior answers. ⇨ cognitive apprenticeship, shaping, Socratic method.

asynchronous learning Also known as location-independent learning. It refers to situations where students learn the same material at different times and locations (such as distance and computer-aided instruction). Synchronous learning, by contrast, has students study together through such means as lectures or labs.

asynchronous learning networks (ALN) A common conference space that is shared by distance learners, using electronic blackboard, e-mail, or chat room to post, read, and respond to messages.

attending Term borrowed from counseling psychology, referring to "the manner of being present with another" (Egan, 1975:67).

authentic assessment Measuring students' mastery of skills in the context of real-life applications.

autobiographical learning A kind of learning that occurs during "life story-telling" (Nelson, 1994, 1997), which encompasses one's reflection on lived experience, critical thinking, and imagining. May bring to awareness some *tacit and symbolic dimensions of knowing. Karpiak (2001) states that "learning and development continue throughout life, and ... both may be enhanced by activities such as autobiographical writing. Because autobiography involves not

only recounting memories and expressions but also finding their larger meaning, and to the extent that the activity expands the individual's knowledge of self and the world, it constitutes learning."

autodidactive learning, autodidaxy Term used in educational research to denote "intentional self-education" (Candy, 1991).

B

banking method Term introduced by *Freire (2000:53) to describe educational systems and practices in which passive learners receive deposits of preselected, ready-made knowledge. The learner's mind is seen as an empty vault into which the riches of approved knowledge are placed. Also referred to as digestive education.

behavior modeling ⇨ modeling.

behavior modification Approach to education, grounded in *behaviorism, which aims to change human behavior through such techniques as positive and negative *reinforcement.

behavioral objectives ⇨ objective.

behaviorism Branch of psychology concerned with the study of observable stimuli and response, at the exclusion of subjective phenomena. ⌒ Burton, et al. (1996). ⇨ behavioristic approach to adult education.

behavioristic approach to adult education Marked by such features as control, *behavior modification, *reinforcement, programmed learning, *behavioral objectives, and *competency-based teacher education (Elias & Merriam, 1995:10).

borrowed knowledge Akin to *received knowledge.

brainmapping ⇨ mindmapping.

bridging knowledge Based on the assumption that teachers hold power over the content and, by extension, the students. Teachers address this power imbalance through bridging knowledge, by explaining and translating concepts to help students move from "not knowing" to "knowing" (Pratt, 1999:136).

buzz group *Task group with three to five members.

C

caucusing, to caucus, to meet in caucus Facilitation technique for use with meeting and learning groups whereby individuals or subgroups perceived to hold special powers (of opinion, expertise, or

authority) are asked to meet separately from the larger group. This allows everyone to work on adjacent tracks and to contribute from unique vantage points.

circle of trust Concept and process developed by Palmer (2004) whereby skilled facilitators help create a quiet, focused, and disciplined space—a circle of trust—to enable participants to experience the paradox of "being alone together," of being present to one another as a "community of solitudes," to explore the intersection of personal and professional lives, make use of stories from their inner-life journeys, reflect on professional practice, and tap insights from various wisdom traditions.

climate, learning climate ⇨ learning environment.

clinical journals Used in practicum placements (e.g., nursing education) where students record personal observations, questions, and incidents; by prior arrangement, instructor may read and comment on entries; useful to help to integrate theory and practice.

closure The process of bringing an event or effort to a conclusion (even temporarily). In some instances (e.g., group discussion, problem-solving task), the facilitator may deliberately resist participants' call for closure, hoping that the resulting tension will cause them to further ponder unresolved issues.

coach, coaching Teaching strategy to enhance *collaborative learning; "involves giving hints or cues, providing feedback, redirecting students' efforts, and helping them use a strategy. A major principle of coaching is to provide the right amount of help when students need it—neither too much, nor too little so that students retain as much responsibility as possible for their own learning" (Tinzman, et al, 1990:5).

cognition Generally refers to the act or process of knowing; the product of such a process, and things thus known and perceived. Psychologists use the term to refer to "any class of mental 'behaviors' (using that term very loosely) where the underlying characteristics are of an abstract nature and involve symbolizing, insight, expectancy, ... imagery, belief, intentionality, problem-solving, and so forth" (Reber, 1985:129).

cognitive apprenticeship A process where newcomers to a craft or profession learn from experienced peers. Stages, not

---

* this term has a separate entry   ⌒ turn to the literature for more   ⇨ see also

necessarily undergone in sequence, may include: *modeling, *approximating, *fading, and generalizing (LeGrand Brandt, 1993). ᴧ̃ Hansman (2001:43-51).

cognitive dissonance Arising from the work of Festinger (1957); refers to "the discomforting awareness of inconsistency between what we know or believe and what we do" (Wulff, 1991:G-5). We try to reduce such discomfort by devaluing the conflicting belief, acquiring new beliefs that change the balance, or removing the conflicting attitude or behavior.

cognitive domain As one of the categories in Bloom's *taxonomy of educational objectives, this domain comprises six levels: *knowledge, comprehension, application, analysis, synthesis, and evaluation.* ⤳ affective domain, psychomotor domain. ᴧ̃ Anderson & Krathwohl (2001).

cognitive modeling ⇨ modeling.

cognitive style Refers to individual ways of "receiving, storing, retrieving, transforming, and transmitting information" (Merriam & Caffarella 1991:159). ⇨ learning styles.

cohesion, cohesiveness (1) Forces (both positive and negative) that cause individuals to maintain their membership in specific groups (Johnson & Johnson, 1991:504). (2) A measure of a person's commitment to the group (Wilson, 1996:350).

cohort Describes participants entering and moving through a training program as a group.

collaborative learning Involves "two or more people laboring together to construct knowledge that is more than, and other than, the individuals involved could have known otherwise" (Peters & Armstrong, 1998:75); teacher and learners sharing knowledge and authority; the teacher assuming various roles (e.g., mediator, model, coach); and students working in heterogeneous work groups (Tinzman, et al, 1990).

communities of practice Self-organized and somewhat informal groups of people who share a common sense of purpose and a desire to learn and know what each other knows; they may meet face-to-face, via e-mail, and/or within larger organizational structures (Hansman, 2001:48). ⇨ learning community.

competency-based education (CBE), **competency-based instruction** (CBI) Grounded in a *behavioristic approach

and characterized by detailed specifications of learning outcomes in behavioral terms, including methods of instruction and type of assessment to measure achievement of predetermined standards. ᴧ̃ Elias & Merriam (1995:93-99).

conditions of learning A way to categorize types or levels of learning, such as verbal information, intellectual skills, cognitive strategies, motor skills, and attitudes. Different internal and external conditions are necessary for each (Gagné, 1985).

congruent, congruity Fundamental to learner-centered teaching, also referred to as *realness, authenticity, or genuineness. "When the facilitator is a real person, being what she is, entering into a relationship with the learner without presenting a front or a façade, she is much more likely to be effective. This means that the feelings that she is experiencing are available to her, available to her awareness, that she is able to live these feelings, be them, and able to communicate if appropriate" (cited in Kirschenbaum & Henderson, 1990:304). ⇨ facilitation.

connected knowing Concept based on the belief "that the most trustworthy knowledge comes from personal experience rather than the pronouncements of authorities" (Belenky, 1997:112).

consensus A type of group decision, according to Schwarz (1994), where "everyone in the group freely agrees with the decision and will support it. If even one person cannot agree …the group does not have consensus (p.83) [thus equalizing] the distribution of power within the group, because each member's concerns must be addressed and each member's support is required" (p.84).

constructivism, constructivist learning theory Proposes that individuals learn by constructing meaning through interacting with and interpreting their environments (Brown, 1998a; originally developed by Bruner, 1966, 1990, in the context of studying language learning in children). The meaning of individual learning is coupled with life experiences and contexts; it is constructed by the learners, not by the teachers; and learning is anchored in the context of real-life situations and problems. Constructivism challenges the technical-rational approach to education by redefining the relationship between the knower and what is known, including what is most

worth knowing and who decides what this is (Dirkx, Amey, & Haston, 1999).

contemplative education Approach based on the belief that the inner lives of teachers and students are vital ingredients in teaching and learning. Chödrön writes that "[t]he path of … our lives altogether has to do with curiosity [and] inquisitiveness. The ground is ourselves; we're here to study ourselves and to get to know ourselves now, not later" (1991:4). ⇨ teacher within.

content Term used by facilitators to distinguish *content* (what the group is working on, the task) from *process* (how the group is working, the climate, the spirit). This separation is, of course, artificial (Pratt, 1998:134); they both occur simultaneously all the time, but the group or the facilitator may want to focus on one over the other at a given moment.

contextual learning Concept rooted in *constructivist learning theory. Emphasizes problem solving; recognizes that teaching and learning need to occur in multiple contexts; assists students in learning how to monitor their learning so that they can become self-regulated learners; anchors teaching in the diverse life context of students; encourages students to learn from each other; employs *authentic assessment (Clifford & Wilson, 2000). Particularly popular in adult literacy, welfare-to-work, workplace education, and family literacy programs (Dirkx, Amey, & Haston, 1999). ᴧ̃ Imel (2000); Brown (1998a).

continuity One of two key dimensions of "learning from experience" envisaged by *Dewey (1938); the other being *interaction. It denotes learning in which the adult learners connect aspects of a new experience with what they already know, in ways that modify that knowledge.

convergent thinking ⇨ divergent thinking.

cooperative education A structured method of instruction whereby students alternate between classroom studies and on-the-job practice related to their academic or occupational objectives.

cooperative learning Small teams made up of students of different levels of ability who engage in various learning activities to study a subject. Team members are responsible not only for their own learning but also for helping teammates learn.

creative thinking According to Brookfield (1983:115-116), creative thinkers are those who reject standardized approaches to problem-solving; have wide-ranging interests; take multiple perspectives; view the world as relative and contextual; frequently use trial-and-error methods; are future-oriented; and trust in their own judgment.

criterion-referenced testing Test items are directly identified with behavioral objectives to measure the extent to which the students have mastered the material. ⇨ competency-based instruction.

critical incident "A brief written report compiled by students about their experience of learning" (Brookfield, 1990a:31).

critical questioning Technique borrowed from psychotherapeutic and qualitative research practices, which aims to elicit the assumptions underlying a person's thoughts and actions (Brookfield, 1987:93). ⇨ critical reflection.

critical reflection To engage in critical reflection requires "moving beyond the acquisition of new knowledge and understanding, into questioning [of] existing assumptions, values, and perspectives (Cranton, 1996b:76). Part of critical reflection is to challenge prevailing social, political, cultural, and professional ways of acting (Brookfield, 1995). ⬿ Stein (2000).

culture of silence According to *Freire, this is a characteristic of oppressed people in colonized countries; they are not heard by the dominant members of their society. The dominant members control the schools and other institutions, thereby effectively silencing the people (Heaney, n.d.). Elements of this occur in learning groups where certain members or subgroups dominate the process and oppress less vocal members.

curriculum, *pl.* curricula. A set of courses making up a program, or a detailed outline for a course.

D

debriefing Originally a military term: to interrogate someone (like a pilot) returning from a mission in order to obtain useful information. In educational context, used during and after a learning activity to cause participants to reflect on aspects such as participation, helpful and hindering behaviors, use of time, resources, etc.

deductive thinking A kind of reasoning, from the general to the specific.

Dewey, John (1859-1952), American philosopher and educator who laid the philosophical foundation for what is today at the core of training and adult education practice: the abandonment of authoritarian methods and an emphasis on experimentation and experience. ⬿ Dewey (1938), Ryan (1995).

digestive education ⇨ banking method.

discursive thinking (1) Thinking broadly, covering a wide field; also rambling. (2) Proceeding to a conclusion through reason (AHCD, 1993:397).

divergent thinking Ways of thinking beyond the predictable and conventional.

diversity training Aims to develop sensitivity and improve working relationships among employees regarding differences in race, gender, and disability. May also deal with such issues as age, educational level, family structure, job function, sexual orientation, ethnicity, and values. ⬿ Brown (2001a) for a summary, with discussion of backlash and resistance.

domains of educational objectives Bloom (1956:7) identifies three kinds: *cognitive,* "which deal with the recall and recognition of knowledge and the development of intellectual abilities and skills;" *affective,* "which describe changes in interest, attitudes, and values, and the development of appreciation;" and *psychomotor,* which have to do with physical skills and abilities.

domains of learning Ways of categorizing learning according to spheres of student activity. Useful information for educational design, delivery, and assessment. Gagné (1972) cites motor skills, verbal information, intellectual skills, cognitive strategies, and attitudes. Anderson & Krathwhol (2001, based on Bloom, 1956), list cognitive, psychomotor, and affective domains. Not recognized by mainstream literature, but possible additions, are *spiritual and *somatic domains.

domesticating education The opposite of *libratory education (Shor & Freire, 1987:172).

dyad A *task group made up of two people. ⇨ triad.

E

e-learning Buzzword for a variety of educational programs accessible on-line.

emancipatory learning self-directed learning.

embodied learning ⇨ somatic learning.

emotional intelligence (EI) A concept popularized —but not originated—by Coleman (1995, 1998), refers to feelings and behavior rather than facts and knowledge (cognitive intelligence) and is concerned with personal and social competencies, including "self-awareness and self-control, motivation and persistence, empathy, and the ability to form mutually satisfying relationships" (Cherniss, 1999:26). Popular education tends to emphasize cognitive learning or knowledge transfer, and discount thinking processes that lead to emotional learning (Sternberg, 1999). ⬿ Brown (1999) for an overview, Paul (1999) for a history.

empathic understanding Term by *Rogers (1961) based on his counseling experience: "When the teacher has the ability to understand the student's reactions from the inside, has a sensitive awareness of the way the process of … learning seems to the student" (Kirschenbaum & Henderson, 1990:311).

empowerment (1) Circumstances intended to help students develop self-awareness, act assertively, speak out in class, take charge of their continuing education, and expand their social and political understanding. (2) *Freire uses the term when discussing the assertion of rights by the oppressed in an (educational) system that tends to favors one group of citizen over another.

energizer Group activity designed to engage participants' curiosity and involvement; may not be directly linked to the task at hand, but meant to raise the energy in the group.

espoused theory Term by Schön (1983) for the "unchallenged conventional wisdom" (Brookfield, 1987:153) of a profession, even though people's everyday actions and attitudes may differ from such prescribed practices. ⇨ theories-in-use.

ethical standards for trainers Industry-generated standards to "provide guidance for … professionals engaged in practice, research, consulting, and instruction, facilitation, and teaching" (AHRD, 1999:1). They address principles of competence, integrity, professional responsibility, respect for people's rights and dignity, concern for others' welfare, and social responsibility (Carter, 2001:1). ⬿ Sork & Welcock (1992), Gordon & Sork (2001).

---

* this term has a separate entry   ⬿ turn to the literature for more   ⇨ see also

ethics Used here to mean the morals of individual action and practice.

experiential learning (EL) A term for a wide range of learning-from-doing approaches. Fenwick (2001:5) describes three EL traditions: 1. phenomenological (reflection begins by analyzing the learner's way of observing, communicating, thinking, and acting); 2. the critical theory tradition (critical self-reflection as a central element of adult learning and development, with special attention to political and social factors that limit development); 3. the situated and action theory traditions (the role of cultural action, criticizing those who divorce the concept from its socio-historical roots).

experiential learning cycle A four-stage model showing the sequential flow of *experiential learning. ᐧᐯ Kolb (1984). ⇨ learning styles.

expressive outcome, expressive objectives Terms by Eisner (1979:103) for learning objectives that cannot be stated in advance of instruction, nor prescribed for all students equally as they pertain to personal learning, arising from creative expressions of an artistic, aesthetic, and analytical nature. In contrast of and to complement *behavioral objectives.

extinguish Term borrowed from *behavior modification, used here to denote teacher actions that aim to limit or curtail "undesirable" student behaviors. ⇨ reinforcement, shaping.

extrinsic motivation "The motivation to engage in an activity as a means to an end. Individuals who are extrinsically motivated work on tasks because they believe that participation will result in desirable outcomes, such as a reward, teacher praise, or avoidance of punishment" (Pintrich & Schunk, 1996).

F

facilitation An approach where the teacher shifts from sole provider of information and keeper of "the right answer" to one who encourages people to "recall, value, talk about, and perhaps critically analyse their own past experience to construct knowledge from it" (Fenwick, 2001:14). *Rogers (1961) sets out certain teacher qualities, or attitudes, that facilitate learning; including realness or *congruity, *acceptance and trust, and *empathic understanding.

fading A phase in the learning process where students gather competence and confidence and the teacher's assistance and other instructional aids can gradually be removed. ⇨ cognitive apprenticeship.

false consensus bias In the context of group work, the problematic belief that other people think and feel very much as we do (Johnson & Johnson, 1991:505).

feedback Pivotal concept in group learning: providing each other with information about responses, behaviors, and progress. Often described as having positive, negative, or neutral characteristics. Feedback tends to be of greatest use to the recipient if it is asked, received, and given in a caring manner, restricted to observable behaviors (instead of speculation and projection), and offered as soon as possible after the action being described. ⇨ reinforcement.

feminist pedagogy Put forward as a "comprehensive perspective that seeks to explain the nature of unequal power relations based on gender, race, and class" (Elias & Merriam, 1995:230). According to hooks (1989), "[f]eminist education is and should be a place where there is a sense of struggle, where there is a visible acknowledgment of the union of theory and practice, where we work together as teachers and students to overcome the estrangement and alienation …[to] engage students in a learning process that makes the world 'more real than less real'" (p.51). Roots of feminist pedagogy are in radical philosophy of education, critical theory, and *humanistic psychology.

force-field analysis A problem-solving tool to help identify forces (e.g., circumstances, dynamics, pressures) which appear to support or resist a proposed solution. Once this is done, the attention shifts to the identification of ways that might help reduce the negative and/or increase the positive forces..

foreshadowing A teacher behavior that points the way, indicates what lies ahead, alerts and motivates students.

formal learning Refers to a prescribed, highly structured, systematic learning procedure, with the content being assigned by the teacher or other educational authority (e.g., textbook, on-line assignment). ⇨ informal learning, incidental learning. ᐧᐯ Marsick & Watkins (2001:25-34).

formative evaluation A kind of evaluation performed during the developmental or "formative stage" of a process, such as course design (Scriven, 1967). It provides feedback regarding the product being developed.

Freire, Paolo Brazilian-born educator (1921-1997), jailed by the military government in 1964 for his "subversive activities"; exiled for 15 years; widely read leader in the struggle for the liberation of the poorest of the poor, the marginalized classes who constitute a "culture of silence" in many lands. Terms associated with Freire's work include *banking method, *domesticating education, critical pedagogy, *libratory education, *problem-posing, *social action learning. ᐧᐯ Elias (1994), Freire (1970, 1974).

G

group behaviors "Actions of a group that are the result of the subtle interworking of the group as a whole, a kind of emergent property and not simply the summation of the separate behaviors of the individuals" (Reber, 1985:310). Groups develop their own style, which can be traced—in part—to certain group behaviors. ⇨ group dynamics.

group-building behaviors Also known as maintenance behaviors, these are contributions by group members to help build group *cohesion and team spirit (Benne & Seats, 1948).

group cohesion ⇨ cohesion.

group dynamics The nature of group life; the study of group life; the relationship of individuals to/in groups, and groups with other groups and organizations.

group effectiveness Success by a group in achieving its goals, maintaining good relationships among members, and adapting to changing circumstances (Johnson & Johnson, 1991:506). Obstacles to success include "a lack of focus and unclear goals for the group work task, tasks that can be done more efficiently by individuals, and a lack of clearly defined roles for group members" (Homan & Poel, cited in Brown, 2001b).

group efficacy A group's expectation of producing valued outcomes through joint efforts (Johnson & Johnson, 1991:506).

group memory A written record of what's being said in a task-oriented group; created by a recorder and openly posted on newsprint for everyone to see; useful

* this term has a separate entry ᐧᐯ turn to the literature for more ⇨ see also

to chart progress and to facilitate review (Quinlivan-Hall & Renner, 1994:27-28).

groupthink Tendency of members in highly cohesive groups led by dynamic leaders to adhere to shared view so strongly that they ignore external information inconsistent with these views (Johnson & Johnson, 1991:506).

H

Hawthorne Effect Term for behavior changes that may occur when individuals and groups know they are being observed.

high-risk pedagogy Approaches that ask student and teacher to challenge limits imposed by society and themselves (Orner, 1996:77).

horizontal student-teacher relationship A view of the teacher as being on equal footing with the student (Freire, 1970), casting them as co-learners and co-guardians of knowing.

humanistic approach to adult education Views learners as engaged in a process of discovery and *self-actualization, striving towards personal enrichment, integration, and psychological development. ⇨ humanistic psychology. ᗺ Elias & Merriam (1995:10), Fenwick (2001:6).

humanistic psychology Largely the creation of Maslow to expand human psychology beyond psychoanalytic and behaviorist approaches. Its main concerns are personal development and interpersonal communications; it entered adult education practice through the work of *Rogers and *Knowles. ⇨ transpersonal psychology.

human potential movement Evolved in the 1960s and early 1970s with an emphasis on personal growth of individuals through encounter groups and sensitivity training. Its theorists (e.g., Allport, Maslow, and *Rogers) focused on a person's open-ended growth rather than reshaping individuals to fit society's demands; an interest in the "here and now," rather than in one's history; a holistic approach concerned with all levels of human being and functioning; and psychological health rather than disturbance (Gale, 2002).

I

incidental learning Defined as "byproduct of some other activity, such as task accomplishment, interpersonal interac-

tion, sensing the organizational structure, trial-and-error experimentation, or even *formal learning" (Marsick & Watkins, 2001:25).

inclusion An aspect of *group dynamics based on the observation by Schutz (1958) that most people share three interpersonal needs: for inclusion, control, and affection.

indigenous education Practice based on such fundamental beliefs as the "continuous development of self-knowledge, on finding life through understanding and participating in the creative process of living, on direct awareness of the natural environment, on knowledge of one's role and responsibility to community, and on cultivating a sensitivity to the spiritual essence of the world" (Cajete, 1994). ⇨ mythopoetic teaching; spirituality in adult education.

individuation Term by Jung (1921) for a lifelong process—most noticeable in the second half of life—"having as its goal the development of the individual personality" (quoted in Jacobi, 1990:94). Individuation involves the discovery of new talents, the "differentiating and becoming aware of the presence of the different selves operating within the psyche" (Dirkx, 2000:1), a sense of *empowerment, confidence, a deeper understanding of one's inner self, and a greater sense of self-responsibility (Boyd, 1991).

informal learning An initiative by an individual or group of learners to set the terms of reference, objectives, process, learning strategies, duration, and ultimate outcome of learning (Livingstone, 1998). ᗺ Imel (2003a) on informal learning and the Internet.

inner teacher ⇨ teacher within.

inquiry method Approach based on the following principles: the teacher does not tell students what they ought to know, uses questioning as major mode of interaction, encourages student-student interaction, and measures success in terms of behavioral changes in the learners (Postman & Weingartner, 1969).

instrument (1) General term for any checklist or inventory. (2) A test that aims to quantify personal traits or preferences, which may be administered in class or online, and may or may not be self-scored. Examples include: *Myers-Briggs® Type Indicator, Pratt's *Teaching Perspectives

Inventory, and Kolb's Learning Styles Inventory. ⇨ standardized test.

interaction One of two key dimensions of learning-from-experience proposed by Dewey (1938); the other is *continuity. Refers to adult learners' presumed preference to interact actively with their environment and test new skills and information in that setting.

interaction diagram, sociogram A graphic representation of interaction patterns, showing who speaks to whom, whose comments yield responses, who is left out of the conversation, and so on. Useful as a feedback device to help participants learn about their own behavior as they work in a group.

intervention A facilitator's act of jumping in to (re-)direct a group's functioning; offering observations about *process, making procedural suggestions, or giving didactic input. ⇨ training commercial. ᗺ Schwarz (1994).

intrinsic motivation Coming from within, as contrasted with *extrinsic motivation, being presented by an outside agent or situation. An intrinsically motivated individual undertakes an activity "for its own sake, for the enjoyment it provides, the learning it permits, or the feelings of accomplishment it evokes" (Lepper, 1988).

I-statement A communication skill, where the sender of a message takes ownership for what he or she is saying. Instead of a guarded "this conversation is getting too confusing," one could say more directly, "I'm getting lost. I can't follow the discussion when several people speak at the same time."

J

Johari Window A model (Luft, 1969) to help deepen the practice of *feedback and *self-disclosure. Offers ways to explore personal communication patterns in the four quadrants of public, private, blind, and unknown.

journals An individual's written reflections on lived experience, taking such forms as *clinical journals, learning log (Brookfield, 1995:55), learning journal (Brookfield, 1990:34), *literature log, *reflective journal. Applications include *autobiographical learning, life planning, self-evaluation, *portfolios, *critical reflection, and meaning-making. Usher & Edwards (1995) criticize journals as "confessionals" which require adults to

---

* this term has a separate entry   ᗺ turn to the literature for more   ⇨ see also

turn on themselves as objects of scrutiny. ↻ Karpiak (2000, 2001) for practical applications, Kerka (1996) for an overview, Rossiter (2000) on personal narrative. ⇨ narrative learning.

just-in-time (JIT) training Term used in corporate settings, referring to as-needed training directly related to tasks and challenges ahead. This in contrast to education for the future, without apparent application.

K

knowledge construction Refers to the process where adult learners actively engage in constructing meaning from the course material within the context of their lives. "Adults integrate new learning by making connections to existing knowledge *schema. They reflect on rich, personal experiences and draw on their previous knowledge and wisdom to make meaning of new material and to understand it in a way that transforms their own previous understanding" (Donaldson & Graham, 1999:27).

Knowles, Malcolm (1913–1997) Major figure in the North American adult education movement who championed *self-directed learning, *learning contracts, and *informal learning; and who proposed *andragogy as a view of teaching and learning unique to adults. Central to andragogy are the adult learner's self-concept, readiness, experience, and motivation. ↻ Knowles, (1978/1990, 1980).

L

lateral thinking Term coined by De Bono (1972) to describe a way of thinking that seeks a solution to an intractable problem through unorthodox methods or elements that would normally be ignored by logical thinking. In contrast to *vertical thinking.

learning audit Term by Brookfield (1995) for a reflective process that assists individuals to "identify the skills, knowledge, and insights they have developed in the recent past" (p. 75), to cause them to think about themselves as learners, to assess their personal and professional development, and to help them plan for the future.

learning career An individual's learning trajectory which depicts the development of attitudes toward learning and the origins of interests, learning styles, and

learning processes (Kerka, 2003a).

learning center May consist of station(s) located around an instructional site (e.g., classroom, workplace, community, lab), each stocked with tools and resources to enable students to pursue various projects of inquiry.

learning circle A group technique where participants are asked to pull their chairs in a circle so they can see and hear each other; deal with one topic or question at a time; and go around the circle so that everyone has an equal opportunity to contribute or pass.

learning community A term with many meanings. In this book, it refers to a group of learners (a class) being guided by a teacher/facilitator with the aim to work cooperatively in support of each others' learning. In the literature, the term frequently is used in conjunction with *on-line learning (Palloff & Pratt, 1999) and *communities of practice: groups that organize informally and that are "resistant to supervision and interference" (Wenger & Snyder, 2000:40). St. Clair (1998) views community as a form of relationship between people, rather than as a collection of things or people. ↻ Imel (2001b).

learning contract Written document which spells out students' and teacher's roles and responsibilities, as well as the process and desired outcome of their work together. ↻ Knowles (1986).

learning disabilities Generally defined as significant difficulties in the acquisition and use of listening, speaking, reading, writing, reasoning, or mathematical abilities (Ohler, et al., 1996). ↻ Kerka (2002) for a list of Web sites.

learning environment *Knowles (1978:111) alerts us to attend to the physical, human/interpersonal, and organizational aspects of a learning setting. The teacher or facilitator is—at least initially—responsible for creating the climate, including such elements as physical comforts, reduction of anxiety, introductions, individual attention, and *group dynamics.

learning needs The requirements of an organization or individual for some kind of education; may be determined with a needs analysis.

learning objective ⇨ objective.

learning styles The literature abounds with attempts to define and measure the

"complex manner in which, and conditions under which, learners most efficiently and most effectively perceive, process, store, and recall what they are attempting to learn" (James & Gardner, 1995:20). ↻ Brown (1998b) for an overview.

learning trajectory ⇨ learning career.

learning-in-action According to Schön, a kind of *experiential learning where "the student discovers that she is expected to learn, by doing, both what [something] is, and how to do it" (1987:83). ⇨ Meno's paradox; swampy lowlands.

lecturette A short didactic presentation, lasting no more than 20 minutes. ⇨ training commercial.

libratory education Arising from the work of *Freire, it "encourages learners to challenge and change the world, not merely uncritically adapt themselves to it. The content and purpose of libratory education is the collective responsibility of learners, teachers, and the community alike who, through dialogue, seek political, as well as economic and personal liberation." (Heaney, n.d.:3). The opposite to libratory is "domesticating" education (Shor & Freire, 1987:172). ⇨ empowerment.

life writing ⇨ autobiographical writing.

lifelong learning A view of learning as uninterrupted from infancy to death. Posited as a "new" term, its roots may be traced to the words of Lindeman (1926:4-5), "The whole of life is learning, therefore education can have no endings," and *Dewey (1929:28), "Education must be reconceived, not as merely a preparation for maturity ... but as a continuous growth in the mind and a continuous illumination of life." ↻ Boud & Garrick (1999), Hayes (1998).

literature log Students' written response to assigned readings. Used in a variety of settings, from adult basic education through graduate study, logs enable readers to enter the literature in their own voice, placing themselves in relation to the text and discovering what they think about it. Entries may be shared with the class to stimulate discussion. Loose-leaf notes may be made accessible to the whole class to become a collaborative journal in which learners and teacher make ongoing comments; over time, the log itself becomes a primary text (Kerka, 1996). ⇨ journals.

---

* this term has a separate entry   ↻ turn to the literature for more   ⇨ see also

loafing, social loafing Term from sociology for the reduction in individual effort when working with others on a group task

M

meaning-making The traditional model of teachers lecturing and students taking notes and memorizing for exams is being replaced with one that has adult learners engage in an "ongoing, continuous process of re-constructing the meaning of [their] experience" (Dirkx, 1998:1) "by establishing and re-working patterns, relationships, and connections" (Ewell, 1997:6). This shift creates new roles for teachers as coach, *facilitator, *mentor, and co-learner. ⇨ transformational learning theory.

Meno's paradox Applies to situations when we seek to learn things the meaning and importance of which we cannot grasp ahead of time. In Plato's *Dialogues*, Meno admits that he does not know what virtue is and asks: "How will you look for something when you don't know in the least what it is? ... even if you come right up against it, how will you know that what you have found is the thing you didn't know?" (1956:128). Schön calls this learning-in-action.

mentor, mentoring An "intense caring relationship in which persons with more experience work with less experienced persons to promote both professional and personal development" (Caffarella, 1993:28). Mentors can act as "interpreters of the environment" (Deloz, 1986:207) to help learners (protégées) navigate unfamiliar context (e.g., preceptors in nursing education). ⌇ Deloz (1986), Zachary (2000).

metamorphic nature of learning A significant personal development that occurs as a result of certain learning activities. ⇨ autobiographical learning, significant personal learning, transformational learning.

metaphors They offer unexpected views of the adult educator's role, including adventure guide, outfitter, fire starter, caregiver (Fenwick, 2000); animator (Boud & Miller, 1998); arranger of contingencies for reinforcement (Skinner, 1968:5); consciousness-raiser, partner (Freire, 1971:63); facilitator of learning (Rogers, 1969:104-105); gardener (Brazier, 1995; Nollman, 1994); guide, pointer-outer (Lindeman, 1956); helper (Benne, 1957); ideal helper (Tough, 1979); leader of group activities (Dewey, 1938:61-66); mediator (Palmer, 1993:29); *mentor, interpreter (Daloz, 1986); midwife (Belenky, 1997:217); model (Bandura, 1969); resource (Knowles, 1978:165); and shepherd (Palmer, 1998).

micro-skills, micro-skills training An approach to learning such skills as interviewing, counseling, and teaching, where complex skills are broken into single, manageable, teachable components. ⌇ Ivey (1999).

mindmapping Visual technique to chart concepts, take notes, plan an essay, and summarize a course or book. Copyrighted term by Buzan, "a mind map consists of a central word or concept; around the central word you draw the 5 to 10 main ideas that relate to that word. You then take each of those words and again draw the 5 to 10 main ideas that relate to each of those words" (Lanzing, 1997). ⌇ Buzan (1995).

minimal encouragers Use of *paralanguage with which we can encourage others to express themselves, using "such things as 'um-hmmm,' repetition of [the other's] words, one-word questions, nods of the head, and a variety of gestures and body postures" (Egan, 1975:71).

modeling (1) Role or behavioral modeling occurs when a learner observes the performance by an accomplished practitioner. (2) Cognitive modeling involves experienced practitioners sharing insider tips with newcomers (LeGrand Brandt, 1993). ⇨ cognitive apprenticeship.

motivation Pivotal concept in most theories of learning; addresses such issues as what makes a person show up for class, pay attention, participate, contribute, do their best, and so on. ⌇ Wlodkowski (1999). ⇨ extrinsic motivation, intrinsic motivation.

motivation to learn Marshall (1987) defines it as "the meaningfulness, value, and benefits of academic tasks to the learner—regardless of whether or not they are intrinsically interesting." ⌇ Lumsden (1994) for an overview.

multiple intelligences (MI) A pluralistic view of intelligence as "the capacity to solve problems or to fashion products that are valued in one or more cultural settings" (Gardner, 1993), suggesting that we possess at least seven different intelligences which operate in varying degrees: linguistic, logical-mathematical, spatial, bodily-kinesthetic, musical, interpersonal, and intrapersonal.

muted group theory A claim that women and members of other subordinate groups are not as free or able as men to say what they wish because their words have been formulated and translated by a male-dominated style of communication (Littlejohn, 1999:75-77).

Myers-Briggs Type Indicator® (MBTI) Popular personality-type inventory; the standard form contains 126 items that determine preferences on four scales: extraversion—introversion; sensing—intuition; thinking—feeling; and judging—perceiving. The various combinations of these preferences result in 16 personality types.

mythopoetic education Arising from tribal traditions, its aims are to reconnect learners to their heritage and distinct place on earth. According to Cajete (1994), this can be achieved through mythopoetic rather than reductionistic teaching methods, including storytelling, sacred art, ritual, immersion in nature, and simply through the daily involvement in the life of the community. Instead of a technical process to be managed by specialists, learning is seen as part of a heroic journey, a challenging quest that each individual undertakes with the support and guidance of the community. ⇨ indigenous education.

N

narrative knowing Bruner (1985) proposes two types of knowing: paradigmatic and narrative. The first treats stories as data and seeks to generate categories out of common elements across a large database. The second takes the same stories, or fragments in the form of events or happenings, and seeks to produce explanatory stories (Polkinghorne, 1995:5).

narrative learning Based on the premise that we are engaged in a lifelong process of self-creation—a constant reworking of our personal story (Randall, 1995:36); "a very natural mode of learning, linked ... to the *meaning-making process" (Clark, 2001:89). ⇨ autobiographical learning, journals, narrative knowing. ⌇ Karpiak (2000), Rossiter (2000, 2002), Renner (2001b).

natural learning Seen as interactive, in that the learner engages spontaneously

---

* this term has a separate entry   ⌇ turn to the literature for more   ⇨ see also

with the environment, selecting the content of learning from what is available from the environment.

needs hierarchy According to Maslow's theory of human motivation (1968), we experience a hierarchy of needs, from basic physical needs to higher needs of emotion and ego. The five levels are: psychological, safety, social, esteem, and *self-actualization. The hierarchy is dynamic; the dominant need is always shifting. Satisfaction is relative; a satisfied need no longer motivates.

negative reinforcement A key concept in *behavior modification, involving the non-rewarding of certain behaviors with the goal of diminishing its chances of recurring. In a training context, it could mean that by not paying attention to it, the teacher can *extinguish certain "undesirable" student behaviors.

nominal group technique (NGT), **nominal group process** (NGP) A five-step group activity aimed at increasing productivity. Members silently list ideas, then, as a group create a master list, clarify ideas, prioritize items through straw vote or rank ordering, and eventually plan for action (based on Wilson, 1996:356). ☙ Quinlivan-Hall & Renner (1994:102).

nonverbal encouragers ⇨ paralanguage.

norm Unspoken rules by which individuals behave in a group.

O

objective, learning objective, behavioral objective "Description of a performance you want learners to be able to exhibit before you consider them competent. An objective describes an intended result of instruction rather than the process of instruction itself" (Mager, 1984). ⇨ expressive outcome, behaviorism.

openness An essential helping trait according to *Rogers (1961): "the more I am open to the realities in me and in the other person, the less do I find myself wishing to rush in to 'fix things'" (p. 21). Zen teachers see it as wisdom: "When you're open, you're able to be one with another person" (Maezumi, 2001). Brookfield (1987) considers openness "the most difficult interpersonal task of adult life. It entails psychological, political, and economic risks to one's self-esteem and livelihood" (p. 253). Daloz (1986) and Belenky (1997) claim that, due to cultural conditioning, being open

and honest comes more easily to women than men.

open group techniques Collective term for approaches that rely on active learner participation, such as brainstorming, *buzz groups, *learning circles, and problem-solving tasks.

outcome, outcome objective Desired result of a unit of instruction. ⇨ objective.

P

paradox of personal growth A "puzzling paradox" (Rogers, 1969) which may be experienced by people making themselves "vulnerable to the possibilities" of reflective practice (Renner, 2001a). Process may be marked by a sense of disorganization, pain of new understandings, feeling of uncertainty, and turmoil within oneself; "all an integral part of the pleasure and satisfaction of being more of oneself ... more fully functioning" (Rogers, 1969:289).

paradoxical intention Technique borrowed from psychotherapy (especially Frankl's *logo-therapy*), wherein the patient is asked to do exactly what she or he is afraid of doing (Reber, 1985:512). In an educational application, this might involve asking someone afraid of public speaking to read aloud a short text while remaining seated.

paralanguage Utterances that lack a written form, e.g., *uh-huh* means *Yes* or *I'm listening to you*; also known as nonverbal or *"minimal" encouragers (Egan, 1975:71).

paraphrasing An interpersonal communication skill, where one person reflects, summarizes, and condenses the essential information and ideas expressed by another. More than mirroring or parroting, paraphrasing requires careful listening to get at the essence of the other's communication. At the same time, it conveys an attitude of cooperation and interest, saying, in a sense, "Here's what I'm hearing—how accurate is that?" ⇨ empathic understanding, perception checking.

peak experience Arising from the work of Maslow, denoting a rare moment of personal achievement, a "high" of self-development, value, and intensity. ⇨ self-actualization.

pedagogy Denotes the education and teaching of children, but also used

regarding education and teaching in general. Many approaches are reported in the literature, including critical (Freire, 1970, McLaren, 1995); exploratory (Britzman & Pitt, 1996); feminist (Tisdell, 1998); situated, *high-risk (Orner, 1996); poisonous (Miller, 1983); or queer pedagogy (Hill, 1995). Because of the term's traditional use and meaning, *Knowles proposes *andragogy as a more fitting term for the education of adults.

peer observation, peer coaching Inviting a colleague into the classroom, asking them to observe and comment on one's teaching behavior, can be a risky yet rewarding under-taking. It ought to be reciprocal, be explained to the students, and be viewed as an opportunity for personal and professional growth. ☙ Brookfield (1995:83-87).

perception-checking An interpersonal communication technique in which a person seeks to determine the accuracy of understanding another's underlying feelings, concerns, or motivation. A simple example might involve a course participant saying "Why do we have to do this in groups?" and the teacher responding, "Do you think it would be better if we did this individually?" By not giving a "because ..." reply, the teacher demonstrates interest in the student's comment and nudges the students to engage actively in a conversation about process. ⇨ empathic understanding, paraphrasing.

performance standard The level of performance on a test, established by external experts, as a goal for students to attain.

persona In Jung's theory, "the social mask or outer attitude a person assumes to meet society's expectations while yet preserving his or her true nature" (Wulff, 1991:G-20). The term is sometimes mistakenly used to mean a false or fake exterior.

personal landscape A term offered by Greene (1978, 1995) to remind teachers to make education meaningful by tapping participants' life stories and lived experiences.

personal learning Type of learning that is self-initiated, with learners selecting the tools, content, and evaluation. ⇨ self-directed learning.

personal space The formal study of space and its use in social and cultural situation, also called proxemics (Hall, 1960).

---

* this term has a separate entry   ☙ turn to the literature for more   ⇨ see also

plateau A period in the learning process when no apparent change occurs.

portfolio A collection of work that documents a student's educational performance or development over time. &⌐ Wonacott (2002).

positive reinforcement Term originating in *behaviorism and *behavior modification; refers to any reward or recognition individuals work to receive. ⇨ negative reinforcement.

possible selves A concept developed by Markus & Nurius (1986) to describe individuals' ideas of what they might become, what they would like to become, and what they fear becoming. It has been applied in research and practice with adolescents exploring career choices, adults in transition, and older adults envisioning and adjusting to life in the "third age" (Kerka, 2003b).

postulate Refers to an assumption that is accepted as true for the purposes of further exploration.

preceptor Term used in medical and nursing education for a process whereby an experienced practitioner works with new staff or students to help them master competencies required in their role, through teaching, counseling, and role modeling. Preceptors support individuals' growth and development for a fixed and limited amount of time. ⇨ preceptorship.

preceptorship Used in nursing and medical education; a period of time, or the experience itself, when a student or inexperienced staff person works with a preceptor in clinical settings to develop specified competences and generally become socialized in work settings, such as a hospital ward or community health unit.

problem-based learning/instruction Used in medical training (also in the training of managers and educational administrators). Students are pointed toward the understanding and resolution of a problem through actual patient cases which serve as stimulus for acquiring basic knowledge needed to understand underlying issues and develop reasoning skills. There are few or no lectures or courses; students are responsible for their own learning to match their prior knowledge and *learning style. ⇨ theme-based learning/instruction.

problem-posing Approach in which knowledge is not seen as the teacher's private property, but "a medium evoking the critical reflection of both teacher and students" (Freire, 1971). Instead of the teacher, for instance, thinking about course content privately and then displaying it publicly for students to store it (*banking), everyone engages in an open process of thinking and talking about what they are thinking. In the process, their roles merge. ⇨ inquiry method.

process When observing and describing the functioning of a *task group, the term is used to describe *how* a group functions, the nature of its activity. This in contrast to *content, which refers to *what* a group accomplishes.

progressive approach to adult education An orientation that focuses on responsibility toward society; views education as a problem-solving instrument of social and political reform (Fenwick, 2001:6).

proxemics ⇨ personal space.

psychometric The measurement of an individual's psychological aspects, such as intelligence, aptitude, and personality.

psychomotor domain Pertains to the learning of such physical skills as coordination, dexterity, manipulation, grace, strength and speed; action that demonstrates fine motor skills (e.g., handling precision instruments) and gross motor skills (e.g., performing athletically). ⇨ taxonomy of learning, affective domain, cognitive domain. &⌐ Anderson & Krathwohl (2001).

Pygmalion effect Situations where the belief in potential creates potential. A study showed that elementary school teachers who were told that a new pupil was particularly bright behaved in a more supportive way, presented more difficult material, allowed more time to answer questions, and provided more feedback to that child. Students receiving this attention improved faster than classmates. Similar results have since been reported in studies involving supervisors and groups of employees (McNatt, 2000).

R

racial identity learning Continuous process of interaction between the individual and the sociocultural milieu; a holistic approach encompassing all aspects of self, not just race or culture (Myers, et al, 1991). As individuals increase their self-understanding and remember their spiritual essence, they transcend the bondage of oppression (Tisdell, et al, 2001).

radical philosophy of adult education An orientation, driven by the desire for societal and individual liberation, that questions and reinterprets the cultural assumptions of experience, and initiates transformative action.

rational learning A general term used for any learning based on logical, conscious reasoning (Reber, 1985:611).

readiness Someone's preparedness to engage in a certain activity or benefit from instruction.

readiness test Tool used to assess the ability to engage in a new type of specific learning. Level of maturity, previous experience, and emotional and mental state are important determinants of readiness.

realness Concept by *Rogers (1961, 1980) which suggests that when the teacher is a real person who enters into a relationship with the learner without presenting a front or a façade, she is much more likely to be effective.

received knowledge A term for knowledge and insights we obtain from others (also known as borrowed knowledge), in contrast to knowledge that results from *self-appropriated learning. &⌐ Belenky (1997).

reciprocity The assumption that others will respond to one's behaviors with similar behaviors.

recurrent training The repeated training for skills that require regular updating and practicing, such as fire drills, first aid, and safety procedures.

reflection An activity in which individuals "recapture their experience, think about it, mull it over and evaluate it" (Boud, et al, 1985:19). ⇨ critical reflection.

reflection-in-action Ways seasoned practitioners solve problems and consider new tasks in the midst of the often chaotic process of performing their craft (Schön, 1983).

reflective essay An expanded entry in a *reflective journal. Students are asked to write a brief essay based on an experience, a group project or field assignment. The essay may require them to reflect on their role (e.g., what they did), and the skills they developed (e.g., learning how to receive feedback).

---

* this term has a separate entry &⌐ turn to the literature for more ⇨ see also

reflective journal A tool for *reflective practice. Students may be asked to respond to fictional and nonfictional texts, making connections between classroom and clinical experience. The aim is to give students an opportunity to challenge the status quo and disagree with teachers—a safe place in which to try out and defend their ideas. Reflective journals are also used to stimulate observation, speculation, doubt, questioning, self-awareness, problem stating, problem solving, emoting, and ideation. ⇨ journals, reflective essay.

reflective practice A mode of functioning that integrates or links thought and action with reflection. It involves thinking about and critically analyzing one's actions with the goal of improving one's professional practice. Individuals assume the perspective of an external observer in order to identify the assumptions and feelings underlying their practice and then speculate about how these assumptions and feelings affect practice (Imel, 1992). ᴓ Brookfield (1995), Cranton (1997).

reinforcement Key concept in *behavior modification: Anything that strengthens a desired response or increases the tendency to make specific responses again. May be external (provided by another person) or intrinsic (generated by the learner). ⇨ extinguishing, negative reinforcement, positive reinforcement, shaping.

relearning Learning anew material that has been forgotten. ⇨ recurrent training.

remedial training Efforts to correct deficiencies or improve students' competence to an acceptable level.

retention The extent and duration of what has been learned during an instructional event.

Rogers, Carl American psychologist and educator (1902-1987) who was a co-founder of the *humanistic psychology movement, which caused a profound shift in psychology, human relations, and education. Rogers advanced the belief that each person has worth, dignity, and the capacity for self-direction. He promoted *self-directed learning and student-centered teaching, which places *facilitation as the essential role of the adult educator since, as Rogers claims (1951), "We cannot teach another person directly; we can only facilitate [their] learning." ᴓ Rogers (1961, 1969),

Kirschenbaum & Henderson (1990).

role modeling ⇨ modeling.

role-play Technique that aims to create direct and vicarious learning opportunities in the classroom. One or more participants act out a scenario which is given to them in advance or developed on the spot; assume roles of actors, audience, or observers; and participate in pre- and post-play analysis. The teacher may act as director, traffic controller, and discussion leader, or delegate these roles to participants.

role reversal A technique used in *role-play. The facilitator asks players to switch and assume each others' parts. Can be useful whenever the development of empathy and sensitivity for another's viewpoint is important (e.g., supervisory training, cross-cultural communications, negotiation, interviewing, and conflict resolution skills).

role-storming A variation on brainstorming where participants assume roles or postures to stimulate creativity.

S

schema, *pl* **schemata** Term used in *transformational learning theory for "a mental codification of experience that includes a particular organized way of perceiving cognitively and responding to a complex situation or set of stimuli" (Merriam-Webster, 2003).

seamless practice Concept borrowed from Zen Buddhism, refers to the flow of one action into another, without jarring interruptions. In adult education, this might be manifested by a teacher's actions being in harmony with her/his *espoused theory.

self-actualization The highest of five levels in Maslow's *needs hierarchy: doing that which maximizes one's potential and fulfills one's innate aspirations (1968).

self-appropriated learning Knowledge that is self-discovered and therefore holds special meaning. As Rogers (1961:276) writes, "The only learning which significantly influences behavior is ...self-appropriated learning." By contrast, ⇨ received knowledge.

self-directed learning (SDL) A process in which learners "take the initiative, with or without the help of others" (Knowles, 1975:18). The term has become amorphous (Jarvis, 1992:130) and continues to resist definition (Kerka, 1999).

Depending on one's viewpoint, the goals of SDL may be seen as: 1. the development of the learner's capacity to be self-directed; 2. the fostering of *transformational learning; or 3. the promotion of *emancipatory learning and social action (Merriam, 2001:9). ⇨ reflective journal. ᴓ Brookfield (1993), Merriam & Caffarella (1999).

self-disclosure The act of revealing one's thoughts and emotions to others. This may be helpful or hindering to open communication, depending on timing and context.

sensitivity training Type of group learning developed in the 1940s and later adapted to T-groups (training groups), encounter groups, and interpersonal skills training at the core of the *human potential movement in the 1970s and 1980s. Remnants have become mainstream techniques in adult education settings (e.g., asking students to "share" and "self-disclose" personal information, "checking-in" at the start of a class, seeking "consensus" and "closure," and generally paying close attention to issues of *process and interpersonal harmony). ⇨ humanistic psychology.

service learning Integrates community service into academic instruction and involves *critical reflection by students. Community-based learning opportunities expand the walls of the classroom beyond the classroom and into the community. ᴓ Lankard (1995), Stanton (1999).

shaping Arising from *behavior modification, the term refers to a teacher's efforts to eliminate undesirable behaviors by *reinforcing, initiating, and strengthening desirable ones. May be done through *approximation. ⇨ reinforcement.

significant personal learning The "coming to a state of critical awareness within personal relationships" (Brookfield, 1987:215-216) with the following characteristics: it is perceived as profoundly important by the learners themselves; is frequently triggered by a major life crisis; entails a redefinition of some aspect of the self; and involves the individual calling into question some of the assumptions underlying the way they conduct personal relationships.

situated learning An approach where knowledge and skills are learned in the contexts that reflect how they are obtained and applied in everyday situa-

---

* this term has a separate entry   ᴓ turn to the literature for more   ⇨ see also

tions. Views learning as a sociocultural phenomenon rather than the acquisition of general information from a decontextualized body of knowledge (Kirshner & Whitson, 1997). Uses *cooperative learning and participative teaching methods. Course content evolves from cues provided by the environment and from dialogue within the *learning community. ᏭᏭ Stern (1998).

situational leadership An approach to group management that stresses that there is no single leadership style that covers all eventualities; as situations and circumstances change, so must a manager's (or facilitator's) style and interventions.

Skinner, B.F. American psychologist (1904-1990) who proposed the principle of *operant conditioning* which states that a "behavior is followed by a consequence, and the nature of the consequence modifies the organism's tendency to repeat the behavior in the future" (Boeree, 1998). Related Skinnerian concepts include aversive stimulus, *behavior modification, *reinforcement, punishment, and *shaping. ᏭᏭ Skinner (1974).

social action learning It typically begins, according to *Freire (1970), with becoming aware of one's oppression and one's implication in it; and can lead to "some of the most powerful learning … as people struggle against oppression, … make sense of what is happening to them and work out ways of doing something about it" (Foley, 1999:1-2). In the classroom, examples include students speaking on behalf of others to air grievances or requesting a say in the running of a course.

sociogram, interaction diagram Graphic representation of the nature and frequency of interaction among group members.

Socratic method Teaching technique credited to Socrates wherein a teacher's systematic questioning aims to elicit something implicitly known by the student. ⇨ inquiry method, tacit knowing.

soft skills Term used in corporate settings, referring to learning which is difficult to quantify: i.e., which does not result in measurable improvement to the bottom line. Examples can be found in interpersonal skills, personal development, and *spirituality.

somatic learning, embodied learning Helps students to integrate their experiential history with their current experience. It "trusts individuals to learn from their ability to attend and to listen to the information they are receiving from the interaction of self with the environment" (Sellers-Young, 1998:176). ᏭᏭ Kerka, (2002) for a summary, Clark (2001) for applications. ⇨ autobiographical learning.

spiritual practice "Any activity that both awakens desire for and provides the means to expand consciousness of Self, Other, and Larger Mystery" (Zimmerman, 1996:6).

spirituality Adult spirituality is typically informed by how one is socialized both religiously and culturally. Yet, they are not the same: religion is an organized community of faith that has written codes of regulatory behavior, whereas spirituality is more about one's personal belief and experience of a higher power or higher purpose (Tisdell, 2001). ⇨ spirituality in adult education, spiritual practice.

spirituality in adult education Concerned with matters of the heart, spirit, and soul in the context of formal education; "about intimacy with our *perceptions* (the experience of having a body); our *thoughts* (the experience of having a mind); and our *emotions* (the experience of having a heart)" (Glazer, 1999). ᏭᏭ Dirkx (1997), Palmer (1983/1993), Tisdell (2000, 2001).

standardized test A written measurement device (*instrument) requiring uniform administration. Interpretation of results may be done by trained experts who use manuals containing norms for the defined reference groups. Tests aim to quantify intelligence, achievement, competence, attitude, or aptitude. Their use is not without controversy, especially when used to classify, rank, or select people.

structured activity Learning tools (such as game, role-play, or simulation) designed to help participants gain certain insights from direct experience. Many structured activities for adult learners are commercially available; good ones contain clear instructions, specify material and time requirements, point to possible outcomes, provide reproducible forms and checklists, offer guidelines for *debriefing activities, and may also provide some theoretical background. ᏭᏭ The *Pfeiffer Annuals*.

structured journals Learning activity for first-time journallers and distance learners. The teacher provides specific questions and sample responses to stimulate recall, reflection, and analysis. ⇨ journals.

superlearning ⇨ accelerated learning.

swampy lowlands Term coined by Schön (1983) in reference to the rough terrain in which practitioners learn from experience—in contrast to the "high road of abstract theory and technical rationality" formulated by academics. ⇨ reflection-in-action.

synchronous learning ⇨ asynchronous learning.

synergy The combined effect of group members that exceeds the sum of their individual efforts.

synthesize The ability to put parts together to form a new whole.

T

tacit knowing "We can know more than we can tell," writes Polany (1967:4). Such knowing is characterized as personal, difficult to articulate fully, experience-based, contextualized, job-specific, held within, both known and unknown to the holder, transferred through conversation and narrative, and capable of becoming explicit knowledge and vice versa. ᏭᏭ Imel (2003b).

talking circle A group technique where participants are given equal time to offer opinions, information, and insights in a nonjudgmental and noncompetitive atmosphere.

task group Commonly used term for small groups given an assignment and specified time period. Often followed by reporting, discussing, and *debriefing.

task-oriented behaviors Individual behaviors exhibited by participants in *task groups; they tend to enhance a group's productivity (Benne & Seats, 1948) and include summarizing, information-giving, and consensus-seeking. ⇨ self-serving behaviors.

taxonomy of learning, taxonomy of educational objectives Classification of levels of intellectual behavior important in learning, developed by Bloom and associates in 1956, resulting in a taxonomy that includes the *cognitive, *psychomotor, and *affective domain. ᏭᏭ Anderson & Krathwohl (2001) for an update.

teachable moment Term credited to Piaget, referring to moments when the

---

* this term has a separate entry   ᏭᏭ turn to the literature for more   ⇨ see also

teacher stretches students' capacity, but stays within what they are capable of understanding. In adult education, the term is commonly used to label moments when the learner is ready and the conditions are right for certain learning and instruction to occur. ⇨ training commercial, lecturette.

teacher within A notion based on "the voice that invites me to honor the nature of my true self" (Palmer, 1998:29), which speaks to the identity and integrity of the person-as-teacher and addresses the basic question: "How can I develop the authority to teach, the capacity to stand my ground amidst the complex forces of both classroom and my own life?" (p. 32).

teaching perspectives Based on research across disciplines and cultures, Pratt (1998) offers five "perspectives" that express the values and assumptions that underlie a teacher's actions: transmission, apprenticeship, developmental, nurturing, and social reform.

Teaching Perspectives Inventory (TPI) Based to measure an individual's *teaching perspectives and is freely available at www.teachingperspectives.com.

teaching point Key point or important materials that a teacher aims to "cover" in a lecture or unit of instruction.

teaching style A teacher's idiosyncratic manner and behavior while working with students. Attempts to devise an *instrument to quantify the elusive matter of personal style have not been successful. ⇨ teaching perspectives.

technological literacy Having knowledge about individual technologies and their development, an understanding of the historical and cultural context of technology, and competencies to "accommodate and cope with rapid and continuous technological change, generate creative and innovative solutions for technological problems, act through technological knowledge both effectively and efficiently, and assess technology and its involvement with the human life world judiciously" (Gagel, 1997:25). ᴕ Wonacott (2001).

theme-based learning/instruction Similar to *problem-based learning in that the curriculum is organized around a central topic or issue. However, it does not necessarily rely on problems of occupational practice; instead themes typically reflect the concrete, everyday lives of the learn-

ers. Grounded in the work of *Freire, themes can be identified by the learners, the teachers, or both teachers and learners working together (Dirkx & Prenger, 1996).

theories-in-use Term by Schön (1983) for the process by which people design and conduct action. Generally, these are approaches that work in certain contexts, can be explained, and may be altered as circumstances change. ⇨ reflective practice, espoused theory.

training commercial Technique proposed by Quinlivan-Hall (1993), whereby the facilitator seizes a * teachable moment and spontaneously offers input before, during, or after a group activity.

transfer of learning (1) In backward-reaching transfer, the student makes connections to prior knowledge. (2) In forward-reaching transfer, the student makes connections to how the information will be used in the future (Woolfolk, 1998:320).

transformational learning Concept by Mezirow (1991) which views *experiential learning as the "bringing of one's assumptions, premises, criteria, and *schemata into consciousness and vigorously critiquing them" (p. 29). Adult learners who encounter a "disorienting dilemma" for which there seems no immediate solution engage in a three-step process. 1. They reflect on the content of the experience (what happened?) which may or may not lead to learning. 2. If they find and test a solution that leads to unsatisfactory outcomes, they may reflect on the process they used (how did it happen?), leading to procedural learning. 3. When they then investigate the deep-seated beliefs and assumptions that guide their approach to problem-solving, critical reflection results (Fenwick, 2001:13). ᴕ Baumgartner (2001:15-24) for recent research and applications; also Cranton (1996b, 1997), Imel (1998), Taylor (1998).

transparent Personal trait of being unconcealed, free from pretence, open to examination and questioning. Could apply to several entities, such as a teacher or student, an educational policy, a course design, or test procedures.

transpersonal psychology Extends from Maslow's work in *humanistic psychology, and is concerned with a variety of phenomena and concepts of cosmic

meaning (Wulff, 1991), such as "peak experiences, ecstatic, mystical experiences, being, essence, bliss, awe, wonder, transcendence of self, spirit, sacralization of everyday life, oneness" (p. 612). Widely viewed as the "fourth force" in the development of psychology, after *behaviorism, classical psychoanalysis, and *humanistic psychology.

triad Three people working as a group. ⇨ dyad.

U

uncertainty reduction theory Provides a rationale for the necessity of icebreakers and introductions in class. States that initial interactions between strangers are characterized by information-seeking aimed at reducing uncertainty through such reciprocal acts as *self-disclosure and nonverbal warmth. ᴕ Littlejohn (1999:260-262).

V

vertical thinking A habitual style of thinking that is logical and linear; in contrast to *lateral thinking. ᴕ De Bono (1972).

vicarious learning Refers here to learning enjoyed by one person through the sympathetic participation in the experience of another. Example: seemingly passive observers in a role-play, video, or story may benefit from the experience of another "actor." Such learning is enhanced by *foreshadowing and *debriefing.

virtual classroom The on-line learning space in which participants and instructor interact.

W

wait time A delay to give students time to ponder after the teacher or another student has posed a question.

Z

zoom principle During a lecture or demonstration, the teacher gives the broad picture before going into details. ⇨ foreshadowing.

* this term has a separate entry   ᴕ turn to the literature for more   ⇨ see also

Notes

Introduction

1 Pratt D.D., & Associates. (1998). *Five perspectives on teaching in adult and higher education*. Melbourne, FL: Krieger Publishing.
2 Kember, D.A. (1997). Reconceptualisation of the research into university academics' conceptions of teaching. *Learning and Instruction*, (7):255-275.
3 Palmer, P.J. (1998). *The courage to teach: exploring the inner landscape of a teacher's life*. San Francisco: Jossey-Bass.

1: Planning a session

1 See also Kemp, J.E. (1990). *The instructional design process*. New York: Harper-Collins; Morrison, G.R., Ross, S. M., & Kemp, J.E. (2003). *Designing effective instruction*. New York: John Wiley; and my own (1988) *The quick instructional planner*. Vancouver, BC.: Training Associates.
2 For more, see Mager, R.F. (1975). *Preparing instructional objectives*. Belmont, CA: Fearon-Pitman.

2: Declaring objectives

1 Mager's books include: *Goal analysis* (1972/1984); *Measuring instructional intent or Got a match?* (1973); *Analyzing performance problems or You really oughta wanna* (1970/1984); and *Preparing instructional objectives* (1975/1984). Originally published by Fearon-Pitman and Lake Publishing, they have been reissued as *The new Mager six-pack* (1997) by the Center for Effective Performance, Atlanta, GA.
2 Mager, R.F. (1972). *Goal analysis*. Belmont, CA: Fearon-Pitman, p. 7.
3 Adapted from Pratt, D.D. (1996). *Course manual for Teaching adults, Adult Education 327*. Vancouver, BC: Distance Education and Technology, University of British Columbia, pp. 63-64.
4 See Glossary for definitions.
5 Mager, R.F. (1975). *Preparing instructional objectives*. Belmont, CA: Fearon-Pitman, p. 93.

6 Mager, *Preparing*, p. 20.
7 Mager, *Preparing*. p. 36.
8 Polanyi, M. (1966). *The tacit dimension*. Garden City, NJ: Doubleday.
9 See my 2001 dissertation, *Vulnerable to possibilities, a journey of self-knowing through personal narrative*. Available on request, renner@gulfislands.com
10 Eisner, E.W. (1979). *The educational imagination: on the design and evaluation of school programs*. New York: Macmillan, p. 99.
11 Adapted from Bloom, B.S. (1956) (Ed.). *Taxonomy of educational objectives: the classification of educational goals: handbook I—cognitive domain*. New York: Longman.
12 Eisner, *The educational imagination*, p. 103.
13 For a full description, see Tinzmann, M.B. et al (1990). What is the collaborative classroom? North Central Regional Educational Laboratory. Retrieved October 3, 2003, from www.ncrel.org
14 Freire, P. (2000). *Pedagogy of the oppressed*. New York: Continuum, p. 53.
15 Fenwick, T.J. (2001). Experiential learning: a theoretical critique from five perspectives. *ERIC Information Series No. 38*, p.14. Retrieved September 28, 2003, from www.ericacve.org

4: Getting packed

1 Rogers, C.R. (1951). *Client-centered therapy*. Boston: Houghton-Mifflin, pp. 388-391.

5: Using icebreakers and energizers

1 Garrison, D.R., & Brook, P. (1992). Getting it right the first session. *Adult Learning*, (August), pp. 25-26.
2 Littlejohn, S.W. (1999). *Theories of human communication (6th ed.)*. Belmont, CA: Wadsworth, pp. 260-262.
3 Adapted from Merman, C.H. (1992). Common concerns checklist. *Training & Development Journal*, (January), p. 70.
4 For more, see Mager, R.F. (1972). *Goal analysis*. Belmont, CA: Fearon-Pitman.
5 Merriam-Webster OnLine Dictionary. Retrieved Oct 18, 2003, from www.m-w.com

6 This image may be freely downloaded from such sites as www.family-crests.com
7 Adapted from an exercise in EDUC 327, conducted by Dan Pratt, University of British Columbia, Summer 1998.
8 Cross, K.P. (1981). *Adults as learners*. San Francisco: Jossey-Bass, pp. 154-157.
9 Excerpted from Imel, S. (1997). A new look at older adults. *ERIC Trends and Issues Alert*. Retrieved October 4, 2003, from www.ericacve.org
10 Neugarten, B.L. (1996). *The meanings of age: selected papers of Bernice L. Neugarten*. Edited by D.A. Neugarten. Chicago: University of Chicago Press, p. 403.
11 Williamson, A. (1997). You're never too old to learn!: third-age perspectives on lifelong learning. *International Journal of Lifelong Education*, (16)3:173-184.

6: Contracting for learning

1 For a rationale and tips on using learning contracts, see Knowles, M. (1978). *The adult learner: a neglected species*. Houston, TX: Gulf Publishing Company, pp. 198-203, and (1975). *Self-directed learning: a guide for learners and teachers*. New York: Association Press.

7: Working in groups

1 Palmer, P.J. (1993). Good talk about good teaching: improving teaching through conversation and community. *Change Magazine*, (25)6:8-13.
2 This variation was suggested by Mardy Wheeler, training director, loss prevention department, Liberty Mutual Insurance Company, Boston, MA.
3 Shaw, M.E. (1976/1980). *Group dynamics: the psychology of small group behavior*. New York: McGraw-Hill, pp. 185-192.

8: Delivering lively lectures

1 Brookfield, S.D. (1991). *The skillful teacher*. San Francisco: Jossey-Bass, p. 75.
2 Brown, G.A., & Bakhar, M.A. (Eds.) (1983). *Styles of lecturing*. Loughborough, UK: Loughborough University Press.

3 Weaver, R.L. Effective lecturing techniques. *The Clearing House,* 55(1):20-33.
4 See also Silberman, M. (1990). *Active training.* Pfeiffer/Wiley, pp. 39-77.
5 Adapted from Detz, J. (1984/1992). *How to write & give a speech.* New York: St. Martin's Press, p. 94.
6 See also Zemke, R. (1991). Humor in training: laugh and the world learns with you – maybe. *Training,* (August), pp. 26-29.
7 Gruner, C.R. Advice to the beginning speaker on using humor: what research tells us. *Communication Education,* 34(2):142-147.

9: Asking beautiful questions
1 Cited in Kloss, R.J. (1988). Toward asking the right questions. *The Clearing House,* (February), pp. 245-248.
2 Boom. B.S, (1956) (Ed.). *Taxonomy of educational objectives: the classification of educational goals: handbook I—cognitive domain.* New York: Longman.
3 Schumaker, D. (1985). But ... do I have time to do it right? In A. Costa (Ed.), *Developing minds: a resource book for teaching thinking,* cited in Kloss, above, p. 247.
4 Adapted and reproduced by permission of Training House, Inc., Princeton, NJ. See copyright page for details.
5 Fairbairn, D.M. (1987). The art of questioning your students. *The Clearing House,* (September), pp. 19-22.
6 Postman, N., & Weingartner, C. (1969). *Teaching as a subversive activity.* New York: Delta Books.

10: Flexing learning styles
1 Kolb, D.A. (1985). *The lerning style inventory: technical manual.* Boston, MA: McBer & Company.
2 Stumpf, S.A., & Friedman, R.D. The learning style inventory: still less than meets the eye. *Academy of Management Review,* 6(2):297-299.
3 See also Kolb, D.A. (1984). *Experiential learning: experience as the source of learning and development.* Englewood Cliffs, NJ: Prentice-Hall.

11: Observing group behavior
1 Adapted from the classic article by Benne, K.D., & Seats, P. (1948). Functional roles of group members. *Journal of Social Issues,* 4:41-49.
2 Schutz, W. (1966). *The interpersonal underworld.* Palo Alto, CA: Science & Behavior Books.

12: Rallying learning circles
1 Zimmerman, J.M. (1996). *The way of council.* Las Vegas, NV: Bramble Books.

13: Brewing brainstorms
1 Adapted from *Mycoted—Creativity & Innovation in Science & Technology.* Retrieved September 10, 2003, from www.mycoted.com
2 Griggs, R.E. (1985). A storm of ideas. *Training,* 22:56.
3 Koberg, D., & Bagnall, J. (1991). *The universal traveler: a soft-systems guide to creativity, problem-solving, & the process of reaching goals.* Los Altos, CA: Crisp Publications, p. 56.

14: Directing role-plays
1 Steinaker, N.W., & Bell, M.R. (1979). *The experiential taxonomy.* New York: Academic Press.
2 Mehrabian, A. (1971). *Silent messages.* Belmont, CA: Wadsworth.
3 Hall, E.T. (1966). *The hidden dimension,* and (1971) *The silent language.* New York: Doubleday.

15: Teaching by demonstration
1 Spaid, O.A. (1986). *The consummate trainer: a practitioner's perspective.* Englewood Cliffs, NJ: Prentice-Hall, p. 156.
2 Clark, R.C. (1989). *Developing technical training.* Reading, MA: Addison-Wesley.
3 Gagné, R.M. (1977/1985). *The conditions of learning.* New York: Holt-Reinhart-Winston.

16: Generating participation
1 Palmer, P.J. (1993). *To know as we are known: education as a spiritual journey.* San Francisco: Harper, p. 80.
2 Cooperrider, D.L., & Srivastva, S. (1987). Appreciative inquiry in organizational life. In R. Woodman & W. Pasmore (Eds.), *Research in organizational change and development.* Greenwich, CT: JAI Press, pp. 129-169.
3 Based on an activity developed by Doug Kerr, president of Tracon Training Consultants Corp. in Vancouver, BC; www.tracontraining.com
4 The stages are based on Cooperrider, D.L., & Whitney, D. (1999). *Appreciative inquiry.* San Francisco: Berrett-Koehler Communications, pp. 6-7. See also Watkins, J.M., & Mohr, B. (2001). *Appreciative inquiry: change at the speed of imagination.* San Francisco: Jossey-Bass.
5 Adapted from Brookfield, S.D. (1995). *Becoming a critically reflective teacher.* San Francisco: Jossey-Bass, p. 150.

6 Based on "ideal knowledge exchange," an activity developed by Mackie Chase, Director, Centre for Intercultural Communication, University of British Columbia.
7 Rogers, C.R. (1969), *Freedom to learn.* Columbus, OH: Merrill, pp. 164-166.

17: Studying cases
1 Adapted from Owenby, P.H. (1992). Making case studies come alive. *Training,* (January), pp. 43-44.
2 Excerpted from Brown, B.L. (1997). Portfolio assessment: missing link in student evaluation. *ERIC Trends and Issues Alert.* Retrieved October 4, 2003, from www.ericacve.org
3 Willis, S. (1996). On the cutting edge of assessment: testing what students can do with knowledge. *Educational Update,* (38)4:4-7.

18: Reading together
1 Palincsar, A.S., & Klenk, L.J. (1991). Dialogues promote reading comprehension. In B. Means, C. Chelemer, & M.S. Knapp (Eds.), *Teaching advanced skills to at-risk students.* San Francisco: Jossey-Bass.
2 Palincsar, A.S., & Brown, A.L. (1985). Reciprocal teaching: activities to promote reading with your mind. In T.L. Harris & E.J. Cooper (Eds.), *Reading, thinking and concept development: strategies for the classroom.* New York: The College Board, pp. 19-20.
3 Cited in Boudah, D.J., & O'Neill, K.J. (1999). Learning strategies. *ERIC/OSEP Digest # E577.* Retrieved October 2, 2003, from www.ericfacility.net
4 Adapted from Knowles, M.S. (1975). *Self-directed learning: a guide for learners and teachers.* New York: Association Press, pp. 105-107.
5 Lindeman, E.C. (1926). *The meaning of adult education.* New York: New Republic, pp. 9-10.
6 Knowles, M.S. (1980). *Modern practice of adult education: from pedagogy to andragogy (revised and updated).* Chicago: Follett Publishing Company/Association Press.
7 Butler, S.J., & Bentley, R. (1992). Literacy through lifewriting. *English Quarterly,* 24(3-4):33-41.
8 Karpiak, I.E. (2000). Writing our life: adult learning and teaching through autobiography. *Canadian Journal of University Continuing Education,* (26)1:31-50.

9 Karpiak, I.E. (2001). Written in earnest: uses of autobiography in learning and development. Paper presented at the Narrative Education Research Conference, Seattle.

21: Individualizing assignments/projects
1 Adapted from Johnson, D.W., & Johnson, F.P. (1987). *Joining together (3rd ed.)*. Englewood Cliffs, NJ: Prentice-Hall, p.17.

22: Using journals
1 Kerka, S. (2002). Journal writing as an adult learning tool. *ERIC Practice Application Brief No. 22*. Retrieved October 1, 2003, from www.ericacve.org
2 Brookfield, S.D. (1995). *Becoming a critically reflective teacher*. San Francisco: Jossey-Bass, p. 97.
3 Adapted from Case Western Reserve University, Frances Payne Bolton School of Nursing. Retrieved October 13, 2003, from http://fpb.cwru.edu/courses/NURS318/ClinicalJournal.htm
4 Adapted from Teachers Net. Retrieved October 22, 2003, from http://teachers.net
5 Based on Zimmerman, J. (1981). Journal as dialogue. *Synergist*, (Fall), pp. 46-49.
6 Based on Norman, J. (1981). Journal as discipline. *Synergist*, (Fall), pp. 46-49.
7 McAlpine, L.(1992). Learning to reflect: using journals as professional conversations. *Adult Learning*, (January), pp. 15-24.

23: Processing feedback
1 Adapted from Realin, J.A. (1989). Making feedback work. *Training & Development Journal*, (July), p. 25.

24: Learning autobiographically
1 Dr. Irene E. Karpiak, University of Oklahoma,www.ou.edu/education/elps/edah/fac_vita/karpiak.htm
2 Nielsen, H.B. (1999). "Black holes" as sites for self-construction. In R. Josselson & A. Lieblich, (Eds.), *Making meaning of narratives*, in *The narrative study of lives*, vol. 6, (pp. 45-75). Thousand Oaks: Sage, p. 50.
3 See, for example, Karpiak, I.E. (2000). Writing our life: adult learning and teaching through autobiography. *Canadian Journal of University Continuing Education*, *26*(1), 31-50; Karpiak, I.E. (2003). The ethnographic, the reflective, and the uncanny: three "tellings" of autobiography. *Journal of Transformative Education, 1*, 2, 99-116.

4 in T. Moore (1996), *The education of the heart*. New York: HarperCollins, p. 58.
5 Cooper, J.E. (1991). Telling our own stories: the reading and writing of journals and diaries. In C. Whitherell & N. Noddings, (Eds.), *Stories lives tell: narrative and dialogue in education,* (pp. 96-112). New York: Teachers College Press.
6 Birren, J.E. & Birren, B.A. (1996). Autobiography: exploring the self and encouraging development. In J.E. Birren et al, (Eds.), *Aging and biography: explorations in adult development*. New York: Springer.
7 Dominicé, P. (2000). *Learning from our lives: using educational biographies with adults*. San Francisco: Jossey-Bass.
8 Hobbs, C. (2005). *Elements of autobiography and life narrative*. New York: Longman Press.
9 Janesick, V.K. (1998). *"Stretching" exercises for qualitative researchers*. Thousand Oaks, CA: Sage.
10 Lao Tzu (1988). *Tao te ching*. Translated by S. Mitchell. New York: Harper-Collins, no. 1 and 14.

25: Designing tests and quizzes
1 Knowles, M. (1989). *The making of an adult educator*. San Francisco: Jossey-Bass.
2 Brookfield, S.D. (1992). Giving helpful evaluations to learners. *Adult Learning*, (June), p. 22. See also *The skillful teacher* by the same author.
3 Adapted from Patton, M.Q. (1991). Beyond evaluation myths. *Adult Learning*, (October), pp. 9-28.
4 Patton, Beyond evaluation myths, p. 28.
5 Based on Gronlund, N.E. (1987). *How to construct achievement tests*. Englewood Cliffs, NJ: Prentice-Hall, pp. 30-43. Check your library for the most recent edition. See also Fenwick,T.J., & Parson, J. (1999). *The art of evaluation*. Toronto, ON: Thompson; and Moran, J.J. (2001). *Assessing adult learning*. Melbourne, FL: Krieger Publishing Co.
6 Gronlund, *How to construct*, pp. 45-46.
7 Gronlund, *How to construct*, pp. 49-50.
8 M. Priestley, M. (1982). *Performance assessment in education & training: alternative techniques*. Englewood Cliffs, NJ: Educational Technology Publ., p. 195.
9 Briefly summarized in Ornstein, A.C. (1992). Essay tests: use, development, and grading. *The Clearing House*, (January/February), pp. 175-177.
10 Brookfield, S.D. (1991). *The skillful teacher*. San Francisco: Jossey-Bass, p. 22.
11 Ornstein, Essay tests, pp. 176-177.

26: Projecting overhead
1 Knowles, M. 1978). *The adult learner*. Houston, TX: Gulf Publishing Company, p. 31.

27: Presenting with PowerPoint
1 Kathryne Roden, University of Oklahoma. PowerPoint is a trademark of Microsoft Corp.
2 Adapted with permission from Dennis Kennedy (www.denniskennedy.com), author of *Ten tips to improve your presentations with PowerPoint*.

28: Flipping charts
1 Expanded from Quinlivan-Hall, D., & Renner, P. (1990). *In search of solutions: sixty ways to guide your problem-solving group*. Vancouver, BC: Training Associates, pp. 25-30.
2 Stuart J. Murphy (2003). *Visual learning, children, and math*. Excerpted from MathStart® Web site. Retrieved May 26, 2004, from http://www.stuartjmurphy.com/visual.html
3 Adapted from Tisdell, E.J. (2001). Spirituality in adult and higher education. *ERIC Digest No. 232*. Retrieved September 23, 2003, from www.ericacve.org
4 Dirkx, J.M. (1997). Nurturing soul in adult learning. In P. Cranton (Ed.), *Transformative learning in action. New Directions for Adult and Continuing Education no. 74*. San Francisco: Jossey-Bass, p. 83.
5 Palmer, P.J. (1998). *The courage to teach*. San Francisco: Jossey-Bass.

30: Assessing the course
1 Gagné, R.M. (1972). Domains of learning. *Interchange*, 3:1-8.

Index

Kerr, Doug: on appreciative inquiry, 88
knowledge-sharing, 9
Knowles, Malcolm: on andragogy, 139; on contracting for learning, 33; on life experience, 102
Kolb, David: on learning styles, 54; on experiential learning cycle, 57

L
layout. *See* seating arrangements
leading questions, 52
learning needs, as icebreaker, 21
Learning Styles Inventory, (Kolb), 57
learning styles, 54
learning: circles, 63, 92
lecture, 40; and humor, 44; best used when, 40; note-taking handout, 45
lecturette, 43; use as part of role-play, 75
lesson planning, 1
Lewin, Kurt: on learning from experience, 112
library assignment, 113
Lindeman, Eduard: on tapping learners' experience, 102
listening triads, as icebreaker, 19

M
Mager, Robert: on instructional objectives, 1-6; on performance and task analysis, 3
magic wand, to generate participation, 92
masking tape, techniques, 145
matador tear, when using flipcharts, 144
meditation, to generate participation, 92
Mehrabian, Albert: on nonverbal behavior, 79
memorable teachers, as an icebreaker, 24; to generate participation, 92
metaphors, as icebreaker, 26
missing pieces, to generate participation, 93
multiple-choice test, 130

N
needs assessment, as icebreaker, 21, 29; to generate participation, 94
negative brainstorming, 70
newsprint. *See* flipchart
nonverbal behavior, 79
note-taking, during lecture, 45

O
objectives, 3: acceptable standard, 5; observable behavior, 6, 80
observable behavior, 5, 80
observer, during role-play, 76; recording from, 77
overhead projector, 135

P
pacing, during demonstration, 81
Palmer, Parker J.: on questions, 37; on silence, 88; on spirituality, 149
panel discussion, 10
parking lot, 60
Parry, Scott: on questions, 47
participation, how to generate, 85

peer teaching, to generate participation, 94
performance analysis, 3
performance feedback, 82; form, 83. *See also* feedback
personal action plan, in group learning, 59
personal space, 79
Polanyi, Michael: on tacit knowing, 6
portfolio assessment, 99
poster session, as icebreaker, 27
Postman, Neil: on creating a climate for inquiry, 53
PowerPoint, 140
Pratt, Daniel D.: on goals and objectives, 4; on teaching perspectives, *x*
precourse checklist, 12
predictable group behaviors, 60
predicting success, as icebreaker, 23
presentations, to generate participation, 94
press conference, as icebreaker, 17
process vs. content, 61
processing ideas, during brainstorming, 72
proxemics, 79
psychomotor domain, 157

Q
questionnaires, for course assessment, 156-160
questions, 46; deadly types, 52; and answers, 44, 94
questions-only rule, 37
quizzes, 129

R
RAP-reading technique, 101
reaction time, changes in adult learners, 31
reading response log, 117
reading together, 100; proactively, 101
reciprocal teaching, 100
recorder, in small groups, 37
recording techniques, with flipchart, 147
remembering names, 16
reporting techniques, in group activities, 38
reverse brainstorming, 70
Roden, Kathryne: on using PowerPoint, 140
Rogers, Carl: on student-centered teaching; 14; on facilitating, 96
role-playing, 74; interventions, 76; developing scripts, 79
role-storming, 70, 95
room setups. *See* seating arrangements

S
scaffolding, 100, 101
Schutz, Will: on group members' needs, 62
scripting a role-play, 79
seating arrangements: for buzz groups, 35; for debates, 106; for guest lectures, 104; for learning circles, 64; with overhead projector, 137; for role-playing, 75
selection-type tests, 130
self-assessment, as icebreaker, 29
self-oriented behaviors, in groups, 61
Shaw, Marvin: on group dynamics, 39

silence, use of, 45, 88, 92
slide layout: with overhead transparencies, 136; with PowerPoint, 141
speedy memo, 85, 87
spend-a-penny, 86, 88
spirituality in adult education, 149
storytelling, to generate participation, 95
structured journal, 117
supply-type tests, 130
synergy, 69

T
table shapes, influence on group dynamics, 39
tacit knowing, 6
talking stick, 67
task analysis, 3
task-oriented behaviors in groups, 60
teachable moments, 82, 90
teacher as: apprentice master, *xi*; collaborator, 9; demonstrator, 80; evaluator, 129, 155; facilitator, 9, 63, 72; lecturer, 40; mediator, 9; nurturer, *xii*; planner, 1; presenter, 135, 140, 144; questioner, 46; social reformer, *xii*; timekeeper, 36; transmitter; *x*
teacher-pleasing questions, 52
Teaching Perspectives Inventory (Pratt), *xiii*
teaching perspectives, *x*
team journal, 116
tests and quizzes, 129
textbook selection, involving students, 112
timekeeper, 36
Tinzman, Margaret: on the collaborative classroom, 9
topsy-turvy, a brainstorming variation, 72
tracking questions, to generate participation, 95
training films, 150
transfer of learning, 83, 84
transparencies, 135
triad, 38
true-false tests, 131

U
uncertainty reduction theory, 17
unfinished statements, as icebreaker, 23

V
videos, as training films, 150
viewing teams, when watching films, 154
vision, change in the adult learner, 31
visualization, to generate participation, 96
visual learning, 144
voting with your feet, to generate participation, 95

W
warm-up activities. *See* icebreakers
whip-around, to generate participation, 96
written tests, benefits, 130

Z
zoom principle, use in presentations, 81